Effective Amazon Machine Learning

Machine learning in the cloud

Alexis Perrier

BIRMINGHAM - MUMBAI

Effective Amazon Machine Learning

First published: April 2017

Production reference: 1210417

Published by Packt Publishing Ltd.
Livery Place
35 Livery Street
Birmingham
B3 2PB, UK.
ISBN 978-1-78588-323-1

www.packtpub.com

Credits

Author

Alexis Perrier

Reviewer

Doug Ortiz

Commissioning Editor

Veena Pagare

Acquisition Editor

Vinay Argekar

Content Development Editor

Cheryl D'sa

Production Coordinator

Arvindkumar Gupta

Copy Editor

Manisha Sinha

Project Coordinator

Nidhi Joshi

Proofreader

Safis Editing

Indexer

Mariammal Chettiyar

Technical Editor

Karan Thakkar

About the Author

Alexis Perrier is a data scientist at Docent Health, a Boston-based startup. He works
with Machine Learning and Natural Language Processing to improve patient experience in
healthcare. Fascinated by the power of stochastic algorithms, he is actively involved in the
data science community as an instructor, blogger, and presenter. He holds a Ph.D. in Signal
Processing from Telecom ParisTech and resides in Boston, MA.

You can get in touch with him on twitter @alexip and by email at
alexis.perrier@gmail.com.

About the Reviewer

Doug Ortiz is an independent consultant who has been architecting, developing, and integrating enterprise solutions throughout his whole career. Organizations that leverage his skillset have been able to rediscover and reuse their underutilized data via existing and emerging technologies, such as Microsoft BI Stack, Hadoop, NoSQL databases, SharePoint, .Net, and related toolsets and technologies.

He is the founder of Illustris, LLC, and can be reached at `dougortiz@illustris.org`.

Interesting aspects of his profession are listed here:

- Has experience integrating multiple platforms and products
- Helps organizations gain a deeper understanding of the value of their current investments in data and existing resources, turning them into useful sources of information
- Has improved, salvaged, and architected projects by utilizing unique and innovative techniques

His hobbies include yoga and scuba diving.

www.PacktPub.com

For support files and downloads related to your book, please visit `www.PacktPub.com`.

Did you know that Packt offers eBook versions of every book published, with PDF and ePub files available? You can upgrade to the eBook version at `www.PacktPub.com` and as a print book customer, you are entitled to a discount on the eBook copy. Get in touch with us at `service@packtpub.com` for more details.

At `www.PacktPub.com`, you can also read a collection of free technical articles, sign up for a range of free newsletters and receive exclusive discounts and offers on Packt books and eBooks.

`https://www.packtpub.com/mapt`

Get the most in-demand software skills with Mapt. Mapt gives you full access to all Packt books and video courses, as well as industry-leading tools to help you plan your personal development and advance your career.

Why subscribe?

- Fully searchable across every book published by Packt
- Copy and paste, print, and bookmark content
- On demand and accessible via a web browser

Customer Feedback

Thanks for purchasing this Packt book. At Packt, quality is at the heart of our editorial process. To help us improve, please leave us an honest review on this book's Amazon page at `https://www.amazon.com/dp/1785883232`.

If you'd like to join our team of regular reviewers, you can e-mail us at `customerreviews@packtpub.com`. We award our regular reviewers with free eBooks and videos in exchange for their valuable feedback. Help us be relentless in improving our products!

This book is dedicated to the love of my life Janne and to our beautiful children Astrid, Léonard and Lucas.

Table of Contents

Preface

Big data and artificial intelligence are ubiquitous part of our everyday lives, fostering a rising, billion-dollar, cloud-based **Machine Learning as a Service (MLaaS)** industry.

Among the several Machine Learning as a Service platforms currently on the market, Amazon Machine Learning stands out for its simplicity. Amazon Machine Learning was launched in April 2015 with a clear goal of lowering the barrier to predictive analytic by offering a service accessible to companies without the need for highly skilled technical resources, while balancing performance and costs. When combined with the depth of the AWS ecosystem, the Amazon Machine Learning platform makes predictive analytics a natural element of the business data pipeline.

This book follows the simplification approach of Amazon Machine Learning with two goals: to give you the core data science knowledge needed to use the service to its full potential and to give you the keys to building a fully featured data pipeline centered around predictive analytics, effectively making predictive analytics the driver of your data driven applications.

What this book covers

Chapter 1, *Introduction to Machine Learning and Predictive Analytics*, this introductory chapter is a general presentation of the Amazon Machine Learning service and the types of predictive analytics problems it can address. We show how the service uses a simple linear model for regression and classification problems, and we present the context for successful predictions with Amazon Machine Learning.

Chapter 2, *Machine Learning Definitions and Concepts*, this chapter explains the machine learning concepts needed to use the Amazon Machine Learning service and fully understand how it works. What are the preparation techniques used when dealing with raw data? How do we evaluate a predictive model? What strategies are available to remediate poor predictive performances?

Chapter 3, *Overview of an Amazon Machine Learning Workflow,* this chapter is an overview of a simple Amazon Machine Learning project. The reader will learn how to get started on the Amazon Machine Learning platform, how to set up an account, and how to secure it. We go through a simple numeric prediction problem based on a classic dataset. We describe how to prepare the data, train and select a model, and make predictions.

Chapter 4, *Loading and Preparing the Dataset,* Amazon ML offers powerful features to transform the data through recipes. Working with a classic dataset, we upload data on S3, implement cross validation, create a schema, and examine available data statistics. We then extend Amazon ML feature engineering and data cleaning capabilities by using Athena, a recently launched AWS SQL service.

Chapter 5, *Model Creation,* in this chapter, we explore the Amazon ML data transformations and how to apply them through recipes. We train and tune models and select the best ones by analyzing different prediction metrics. We present insights into the Stochastic Gradient Descent algorithm, and the use of different types of regularization. Finally, we analyze the training logs to better understand what goes on under the Amazon ML hood during model training.

Chapter 6, *Predictions and Performances,* we apply our newly trained models to make predictions on previously unseen data, and we make a final assessment of their performance and robustness. We show how to make batch predictions on a given dataset and how to set up a real-time endpoint for streaming predictions.

Chapter 7, *Command Line and SDK,* using the AWS web interface to manage and run your projects is time-consuming. In this chapter, we move away from the web interface and start running our projects via the command line with the AWS Command Line Interface (AWS CLI) and the Python SDK with the Boto3 library. We use our new powers to implement cross validation and recursive feature selection.

Chapter 8, *Creating Datasources from Redshift,* in this chapter, we will use the power of SQL queries to address non-linear datasets. Creating datasources in Redshift gives us the potential for upstream SQL based feature engineering prior to datasource creation. We explore how to upload data from S3 to Redshift, access the database, run queries, and export results.

Chapter 9, *Building a Streaming Data Analysis Pipeline,* in the final chapter of the book, we extend Amazon ML capabilities by integrating with other AWS services. We build a fully featured streaming data flow integrating AWS Kinesis, Lambda, Redshift, and Machine Learning to implement real time tweets classification.

What you need for this book

This book requires an AWS account, and the ability to run Python 3 (3.5) code examples. We use the latest Anaconda distribution (conda 4.3). The reader should also be able to run basic shell commands in a terminal. Note that the Amazon Machine Learning service is not part of the free tier AWS offer.

Who this book is for

This book is for Python developers who want to build real-world artificial intelligence applications. This book is friendly to Python beginners, but being familiar with Python would be useful to play around with the code. It will also be useful for experienced Python programmers who are looking to use artificial intelligence techniques in their existing technology stacks.

Conventions

In this book, you will find a number of text styles that distinguish between different kinds of information. Here are some examples of these styles and an explanation of their meaning.

Code words in text, database table names, folder names, filenames, file extensions, pathnames, dummy URLs, user input, and Twitter handles are shown as follows: "Set original weight estimation at `w_0 = 100g` to initialize and a counter."

A block of code is set as follows:

```
# Create datasource for training
resource = name_id_generation('DS', 'training', trial)
print("Creating datasources for training (%s)"% resource['Name'] )
```

Any command-line input or output is written as follows:

```
$ aws s3 cp data/titanic.csv s3://aml.packt/data/ch9/
```

New terms and **important words** are shown in bold. Words that you see on the screen, for example, in menus or dialog boxes, appear in the text like this: "Examples of reinforcement learning applications include **AlphaGo**, Google's world championship Go algorithm, self-driving cars, and semi-autonomous robots."

Warnings or important notes appear in a box like this.

 Tips and tricks appear like this.

Reader feedback

Feedback from our readers is always welcome. Let us know what you think about this book-what you liked or disliked. Reader feedback is important for us as it helps us develop titles that you will really get the most out of.

To send us general feedback, simply e-mail feedback@packtpub.com, and mention the book's title in the subject of your message.

If there is a topic that you have expertise in and you are interested in either writing or contributing to a book, see our author guide at www.packtpub.com/authors.

Customer support

Now that you are the proud owner of a Packt book, we have a number of things to help you to get the most from your purchase.

Downloading the example code

You can download the example code files for this book from your account at http://www.packtpub.com. If you purchased this book elsewhere, you can visit http://www.packtpub.com/support and register to have the files e-mailed directly to you.

You can download the code files by following these steps:

1. Log in or register to our website using your e-mail address and password.
2. Hover the mouse pointer on the **SUPPORT** tab at the top.
3. Click on **Code Downloads & Errata**.
4. Enter the name of the book in the **Search** box.
5. Select the book for which you're looking to download the code files.
6. Choose from the drop-down menu where you purchased this book from.
7. Click on **Code Download**.

Once the file is downloaded, please make sure that you unzip or extract the folder using the latest version of:

- WinRAR / 7-Zip for Windows
- Zipeg / iZip / UnRarX for Mac
- 7-Zip / PeaZip for Linux

The code bundle for the book is also hosted on GitHub at `https://github.com/PacktPubl ishing/Effective-Amazon-Machine-Learning`. We also have other code bundles from our rich catalog of books and videos available at `https://github.com/PacktPublishing/`. Check them out!

Errata

Although we have taken every care to ensure the accuracy of our content, mistakes do happen. If you find a mistake in one of our books-maybe a mistake in the text or the code-we would be grateful if you could report this to us. By doing so, you can save other readers from frustration and help us improve subsequent versions of this book. If you find any errata, please report them by visiting `http://www.packtpub.com/submit-errata`, selecting your book, clicking on the **Errata Submission Form** link, and entering the details of your errata. Once your errata are verified, your submission will be accepted and the errata will be uploaded to our website or added to any list of existing errata under the Errata section of that title.

To view the previously submitted errata, go to `https://www.packtpub.com/books/conten t/support`and enter the name of the book in the search field. The required information will appear under the **Errata** section.

Piracy

Piracy of copyrighted material on the Internet is an ongoing problem across all media. At Packt, we take the protection of our copyright and licenses very seriously. If you come across any illegal copies of our works in any form on the Internet, please provide us with the location address or website name immediately so that we can pursue a remedy.

Please contact us at copyright@packtpub.com with a link to the suspected pirated material.

We appreciate your help in protecting our authors and our ability to bring you valuable content.

Questions

If you have a problem with any aspect of this book, you can contact us at questions@packtpub.com, and we will do our best to address the problem.

1
Introduction to Machine Learning and Predictive Analytics

As artificial intelligence and big data have become a ubiquitous part of our everyday lives, cloud-based machine learning services are part of a rising billion-dollar industry. Among the several services currently available on the market, Amazon Machine Learning stands out for its simplicity. Amazon Machine Learning was launched in April 2015 with a clear goal of lowering the barrier to predictive analytics by offering a service accessible to companies without the need for highly skilled technical resources.

This introductory chapter is a general presentation of the Amazon Machine Learning service and the types of predictive analytics problems it can solve. The Amazon Machine Learning platform distinguishes itself by its simplicity and straightforwardness. However, simplicity often implies that hard choices have been made. We explain what was sacrificed, why these choices make sense, and how the resulting simplicity can be extended with other services in the rich data-focused AWS ecosystem.

We explore what types of predictive analytics projects the Amazon Machine Learning platform can address and how it uses a simple linear model for regression and classification problems. Before starting a predictive analytics project, it is important to understand what context is appropriate and what constitutes good results. We present the context for successful predictions with **Amazon Machine Learning** (**Amazon ML**).

The reader will understand what sort of problems Amazon ML can address and the assumptions with regard to the underlying data. We show how Amazon ML solves linear regression and classification problems with a simple linear model and why that makes sense. Finally, we present the limitations of the platform.

This chapter addresses the following topics:

- What is Machine Learning as a Service (MLaaS) and why does it matter?
- How Amazon ML successfully leverages linear regression, a simple and powerful model
- What is predictive analytics and what types of regression and classification problems can it address?
- The necessary conditions the data must verify to obtain reliable predictions
- What's missing from the Amazon ML service?

Introducing Amazon Machine Learning

In the emerging MLaaS industry, Amazon ML stands out on several fronts. Its simplicity, allied to the power of the AWS ecosystem, lowers barriers to entry in machine learning for companies while balancing out performances and costs.

Machine Learning as a Service

Amazon Machine Learning is an online service by **Amazon Web Services** (**AWS**) that does supervised learning for predictive analytics.

Launched in April 2015 at the AWS summit, Amazon ML joins a growing list of cloud-based machine learning services, such as Microsoft Azure, Google prediction, IBM Watson, Prediction IO, BigML, and many others. These online machine learning services form an offer commonly referred to as **Machine Learning as a Service** or **MLaaS** following a similar denomination pattern of other cloud-based services such as **SaaS**, **PaaS**, and **IaaS** respectively for Software, Platform, or Infrastructure as a Service.

Studies show that MLaaS is a potentially big business trend. ABI research, a business intelligence consultancy, estimates machine learning-based data analytics tools and services revenues to hit nearly $20 billion in 2021 as MLaaS services take off as outlined in this business report: http://iotbusinessnews.com/2016/08/01/39715-machine-learning-iot-enterprises-spikes-advent-machine-learning-service-models/

Eugenio Pasqua, Research Analyst at *ABI Research*, said the following:

> *"The emergence of the Machine-Learning-as-a-Service (MLaaS) model is good news for the market, as it cuts down the complexity and time required to implement machine learning and thus opens the doors to an increase in its adoption level, especially in the small-to-medium business sector."*

The increased accessibility is a direct result of using an API-based infrastructure to build machine-learning models instead of developing applications from scratch. Offering efficient predictive analytics models without the need to code, host, and maintain complex code bases lowers the bar and makes ML available to smaller businesses and institutions.

Amazon ML takes this democratization approach further than the other actors in the field by significantly simplifying the predictive analytics process and its implementation. This simplification revolves around four design decisions that are embedded in the platform:

- A limited set of tasks: binary classification, multi classification and regression
- A single linear algorithm
- A limited choice of metrics to assess the quality of the prediction
- A simple set of tuning parameters for the underlying predictive algorithm

That somewhat constrained environment is simple enough while addressing most predictive analytics problems relevant to business. It can be leveraged across an array of different industries and use cases.

Leveraging full AWS integration

The AWS data ecosystem of pipelines, storage, environments, and Artificial Intelligence (AI) is also a strong argument in favor of choosing Amazon ML as a business platform for its predictive analytics needs. Although Amazon ML is simple, the service evolves to greater complexity and more powerful features once it is integrated in a larger structure of AWS data related services.

AWS is already a major actor in cloud computing. Here's what an excerpt from *The Economist, August 2016* has to say about AWS (http://www.economist.com/news/busines s/21705849-how-open-source-software-and-cloud-computing-have-set-up-it-indus try):

> *AWS shows no sign of slowing its progress towards full dominance of cloud computing's wide skies. It has ten times as much computing capacity as the next 14 cloud providers combined, according to Gartner, a consulting firm. AWS's sales in the past quarter were about three times the size of its closest competitor, Microsoft's Azure.*

This gives an edge to Amazon ML, as many companies that are using cloud services are likely to be already using AWS. Adding simple and efficient machine learning tools to the product offering mix anticipates the rise of predictive analytics features as a standard component of web services. Seamless integration with other AWS services is a strong argument in favor of using Amazon ML despite its apparent simplicity.

The following architecture is a case study taken from an AWS *January 2016* white paper titled *Big Data Analytics Options on AWS* (http://d0.awsstatic.com/whitepapers/Big_Da ta_Analytics_Options_on_AWS.pdf), showing a potential AWS architecture for sentiment analysis on social media. It shows how Amazon ML can be part of a more complex architecture of AWS services:

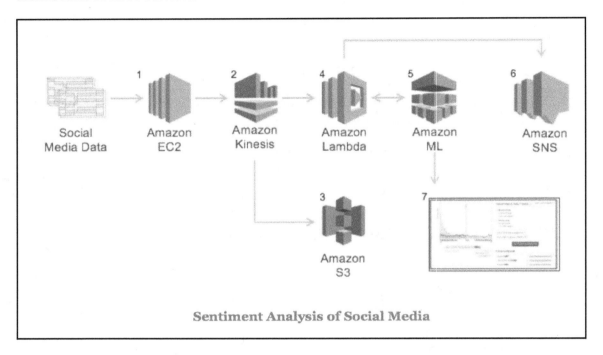

Sentiment Analysis of Social Media

Comparing performances

Keeping systems and applications simple is always difficult, but often worth it for the business. Examples abound with overloaded UIs bringing down the user experience, while products with simple, elegant interfaces and minimal features enjoy widespread popularity. The *Keep It Simple* mantra is even more difficult to adhere to in a context such as predictive analytics where performance is key. This is the challenge Amazon took on with its Amazon ML service.

A typical predictive analytics project is a sequence of complex operations: getting the data, cleaning the data, selecting, optimizing and validating a model and finally making predictions. In the scripting approach, data scientists develop codebases using machine learning libraries such as the Python **scikit-learn** library or **R** packages to handle all these steps from data gathering to predictions in production. As a developer breaks down the necessary steps into modules for maintainability and testability, Amazon ML breaks down a predictive analytics project into different entities: datasource, model, evaluation and predictions. It's the simplicity of each of these steps that makes AWS so powerful to implement successful predictive analytics projects.

Engineering data versus model variety

Having a large choice of algorithms for your predictions is always a good thing, but at the end of the day, domain knowledge and the ability to extract meaningful features from clean data is often what wins the game.

Kaggle is a well-known platform for predictive analytics competitions, where the best data scientists across the world compete to make predictions on complex datasets. In these predictive competitions, gaining a few decimals on your prediction score is what makes the difference between earning the prize or being just an extra line on the public leaderboard among thousands of other competitors. One thing Kagglers quickly learn is that choosing and tuning the model is only half the battle. Feature extraction or how to extract relevant predictors from the dataset is often the key to winning the competition.

In real life, when working on business related problems, the quality of the data processing phase and the ability to extract meaningful signal out of raw data is the most important and time consuming part of building an efficient predictive model. It is well know that "*data preparation accounts for about 80% of the work of data scientists*" (http://www.forbes.com/sit es/gilpress/2016/03/23/data-preparation-most-time-consuming-least-enjoyable-d ata-science-task-survey-says/). Model selection and algorithm optimization remains an important part of the work but is often not the deciding factor when implementation is concerned.

A solid and robust implementation that is easy to maintain and connects to your ecosystem seamlessly is often preferred to an overly complex model developed and coded in-house, especially when the scripted model only produces small gains when compared to a service based implementation.

Amazon's expertise and the gradient descent algorithm

Amazon has been using machine learning for the retail side of its business and has build a serious expertise in predictive analytics. This expertise translates into the choice of algorithm powering the Amazon ML service.

The **Stochastic Gradient Descent** (**SGD**) algorithm is the algorithm powering Amazon ML linear models and is ultimately responsible for the accuracy of the predictions generated by the service. The SGD algorithm is one of the most robust, resilient, and optimized algorithms. It has been used in many diverse environments, from signal processing to deep learning and for a wide variety of problems, since the 1960s with great success. The SGD has also given rise to many highly efficient variants adapted to a wide variety of data contexts. We will come back to this important algorithm in a later chapter; suffice it to say at this point that the SGD algorithm is the Swiss army knife of all possible predictive analytics algorithm.

Several benchmarks and tests of the Amazon ML service can be found across the web (Amazon, Google and Azure: `https://blog.onliquid.com/machine-learning-services -2/` and Amazon versus **scikit-learn**: `http://lenguyenthedat.com/minimal-data-scienc e-2-avazu/`). Overall results show that the Amazon ML performance is on a par with other MLaaS platforms, but also with scripted solutions based on popular machine learning libraries such as `scikit-learn`.

For a given problem in a specific context and with an available dataset and a particular choice of a scoring metric, it is probably possible to code a predictive model using an adequate library and obtain better performances than the ones obtained with Amazon ML. But what Amazon ML offers is stability, absence of coding, and a very solid benchmark record, as well as a seamless integration with the Amazon Web Services ecosystem that already powers a large portion of the Internet.

Pricing

As with other MLaaS providers and AWS services, Amazon ML only charges for what you consume.

The cost is broken down into the following:

- An hourly rate for the computing time used to build predictive models
- A prediction fee per thousand prediction samples
- And in the context of real-time (streaming) predictions, a fee based on the memory allocated upfront for the model

The computational time increases as a function of the following:

- The complexity of the model
- The size of the input data
- The number of attributes
- The number and types of transformations applied

At the time of writing, these charges are as follows:

- $0.42 per hour for data analysis and model building fees
- $0.10 per 1,000 predictions for batch predictions
- $0.0001 per prediction for real-time predictions
- $0.001 per hour for each 10 MB of memory provisioned for your model

These prices do not include fees related to the data storage (S3, Redshift, or RDS), which are charged separately.

During the creation of your model, Amazon ML gives you a cost estimation based on the data source that has been selected.

The Amazon ML service is not part of the AWS free tier, a 12-month offer applicable to certain AWS services for free under certain conditions.

Understanding predictive analytics

Data Science, predictive analytics, machine learning -- these terms are used in many ways and sometimes overlap each other. What they actually refer to is not always obvious.

Data science is one of the most popular technical domains whose trend erupted after the publication of the often cited *Harvard Business Review* article of October 2012, *Data Scientist: The Sexiest Job of the 21st Century* (https://hbr.org/2012/10/data-scientist-the-sexiest-job-of-the-21st-century). Data science can be seen as an evolution from data mining and data analytics. Data mining is about exploring data to discover patterns that potentially lead to decisions and actions at the business level. Data science englobes data analytics and regroups a wider scope of domains, such as statistics, data visualization, predictive analytics, software engineering, and so on, under one very large umbrella.

Predictive analytics is the art of predicting future events based on past observations. It requires your data to be organized in a certain way with predictor variables and outcomes well identified. As the Danish politician *Karl Kristian Steincke* once said, "*Making predictions is difficult especially about the future.*" (This quote has also been attributed to Niels Bohr, Yogi Berra and others by `http://quoteinvestigator.com/2013/10/20/no-predict/`). Predictive analytics applications are diverse and far ranging: predicting consumer behavior, natural events (weather, earthquakes, and so on), people's behavior or health, financial markets, industrial applications, and so on. Predictive analytics relies on supervised learning, where data and labels are given to train the model.

Machine learning comprises the tools, methods, and concepts for computers to optimize models used for predictive analytics or other goals.

Machine learning's scope is much larger than predictive analytics. Three different types of machine learning are usually considered:

- **Supervised learning:** Assumes that a certain amount of training data with known outcomes is available and can be used to train the model. Predictive analytics is part of supervised learning.
- **Unsupervised learning:** Is about finding patterns in existing data without knowing the outcome. Clustering customer behavior or reducing the dimensions of the dataset for visualization purposes are examples of unsupervised learning.
- **Reinforcement learning:** Is the third type of machine learning, where agents learn to act on their own when given a set of rules and a specific reward schema. Examples of reinforcement learning applications include **AlphaGo**, Google's world championship Go algorithm, self-driving cars, and semi-autonomous robots. AlphaGo learned from thousands of past games and was able to beat the world Go champion in March 2016 (`https://www.wired.com/2016/03/go-grand master-lee-sedol-grabs-consolation-win-googles-ai/`). A classic reinforcement learning implementation follows this schema, where an agent adapts its actions on an environment based on the resulting rewards:

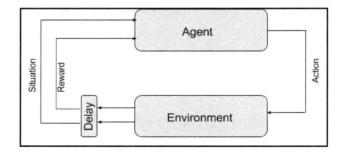

The difference between supervised and unsupervised learning in the context of binary classification and clustering is illustrated in the following two figures:

- For **supervised learning**, the original dataset is composed of two classes (squares and circles), and we know from the start to which class each sample belongs. Giving that information to a binary classification algorithm allows for a somewhat optimized separation of the two classes. Once that separating frontier is known, the model (the line) can be used to predict the class of new samples depending on which side the sample ends up being:

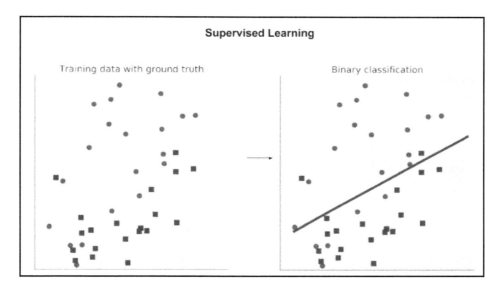

- In **unsupervised learning**, the different classes are not known. There is no ground truth. The data is given to an algorithm along with some parameters, such as the number of classes to be found, and the algorithm finds the best set of clusters in the original dataset according to a defined criteria or metric. The results may be very dependent on the initialization parameters. There is no truth, no accuracy, just an interpretation of the data. The following figure shows the results obtained by a clustering algorithm asked to find three classes in the original data:

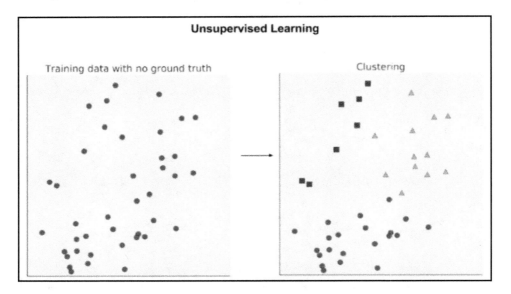

The reader will notice at this point that the book is titled Amazon Machine Learning and not Amazon Predictive Analytics. This is a bit misleading, as machine learning covers many applications and problems besides predictive analytics. However, calling the service machine learning leaves the door open for Amazon to roll out future services that are not focused on predictive analytics. The following figure maps out the relationships between data science terms:

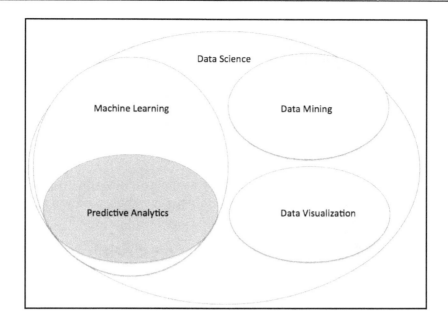

Building the simplest predictive analytics algorithm

Predictive analytics can be very simple. We introduce a very simple example of a predictive model in the context of binary classification based on a simple threshold.

Imagine that a truck transporting small oranges and large grapefruits runs off the road; all the boxes of fruits open up, and all the fruits end up mixed together. Equipped with a simple weighing scale and a way to roll the fruits out of the truck, you want to be able to separate them automatically based on their weights. You have some information on the average weights of small oranges (96g) and large grapefruits (166g).

 According to the USDA, the average weight of a medium-sized orange is 131 grams, while a larger orange weighs approximately 184 grams, and a smaller one around 96 grams.

- Large grapefruit (approx 4-1/2" dia) 166g
- Medium grapefruit (approx 4" dia) 128g
- Small grapefruit (approx 3-1/2" dia) 100g

Your predictive model is the following:

- You arbitrarily set a threshold of 130g
- You weigh each fruit
- If the fruit weighs more than 130g, it's a grapefruit; otherwise it's an orange

There! You have a robust reliable, predictive model that can be applied to all your mixed up fruits to separate them. Note that in this case, you've set the threshold with an educated guess. There was no machine learning involved.

In machine learning, the models learn by themselves. Instead of setting the threshold yourself, you let your program evolve and calculate the weight separation threshold of fruits by itself.

For that, you would set aside a certain number of oranges and grapefruits. This is called the training dataset. It's important that this training dataset has roughly the same number of oranges and grapefruits.

And you let the machine decide the threshold value by itself. A possible algorithm could be along these lines:

1. Set original weight estimation at $w\_0 = 100g$ to initialize and a counter $k = 0$
2. For each new fruit in the training dataset, adjust the weight estimation according to the following:

```
For each new fruit_weight:
    w(k+1) = (k*w(k) + fruit_weight)/ (k+1)
    k = k+1
```

Assuming that your training dataset is representative of all the remaining fruits and that you have enough fruits, the threshold would converge under certain conditions to the best average between all the fruit weights. A value which you use to separate all the other fruits depending on whether they weight more or less than the threshold you estimated. The following plot shows the convergence of this crude algorithm to estimate the average weight of the fruits:

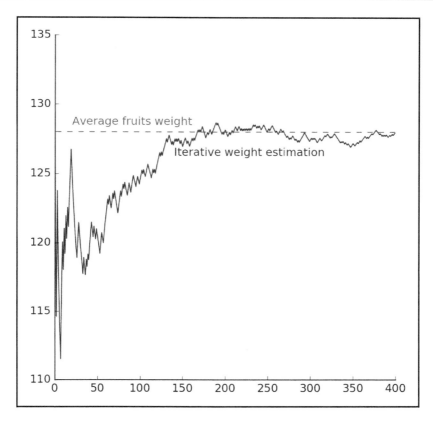

This problem is a typical binary classification model. If we had not two but three types of fruits (lemons, oranges, and grapefruit), we would have a multiclass classification problem.

In this example, we only have one predictor: the weight of the fruit. We could add another predictor such as the diameter. This would result in what is called a multivariate classification problem.

In practice, machine learning uses more complex algorithms such as the SGD, the linear algorithm used by Amazon ML. Other classic prediction algorithms include Support Vector Machines, Bayes classifiers, Random forests and so on. Each algorithm has its strength and set of assumptions on the dataset.

Regression versus classification

Amazon ML does two types of predictive analytics: classification and **regression**.

As discussed in the preceding paragraph, classification is about predicting a finite set of labels or categories for a given set of samples.

- In the case of two classes, the problem is called Binary classification
- When there are more than two classes and the classes are mutually exclusive, the problem is a multiclass classification problem
- If the samples can belong to several classes at once, we talk about a multilabel classification problem

In short, classification is the prediction of a finite set of classes, labels, categories.

- Examples of Binary classification are: buying outcome (yes/no), survival outcome (yes/no), anomaly detection (spam, bots), and so on
- Examples of multiclass classification are: classifying object in images (fruits, cars, and so on), identifying a music genre, or a movement based on smartphone sensors, document classification and so on

In regression problems, the outcome has continuous values. Predicting age, weight, stock prices, salaries, rainfall, temperature, and so forth are all regression problems. We talk about multiple regression when there are several predictors and multivariate regression when the predictions predict several values for each sample. Amazon ML does univariate regression and classification, both binary and multiclass, but not multilabel.

Expanding regression to classification with logistic regression

Amazon ML uses a linear regression model for regression, binary, and multiclass predictions. Using the **logistic regression** model extends continuous regression to classification problems.

A simple regression model with one predictor is modeled as follows:

$$y = a \times x + b$$

Here, x is the predictor, y is the outcome, and (a, b) are the model parameters. Each predicted value y is continuous and not bounded. How can we use that model to predict classes which are by definition categorical values?

Take the example of binary predictions. The method is to transform the continuous predictions that are not bounded into probabilities, which are all between 0 and 1. We then associate these probabilities to one of the two classes using a predefined threshold. This model is called the **logistic regression** model–misleading name as logistic regression is a classification model and not a regression one.

To transform continuous not bounded values into probabilities, we use the `sigmoid` function defined as follows:

$$f(y) = \frac{1}{1+e^{-y}}$$

This function transforms any real number into a value within the *[0,1]* interval. Its output can, therefore, be interpreted as a probability:

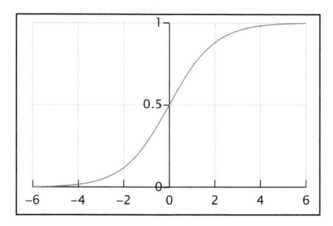

In conclusion, the way to do binary classification with a regression model is as follows:

1. Build the regression model, and estimate the real valued outcomes y.
2. Use the predicted value y as the argument of the `sigmoid` function. The result $f(y)$ is a probability measure of belonging to one of the two classes.
3. Set a threshold T in [0,1]. All predicted samples with a probability $f(y) > T$ belong to one class, others belong to the other class. The default value for $T = 0.5$.

Logistic regression is, by nature, a Binary classifier. There are several strategies to transform a binary classifier into a multi class classifier.

The **one versus all (OvA)** technique consists in selecting one class as positive and all the others as negative to go back to a binary classification problem. Once the classification on the first class is carried out, a second class is selected as the positive versus all the others as negative. This process is repeated N-1 times when there are N classes to predict. The following set of plots shows:

- The original datasets and the classes for all the samples
- The result of the first Binary classification (circles versus all the others)
- The result of the second classification that separates the squares and the triangles

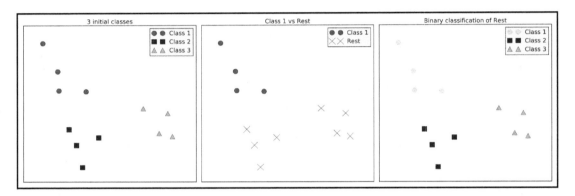

Extracting features to predict outcomes

That available data needs to be accessible and meaningful in order for the algorithm to extract information.

Let's consider a simple example. Imagine that we want to predict the market price of a house in a given city. We can think of many variables that would be predictors of the price of a house: the number of rooms or bathrooms, the neighborhood, the surface, the heating system, and so on. These variables are called features, attributes, or predictors. The value that we want to predict is called the outcome or the target.

If we want our predictions to be reliable, we need several features. Predicting the price of a house based on its surface alone would not be very efficient. Many other factors influence the price of a house and our dataset should include as many as possible (with conditions).

It's often possible to add large numbers of attributes to a model to try to improve the predictions. For instance, in our housing pricing prediction, we could add all the characteristics of the house (bathroom, superficies, heating system, the number of windows). Some of these variables would bring more information to our pricing model and increase the accuracy of our predictions, while others would just add noise and confuse the algorithm. Adding new variables to a predicting model does not always improve the predictions.

In order to make reliable predictions, each of the new features you bring to your model must bring some valuable piece of information. However, this is also not always the case. As we will see in `Chapter 2`, *Machine Learning Definitions and Concepts*, correlated predictors can hurt the performances of the model.

Predictive analytics is built on several assumptions and conditions:

- The value you are trying to predict is predictable and not just some random noise.
- You have access to data that has some degree of association to the target.
- The available dataset is large enough. Reliable predictions cannot be inferred from a dataset that is too small. (For instance, you can define and therefore predict a line with two points but you cannot infer data that follows a sine curve from only two points.)
- The new data you will base future predictions on is similar to the one you parameterized and trained your model on.

You may have a great dataset, but that does not mean it will be efficient for predictions.

These conditions on the data are very general. In the case of SGD, the conditions are more constrained.

Diving further into linear modeling for prediction

Amazon ML is based on linear modeling. Recall the equation for a straight line in the plan:

$$y = a \times x + b$$

This linear equation with coefficients (*a, b*) can be interpreted as a predictive linear model with *x* as the predictor and *y* as the outcome. In this simple case, we have two parameters (*a, b*) and one predictor *x*. An example can be that of predicting the height of children with respect to their weight and find some a and b such that the following equation is true:

$$Height = a \times Weight + b$$

Let's consider the classic *Lewis Taylor (1967)* dataset with 237 samples of children's age, weight, height, and gender (https://v8doc.sas.com/sashtml/stat/chap55/sect51.htm) and focus on the relation between the height and weight of the children. In this dataset, the optimal regression line follows the following equation:

$$Height = 0.16 \times Weight + 45.4$$

The following figure illustrates the height versus weight dataset and the associated linear regression:

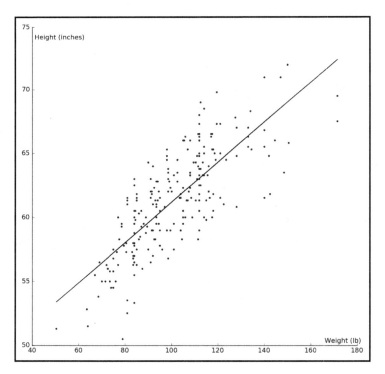

Consider now that we have not one predictor but several, and let's generalize the preceding linear equation to N predictors denoted by $\{x_1, \ldots, x_n\}$ and N +1 coefficients or $\{w_0, w_1, \ldots, w_n\}$ weights. The linear model can be written as follows:

$$\hat{y} = w_0 + \sum_{i=1}^{N} w_i x_i$$

Here, $\hat{y}$ denotes the predicted value, (y would correspond to the true value to be predicted). To simplify notations, we will assume for the rest of the book the coefficient $w_o = 0$.

This equation can be rewritten in vector form as follows:

$$\hat{y} = W X^T$$

Where T is the transpose operator, X = $\{x_1, \ldots, x_n\}$ and W= $\{w_1, \ldots, w_n\}$ are the respective vectors of predictors and model weights. Under certain conditions, the coefficients w_i can be calculated precisely. However, for a large number of samples N, these calculations are expensive in terms of required computations as they involve inverting matrices of dimension N, which for large datasets is costly and slow. As the number of samples grows, it becomes more efficient to estimate these model coefficients via an iterative process.

The Stochastic Gradient Descent algorithm iteratively estimates the coefficients $\{w_0, w_1, \ldots, w_n\}$ of the model. At each iteration, it uses a random sample of the training dataset for which the real outcome value is known. The SGD algorithm works by minimizing a function of the prediction error:

$$error = y - \hat{y} = y - W X^T$$

Functions that take the prediction error as argument are also called **loss functions**. Different loss functions result in different algorithms. A convex loss function has a unique minimum, which corresponds to the optimal set of weights for the regression problem. We will come back to the SGD algorithm in details in later chapters. Suffice to say for now that the SGD algorithm is especially well-suited to deal with large datasets.

There are many reasons to justify selecting the SGD algorithm for general purpose predictive analysis problems:

- It is robust
- Its convergence properties have been extensively studied and are well known
- It is well adapted to optimization techniques
- It has many extensions and variants
- It has low computational cost
- It can be applied to regression, classification, and streaming data

Some weaknesses include the following:

- The need to properly initialize its parameters
- A convergence rate dependent on a parameter called the learning rate

Validating the dataset

Not all datasets lend themselves to linear modeling. There are several conditions that the samples must verify for your linear model to make sense. Some conditions are strict, others can be relaxed.

In general, linear modeling assumes the following conditions (http://www.statisticssol utions.com/assumptions-of-multiple-linear-regression/):

- **Normalization/standardization**: Linear regression can be sensitive to predictors that exhibit very different scales. This is true for all loss functions that rely on a measure of the distance between samples or on the standard deviations of samples. Predictors with higher means and standard deviations have more impact on the model and may potentially overshadow predictors with better predictive power but more constrained range of values. Standardization of predictors puts all the predictors on the same level.
- **Independent and identically distributed (i.i.d.)**: The samples are assumed to be independent from each other and to follow a similar distribution. This property is often assumed even when the samples are not that independent from each other. In the case of time series where samples depend on previous values, using the sample to sample difference as the data is often enough to satisfy the independence assumption. As we will see in Chapter 2, *Machine Learning Definitions and Concepts,* confounders and noise will also negatively impact linear regression.

- **No multicollinearity**: Linear regression assumes that there is little or no multicollinearity in the data, meaning that one predictor is not a linear composition of other predictors. Predictors that can be approximated by linear combinations of other predictors will confuse the model.
- **Heteroskedasticity**: The standard deviation of a predictor is constant across the whole range of its values.
- **Gaussian distribution of the residuals**: This is more than a posteriori validation that the linear regression is valid. The residuals are the differences between the true values and their linear estimation. The linear regression is considered relevant if these residuals follow a Gaussian distribution.

These assumptions are rarely perfectly met in real-life datasets. As we will see in `Chapter 2`, *Machine Learning Definitions and Concepts*, there are techniques to detect when the linear modeling assumptions are not respected, and subsequently to transform the data to get closer to the ideal linear regression context.

Missing from Amazon ML

Amazon ML offers supervised learning predictions for classification (binary and multiclass) and regression problems. It offers some very basic visualization of the original data and has a preset list of data transformations, such as binning or normalizing the data. It is efficient and simple. However, several functionalities that are important to the data scientist are unfortunately missing from the platform. Lacking these features may not be a deal breaker, but it nonetheless restricts the scope of problems Amazon ML can be applied to.

Some of the common machine learning features Amazon ML does not offer are as follows:

- **Unsupervised learning**: It is not possible to do clustering or dimensionality reduction of your data.
- **A choice of models beside linear models**: Non-linear Support Vector Machines, any type of Bayes classification, neural networks, and tree, based algorithms (decision trees, random forests, or boosted trees) are all absent models. All predictions, all experiments will be built on linear regression and logistic regression with the SGD.
- Data visualization capabilities are reduced to histograms and density plots.
- **A choice of metrics**: Amazon ML uses F1-score and ROC-AUC metrics for classification, and MSE for regression. It is not possible to assess the model performance with any other metric.
- You cannot download your trained model and use it anywhere else than Amazon ML.

Finally, although it is not possible to directly use your own scripts (R, Python, Scala, and so on) within the Amazon ML platform, it is possible and recommended to use other AWS services, such as AWS Lambda, to preprocess the datasets. Data manipulation beyond the transformations available in Amazon ML can also be carried out with SQL if your data is stored in one of the AWS SQL enabled services (Athena, RDS, Redshift, and others).

The statistical approach versus the machine learning approach

In 2001, *Leo Breiman* published a paper titled *Statistical Modeling: The Two Cultures* (http://p rojecteuclid.org/euclid.ss/1009213726) that underlined the differences between the statistical approach focused on validation and explanation of the underlying process in the data and the machine learning approach, which is more concerned with the results.

Roughly put, a classic statistical analysis follows steps such as the following:

1. A hypothesis called the null hypothesis is stated. This null hypothesis usually states that the observation is due to randomness.
2. The probability (or p-value) of the event under the null hypothesis is then calculated.
3. If that probability is below a certain threshold (usually $p < 0.05$), then the null hypothesis is rejected, which means that the observation is not a random fluke.

 p> 0.05 does not imply that the null hypothesis is true. It only means that you cannot reject it, as the probability of the observation happening by chance is not large enough.

This methodology is geared toward explaining and discovering the influencing factors of the phenomenon. The goal here is to establish/build a somewhat static and fully known model that will fit observations as well as possible and, therefore, will be able to predict future patterns, behaviors, and observations.

In the machine learning approach, in predictive analytics, an explicit representation of the model is not the focus. The goal is to build the best model for the prediction period, and the model builds itself from the observations. The internals of the models are not explicit. This machine learning approach is called a black box model.

By removing the need for explicit modeling of the data, the ML approach has a stronger potential for predictions. ML is focused on making the most accurate predictions possible by minimizing the prediction error of a model at the expense of explainability.

Summary

In this introductory chapter, we presented the techniques used by the Amazon ML service. Although Amazon ML offers fewer features than other machine learning workflows, Amazon ML is built on a solid ground, with a simple yet very efficient algorithm driving its predictions.

Amazon ML does not offer to solve any type of automated learning problems and will not be adequate in some contexts and some datasets. However, its simple approach and design will be sufficient for many predictive analytics projects, on the condition that the initial dataset is properly preprocessed and contains relevant signals on which predictions can be made.

In Chapter 2, *Machine Learning Definitions and Concepts*, we will dive further into techniques and concepts used in predictive analytics.

More precisely, we will present the most common techniques used to improve the quality of raw data; we will spot and correct common anomalies within a dataset; we will learn how to train and validate a predictive model and how to improve the predictions when faced with poor predictive performance.

Machine Learning Definitions and Concepts

This chapter offers a high-level definition and explanation of the machine learning concepts needed to use the Amazon Machine Learning (Amazon ML) service and fully understand how it works. The chapter has three specific goals:

- Listing the main techniques to improve the quality of predictions used when dealing with raw data. You will learn how to deal with the most common types of data problems. Some of these techniques are available in Amazon ML, while others aren't.
- Presenting the predictive analytics workflow and introducing the concept of cross validation or how to split your data to train and test your models.
- Showing how to detect poor performance of your model and presenting strategies to improve these performances.

The reader will learn the following:

- How to spot common problems and anomalies within a given dataset
- How to extract the most information out of a dataset in order to build robust models
- How to detect and improve upon poor predictive performance

What's an algorithm? What's a model?

Before we dive into data munging, let's take a moment to explain the difference between an algorithm and a model, two terms we've been using up until now without a formal definition.

Consider the simple linear regression example we saw in `Chapter 1`, *Introduction to Machine Learning and Predictive Analytics* — the linear regression equation with one predictor:

$$\hat{y} = ax + b$$

Here, x is the variable, $\hat{y}$ the prediction, not the real value, and *(a,b)* the parameters of the linear regression model:

- The conceptual or theoretical model is the representation of the data that is the most adapted to the actual dataset. It is chosen at the beginning by the data scientist. In this case, the conceptual model is the linear regression model, where the prediction is a linear combination of a variable. Other conceptual models include decision trees, naive bayes, neural networks, and so on. All these models have parameters that need to be tuned to the actual data.
- The algorithm is the computational process that will calculate the optimal parameters of the conceptual model. In our simple linear regression case, the algorithm will calculate the optimal parameters a and b. Here optimal means that it gives the best predictions given the available dataset.
- Finally, the predictive model corresponds to the conceptual model associated with the optimal parameters found for the available dataset.

In reality, no one explicitly distinguishes between the conceptual model and the predictive model. Both are called the model.

In short, the algorithm is the method of learning, and the model is what results form the learning phase. The model is the conceptual model (trees, svm, linear) trained by the algorithm on your training dataset.

Dealing with messy data

As the dataset grows, so do inconsistencies and errors. Whether as a result of human error, system failure, or data structure evolutions, real-world data is rife with invalid, absurd, or missing values. Even when the dataset is spotless, the nature of some variables need to be adapted to the model. We look at the most common data anomalies and characteristics that need to be corrected in the context of Amazon ML linear models.

Classic datasets versus real-world datasets

Data scientists and machine-learning practitioners often use classic datasets to demonstrate the behavior of certain models. The **Iris** dataset, composed of 150 samples of three types of iris flowers, is one of the most commonly used to demonstrate or to teach predictive analytics. It has been around since 1936!

The **Boston housing** dataset and the **Titanic** dataset are other very popular datasets for predictive analytics. For text classification, the **Reuters** or the **20 newsgroups** text datasets are very common, while image recognition datasets are used to benchmark deep learning models. These classic datasets are used to establish baselines when evaluating the performances of algorithms and models. Their characteristics are well known, and data scientists know what performances to expect.

These classic datasets can be downloaded:

- **Iris**: http://archive.ics.uci.edu/ml/datasets/Iris
- **Boston housing**: https://archive.ics.uci.edu/ml/datasets/Housing
- **Titanic dataset**: https://www.kaggle.com/c/titanic or http://biostat.mc.vanderbilt.edu/wiki/pub/Main/DataSets/
- **Reuters**: https://archive.ics.uci.edu/ml/datasets/Reuters-21578+Text+Categorization+Collection
- **20 newsgroups**: http://scikit-learn.org/stable/datasets/twenty_newsgroups.html
- **Image recognition and deep learning**: http://deeplearning.net/datasets/

However, classic datasets can be weak equivalents of real datasets, which have been extracted and aggregated from a diverse set of sources: databases, APIs, free form documents, social networks, spreadsheets, and so on. In a real-life situation, the data scientist must often deal with messy data that has missing values, absurd outliers, human errors, weird formatting, strange inputs, and skewed distributions.

The first task in a predictive analytics project is to clean up the data. In the following section, we will look at the main issues with raw data and what strategies can be applied. Since we will ultimately be using a linear model for our predictions, we will process the data with that in mind.

Assumptions for multiclass linear models

For a linear model to offer reliable predictions, predictors must satisfy a certain number of conditions. These conditions are known as the *Assumptions of Multiple Linear Regression* (htt p://www.statisticssolutions.com/assumptions-of-multiple-linear-regression/):

- **Linear relationship**: The predictors should have some level of linear relationship with the outcome
- **Multivariate normality**: The predictors should follow a Gaussian distribution
- **No or little multicollinearity**: The predictors should not be correlated to one another
- **Homoscedasticity**: The variance of each predictor should remain more or less constant across the whole range of values

Of course, these assumptions are seldom verified. But there are ways to transform the data to approach these optimal conditions.

Missing values

Data aggregation, extraction, and consolidation is often not perfect and sometimes results in missing values. There are several common strategies to deal with missing values in datasets:

- Removing all the rows with missing values from the dataset. This is simple to apply, but you may end up throwing away a big chunk of information that would have been valuable to your model.
- Using models that are, by nature, not impacted by missing values such as decision tree-based models: random forests, boosted trees. Unfortunately, the linear regression model, and by extension the SGD algorithm, does not work with missing values (http://facweb.cs.depaul.edu/sjost/csc423/documents/mis sing_values.pdf).

- Imputing the missing data with replacement values; for example, replacing missing values with the median, the average, or the harmonic mean of all the existing values, or using clustering or linear regression to predict the missing values. It may be interesting to add the information that these values were missing in the first place to the dataset.

In the end, the right strategy will depend on the type of missing data and of course, the context. While replacing missing blood pressure numbers in a patient medical record by some average may not be acceptable in a healthcare context, replacing missing age values by the average age in the Titanic dataset is definitely adapted to a data science competition.

However, Amazon ML's documentation is not 100% clear on the strategy used to deal with missing values:

> *If the target attribute is present in the record, but a value for another numeric attribute is missing, then Amazon ML overlooks the missing value. In this case, Amazon ML creates a substitute attribute and sets it to 1 to indicate that this attribute is missing.*

In the case of missing values, a new column is created with a Boolean flag to indicate that the value was missing in the first place. But it is not clear whether the whole row or sample is dismissed or overlooked or if just the cell is removed. There is no mention of any type of imputation.

Normalization

Machine learning algorithms incrementally update the model parameters by minimizing the error between the real value and the one predicted with the last iteration's parameters. To measure this prediction error we introduce the concept of loss functions. A loss function is a measure of the prediction error. For a certain algorithm, using different loss functions will create variants of the algorithm. Most common loss functions use the **L2** or the **L1** norm to measure the error:

- **L2 norm:**

$$||\hat{y} - y||_2^2 = \sum_{i=1}^{n} (\hat{y_i} - y_i)^2$$

● **L1 norm:**

$$||\hat{y} - y||_1 = \sum_{i=1}^{n} |\hat{y}_i - y_i|$$

Where y_i and $\hat{y}$ are the real and predicted values of the samples.

The measure of the prediction error can end up being skewed when the different predictors differ by an order of magnitude. The large predictors obfuscate the importance of the smaller valued ones, thus making it difficult to infer the relative importance of each predictor in the model. This impacts how the respective weights of the linear model converge to their optimal value and as a consequence the performance of the algorithm. Predictors with the highest magnitude will end up dominating the model even if the predictor has little predictive power with regard to the real outcome value. Normalizing the data is a way to mitigate that problem by forcing the predictors to all be on the same scale.

There are two common types of normalization; data can be normalized or standardized:

- The **min-max normalization**, or **normalization**, which sets all values between *[0,1]*:

$$x = \frac{x - min(x)}{max(x) - min(x))}$$

- The **z-score normalization**, or **standardization**, which normalizes with respect to the standard deviation. All predictors will have a mean of 0 and a standard deviation of 1:

$$x = \frac{x - mean(x)}{std(x)}$$

The tree-based methods (decision trees, random forests, boosted trees) are the only machine learning models whose performance is not improved by normalization or standardization. All other distance/variance-based predictive algorithms may benefit from normalization. It has been shown that standardization is particularly useful for SGD, as it ensures that all the weights will be adapted at the same speed.

Efficient BackProp Yann A. LeCun et al. in Neural Networks: Tricks of the Trade pp. 9-48, Springer Verlag

Amazon ML offers z-score standardization as part of the available data transformations.

Imbalanced datasets

Dealing with imbalanced datasets is a very common classification problem.

Consider a Binary classification problem. Your goal is to predict a positive versus a negative class. The ratio between the two classes is highly skewed in favor of the positive class. This situation is frequently encountered in the following instance:

- In a medical context where the positive class corresponds to the presence of cancerous cells in people out of a large random population
- In a marketing context where the positive class corresponds to prospects buying an insurance while the majority of people are not buying it

In both these cases, we want to detect the samples in the minority class, but they are overwhelmingly outnumbered by the samples in the majority (negative) class. Most predictive models will be highly biased toward the majority class.

In the presence of highly imbalanced classes, a very simplistic model that always predicts the majority class and never the minority one will have excellent accuracy but would never detect the important and valuable class. Consider for instance a dataset composed of 1,000 samples, with 50 positive samples that we want to detect or predict and 950 negative ones of little interest. That simplistic model has an accuracy rate of 95% which is obviously a decent accuracy even though that model is totally useless. This problem is known as the **Accuracy paradox** (https://en.wikipedia.org/wiki/Accuracy_paradox).

A straightforward solution would be to gather more data, with a focus on collecting samples of the minority class and in order to balance out the two classes. But that's not always a possibility.

There are many other strategies to deal with imbalanced datasets. We will briefly look at some of the most common ones. One approach is to resample the data by under sampling or oversampling the available data:

- **Undersampling** consists in discarding most samples in the majority class in order to tilt back the minority/majority class ratio toward *50/50*. The obvious problem with that strategy is that a lot of data is discarded and along with that, meaningful signal for the model. This technique can be useful in the presence of large enough datasets.
- **Oversampling** consists in duplicating samples that belong to the minority class. Contrary to under sampling, there is no loss of data with that strategy. However, oversampling adds extra weight to certain patterns from the minority class, which may not bring useful information to the model. Oversampling adds noise to the model. Oversampling is useful when the dataset is small and you can't afford to leave some data out.

Under sampling and oversampling are two simple and easy-to-implement methods that are useful in establishing a baseline. Another widely-used method consists in creating synthetic samples from the existing data. A popular sample creation technique is the **SMOTE** method, which stands for **Synthetic Minority Over-Sampling Technique**. SMOTE works by selecting similar samples (with respect to some distance measure) from the minority class and adding perturbations on the selected attributes. SMOTE then creates new minority samples within clusters of existing minority samples. SMOTE is less of a solution in the presence of high-dimensional datasets.

The **imbalanced library** in Python (`http://github.com/scikit-learn-contrib/imbalanced-learn`) or the **unbalanced package** in R (`https://cran.r-project.org/web/packages/unbalanced/index.html`) both offer a large set of advanced techniques on top of the ones mentioned.

Note that the choice of the metric used to assess the performances of the model is particularly important in the context of an imbalanced dataset. The accuracy rate, which is defined as the ratio of correctly predicted samples to the total number of samples is the most straightforward metric in classification problems. But as we have seen, this accuracy rate is not a good indicator of the model's predictive power in the presence of a highly skewed class distribution.

In such a context, two metrics are recommended:

- **Cohen's kappa:** A robust measure of the agreement between real and predicted classes (`https://en.wikipedia.org/wiki/Cohen%27s_kappa`)
- **The F1 score**: The harmonic mean between Precision and Recall (`https://en.wikipedia.org/wiki/F1_score`)

The F1 score is the metric used by Amazon ML to assess the quality of a classification model. We give the definition of the F1-score under the *Evaluating the performance of your model* section at the end of this chapter.

Addressing multicollinearity

The following is the definition of multicollinearity according to Wikipedia (`https://en.wikipedia.org/wiki/Multicollinearity`):

Multicollinearity is a phenomenon in which two or more predictor variables in a multiple regression model are highly correlated, meaning that one can be linearly predicted from the others with a substantial degree of accuracy.

Basically, let's say you have a model with three predictors:

$$\hat{y} = w_1 x_1 + w_2 x_2 + w_3 x_3$$

And one of the predictors is a linear combination (perfect multicollinearity) or is approximated by a linear combination (near multicollinearity) of two other predictors.

For instance: $x_3 = a x_1 + b x_2 + \epsilon$

Here, ϵ is some noise variable.

In that case, changes in x_1 and x_2 will drive changes in x_3, and as a consequence, w_3 will be tied to w_1 and w_2. The information already contained in x_1 and x_2 will be shared with the third predictor x_3, which will cause high uncertainty and instability in the model. Small changes in the predictors' values will bring large variations in the coefficients. The regression may no longer be reliable. In more technical terms, the standard errors of the coefficient would increase, which would lower the significance of otherwise important predictors.

There are several ways to detect multicollinearity. Calculating the correlation matrix of the predictors is a first step, but that would only detect collinearity between pairs of predictors.

A widely used detection method for multicollinearity is to calculate the **variance inflation factor** or **VIF** for each of the predictors:

$$\text{VIF}_i = \frac{1}{1 - R_i^2}$$

Here, R_i^2 is the coefficient of determination of the regression equation in step one, with x_i on the left-hand side and all other predictor variables (all the other X_j for $j! = i$ variables) on the right-hand side.

A large value for one of the VIFs is an indication that the variance (the square of the standard error) of a particular coefficient is larger than it would be if that predictor was completely uncorrelated with all the other predictors. For instance, a VIF of 1.8 indicates that the variance of a predictor is 80% larger than what it would be in the uncorrelated case.

Once the attributes with high collinearity have been identified, the following options will reduce collinearity:

- Removing the high collinearity predictors from the dataset
- Using **Partial Least Squares Regression (PLS)** or **Principal Components Analysis (PCA)**, regression methods (`https://en.wikipedia.org/wiki/Princi pal_component_analysis`); PLS and PCA will reduce the number of predictors to a smaller set of uncorrelated variables

Unfortunately, detection and removal of multicollinear variables is not available from the Amazon ML platform.

Detecting outliers

Given a variable, outliers are values that are very distant from other values of that variable. Outliers are quite common, and often caused by human or measurement errors. Outliers can strongly derail a model.

To demonstrate, let's look at two simple datasets and see how their mean is influenced by the presence of an outlier.

Consider the two datasets with few samples each: *A = [1,2,3,4]* and *B = [1,2,3,4, 100]*. The 5th value in the B dataset, 100, is obviously an outlier: *mean(A) = 2.5*, while *mean(B) = 22*. An outlier can have a large impact on a metric. Since most machine learning algorithms are based on distance or variance measurements, outliers can have a high impact on the performance of a model.

Multiple linear regression is sensitive to outlier effects, as shown in the following graph where adding a single outlier point derails the solid regression line into the dashed one:

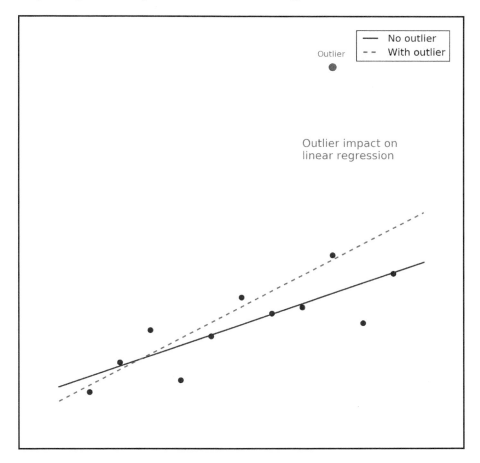

Removing the samples associated with the outliers is the simplest solution.

Another solution can be to apply **quantile binning** to the predictor by splitting the values into N ordered intervals or bins, each approximately containing an equal number of samples. This will transform a numeric (continuous) predictor into a categorical one. For example, [1,2,3,4,5,6,7,8,9,10,11,100] split into three equally sized bins becomes [*1,1,1,1,2,2,2,2,3,3,3,3*]; the outlier value 100 has been included in the third bin and hidden.

The downside of quantile binning is that some granularity of information is lost in the process, which may degrade the performance of the model.

Quantile binning is available as a data transformation process in Amazon ML and is also used to quantify non-linearities in the original dataset.

In fact, **Quantile Binning** (**QB**) is applied by default by Amazon ML to all continuous variables that do not exhibit a straightforward linear relation to the outcome. In all our trials, and contrary to our prior assumptions, we have found that QB is a very efficient data transformation in the Amazon ML context.

Accepting non-linear patterns

A linear regression model implies that the outcome can be estimated by a linear combination of the predictors. This, of course, is not always the case, as features often exhibit nonlinear patterns.

Consider the following graph, where Y axis depends on X axis but the relationship displays an obvious quadratic pattern. Fitting a line ($y = aX + b$) as a prediction model of Y as a function of X does not work:

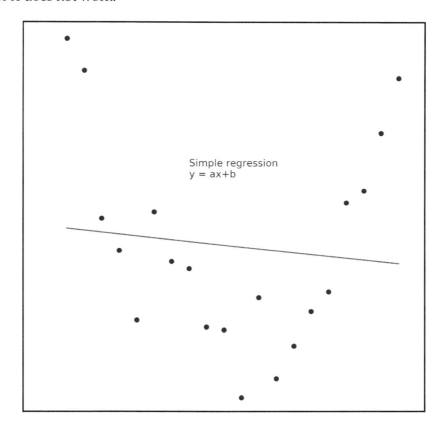

Some models and algorithms are able to naturally handle non-linearities, for example, tree-based models or support vector machines with non-linear kernels. Linear regression and SGD are not.

Transformations: One way to deal with these nonlinear patterns in the context of linear regression is to transform the predictors. In the preceding simple example, adding the square of the predictor X to the model would give a much better result. The model would now be of the following form:

$$y = ax + bx^2 + c$$

And as shown in the following diagram, the new quadratic model fits the data much better:

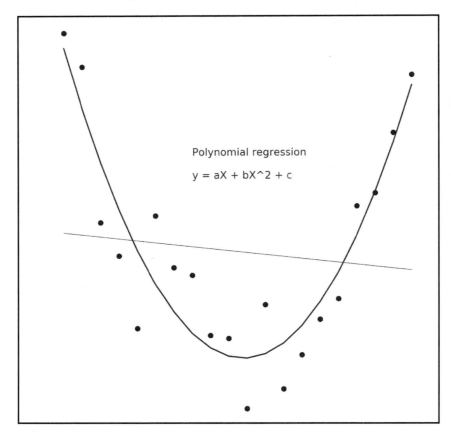

Polynomial regression

y = aX + bX^2 + c

We are not restricted to the quadratic case, and a power function of higher order can be used to transform existing attributes and create new predictors. Other useful transformations could include taking the logarithm, exponential, sine and cosine, and so on. The **Boxcox transformation**
(http://onlinestatbook.com/2/transformations/box-cox.html) is worth citing at this point. It's an efficient data transformation that reduces skewness and kurtosis of a variable distribution. It reshapes the variable distribution into one closer to a Gaussian distribution.

Splines are an excellent and more powerful alternative to polynomial interpolation. Splines are piece-wise polynomials that join smoothly. At their simplest level, splines consists of lines that are connected together at different points. Splines are not available in Amazon ML.

Quantile binning is the Amazon ML solution to non-linearities. By splitting the data into N bins, you remove any non-linearities in the bin's intervals. Although binning has several drawbacks (`http://biostat.mc.vanderbilt.edu/wiki/Main/CatContinuous`), the main one being that information is discarded in the process, it has been shown to generate excellent prediction performance in the Amazon ML platform.

Adding features?

In general, adding new features that are correlated in some ways to the outcome brings information and improves a model. However, adding too many features with little predictive power may end up bringing confusion to that same model and in the end degrading its performance.

Feature selection by removal of the least interesting features is worth trying when the sample size is small compared to the number of features; it leads to too few observations or too many features. There are different strategies (`http://machinelearningmastery.com/an-introduction-to-feature-selection/`) to identify and remove weak features. Selecting features based on their correlation with the outcome and discarding features with little or no correlation with the outcome will usually improve your model.

Preprocessing recapitulation

The following table recapitulates the different issues that one can find in raw data and whether Amazon ML offers ways to deal with them:

	Linear model sensitivity	Available on Amazon ML
Missing values	Yes	Dealt with automatically
Standardization	Yes	z-score standardization
Outliers	Yes	Quantile binning
Multicollinearity	Yes	No
Imbalanced datasets	Yes	Uses the right metric F1 Score No sampling strategy (may exist in background)
Non linearities	Yes	Quantile binning

The predictive analytics workflow

We have been talking about training the model. What does that mean in practice?

In supervised learning, the dataset is usually split into three non-equal parts: training, validation, and test:

Training 60%	Validation 20%	Test 20%

- The **training** set on which you train your model. It has to be big enough to give the model as much information on the data as possible. This subset of the data is used by the algorithm to estimate the best parameters of the model. In our case, the SGD algorithm will use that training subset to find the optimal weights of the linear regression model.

- The **validation** set is used to assess the performance of a trained model. By measuring the performance of the trained model on a subset that has not been used in its training, we have an objective assessment of its performance. That way we can train different models with different meta parameters and see which one is performing the best on the validation set. This is also called model selection. Note that this creates a feedback loop, since the validation dataset now has an influence on your model selection. Another model may have performed worse on that particular validation subset but overall better on new data.

- The **test** set corresponds to data that is set aside until you have fully optimized your features and model. The test subset is also called the **held-out** dataset.

In real life, your model will face previously unforeseen data, since the ultimate *raison d'etre* for a model is to predict unseen data. Therefore, it is important to assess the performance of the model on data it has never encountered before. The held-out dataset is a proxy for yet unseen data. It is paramount to leave this dataset aside until the end. It should never be used to optimize the model or the data attributes.

These three subsets should be large enough to represent the real data accurately. More precisely, the distribution of all the variables should be equivalent in the three subsets. If the original dataset is ordered in some way, it is important to make sure that the data is shuffled prior to the train, validation, test split.

As mentioned previously, the model you choose based on its performance on the validation set may have had a positive bias toward that particular dataset. In order to minimize such a dependency, it is common to train and evaluate several models with the same parameter settings and to average the performance of the model over several training validation dataset pairs. This reduces the model selection dependence with regard to the specific distribution of variables in the validation dataset.

This third-split method is basic and as we've seen, the model could end up being dependent on some specificities of the validation subset. Cross-validation is a standard method to reduce that dependency and improve our model selection. Cross validation consists in carrying out several training/validation split and averaging the model performance on the different validation subsets. The most frequent cross validation technique is k-fold cross validation which consists in splitting the dataset in K-chunks, recursively using each part as validation and the k-1 other parts as training. Other cross validation techniques include Monte-Carlo cross validation where the different training and validation sets are randomly sampled from the initial dataset. We will implement Monte Carlo cross validation in a later chapter. Cross validation is not a feature included in the Amazon ML service and needs to be implemented programatically. In Amazon ML, the training and evaluation of a model is done on one training-validation split only.

Training and evaluation in Amazon ML

In the context of Amazon ML, the model is linear regression and the algorithm the **Stochastic Gradient Descent** (**SGD**) algorithm. This algorithm has one main meta parameter called the learning rate and often noted α, which dictates how much of a new sample is taken into account for each iterative update of the weights. A larger learning rate makes the algorithm converge faster but stabilizes further from the optimal weights, while a smaller learning induces a slower convergence but a more precise set of regression coefficients.

Given a training and a validation dataset, this is how Amazon ML tunes and select the best model:

- Amazon trains several models, each with a different learning rate
- For a given a learning rate:
    - The training dataset allows the SGD to train the model by finding the best regression coefficients
    - The model is used on the validation dataset to make predictions
- By comparing the quality of the predictions of the different models on that validation set, Amazon ML is able to select the best model and the associated best learning rate
- The held-out set is used as final confirmation that the model is reliable

Usual splitting ratios for the training, validation, and held-out subsets are as follows:

- Training : *70%* validation and held-out 15% each

- Training : *60%* validation and held-out 20% each

Shuffling: It is important to make sure that the predictors and the outcome follow the same distribution in all three subsets. Shuffling the data before splitting it is an important part of creating reliable training, validation, and held-out subsets.

It is important to define the data transformations on the training dataset and apply the transformation parameters on the validation and held-out subsets so that the validation and held-out subsets do not leak information back in the training set.

Take standardization as an example: the standard deviation and the mean of the predictors should be calculated on the training dataset. And these values then applied to standardize the validation and held-out sets. If you use the whole original dataset to calculate the mean and SGD, you leak information from the held-out set into the training set.

A common Supervised Predictive Analytics workflow follows these steps - Let's assume we have an already extracted dataset and that we have chosen a metric to assess the quality of our predictions:

1. Building the dataset
    - Cleaning up and transforming the data to handle noisy data issues
    - Creating new predictors
    - Shuffling and splitting the data into a training, a validation and a held-out set

2. Selecting the best model
    - Choosing a model (linear, tree-based, bayesian , ...)
    - Repeat for several values of the meta parameters:
        - Train the model on the training set
        - Assess the model performance on the validation set

3. Repeat steps 1 and 2 with new data, new predictors, and other model parameters until you are satisfied with the performances of your model. Keep the best model.

4. Final test of the model on the held-out subset.

 In the context of Amazon ML, there is no possibility to choose a model (step 2) other than a linear regression one (logistic regression for classification).

Identifying and correcting poor performances

A performant predictive model is one that produces reliable and satisfying predictions on new data. There are two situations where the model will fail to consistently produce good predictions, and both depend on how the model is trained. A poorly trained model will result in underfitting, while an overly trained model will result in overfitting.

Underfitting

Underfitting means that the model was poorly trained. Either the training dataset did not have enough information to infer strong predictions, or the algorithm that trained the model on the training dataset was not adequate for the context. The algorithm was not well parameterized or simply inadequate for the data.

If we measure the prediction error not only on the validation set but also on the training set, the prediction error will be large if the model is underfitting. Which makes sense: if the model cannot predict the training, it won't be able to predict the outcomes in the validation set it has not seen before. Underfitting basically means your model is not working.

Common strategies to palliate this problem include:

- Getting more data samples – If the problem comes from a dataset that is too small or does not contain sufficient information, getting more data may improve the model performance.
- Adding more features, raw or via feature engineering – by taking the log, squaring, binning, using splines or power functions. Adding many features and seeing how that improves the predictions.
- Choosing another model – Support Vector Machine, Random Forest, Boosted trees, Bayes classifiers all have different strengths in different contexts.

Overfitting

Overfitting occurs when the model was so well trained that it fits the training data too perfectly and cannot handle new data.

Say you have a unique predictor of an outcome and that the data follows a quadratic pattern:

1. You fit a linear regression on that data $y = w_1x$, the predictions are weak. Your model is underfitting the data. There is a high error level on both the training error and the validation dataset.
2. You add the square of the predictor in the model $y = w_1x + w_2x^2$ and find that your model makes good predictions. The error on both the training and the validation datasets are equivalent and lower than for the simpler model.
3. If you increase the number and power of polynomial features so that the model is now $y = w_1x + w_2x^2 + \cdots + w_nx^n$, you end up fitting the training data too closely. The model has a very low prediction error on the training dataset but is unable to predict anything on new data. The prediction error on the validation dataset remains high.

This is a case of overfitting.

The following graph shows an example of an overfitting model with regard to the previous quadratic dataset, by setting a high order for the polynomial regression (*n* = *16*). The polynomial regression fits the training data so well it would be incapable of any predictions on new data whereas the quadratic model (*n* = 2) would be more robust:

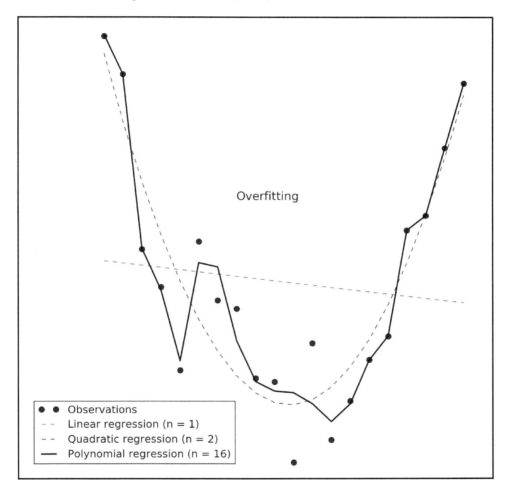

The best way to detect overfitting is, therefore, to compare the prediction errors on the training and validation sets. A significant gap between the two errors implies overfitting. A way to prevent this overfitting from happening is to add constraints on the model. In machine learning, we use regularization.

Regularization on linear models

The Stochastic Gradient Descent algorithm (SGD) finds the optimal weights $\{w_i\}$ of the model by minimizing the error between the true and the predicted values on the N training samples:

$$E(w) = \frac{1}{N} \sum_{j=1}^{N} ||y_j - \hat{y}_j||_2$$

$$E(w) = \frac{1}{N} \sum_{j=1}^{N} ||y_j - \sum_{i=1}^{n} w_i x_i||_2$$

Where $\hat{y}_j$ and y_j for $j \in [1, \cdots, N]$ are the predicted values, $\hat{y}_i$ the real values to be predicted; we have N samples, and each sample has n dimensions.

Regularization consists of adding a term to the previous equation and to minimize the regularized error:

$$E(w) = \frac{1}{N} \sum_{j=1}^{N} ||y_j - \hat{y}_j||_2 + \lambda R(w)$$

The λ parameter helps quantify the amount of regularization, while $R(w)$ is the regularization term dependent on the regression coefficients.

There are two types of weight constraints usually considered:

- L2 regularization as the sum of the squares of the coefficients:

$$R(w) = \frac{1}{2} \sum_{i=1}^{n} w_i^2$$

- L1 regularization as the sum of the absolute value of the coefficients:

$$R(w) = \sum_{i=1}^{n} |w_i|$$

The constraint on the coefficients introduced by the regularization term $R(w)$ prevents the model from overfitting the training data. The coefficients become tied together by the regularization and can no longer be tightly leashed to the predictors. Each type of regularization has its characteristic and gives rise to different variations on the SGD algorithm, which we now introduce:

L2 regularization and Ridge

L2 regularization prevents the weights $\{w_i\}$ from being too spread. The smaller weights that rise up for non-correlated though potentially meaningful, features will not become insignificant when compared to the weights associated to the important correlated features. L2 regularization will enforce similar scaling of the weights. A direct consequence of L2 regularization is to reduce the negative impact of collinearity, since the weights can no longer diverge from one another.

The Stochastic Gradient Descent algorithm with L2 regularization is known as the **Ridge algorithm**.

L1 regularization and Lasso

L1 regularization usually entails some loss of predictive power of the model.

One of the properties of L1 regularization is to force the smallest weights to 0 and thereby reduce the number of features taken into account in the model. This is a desired behavior when the number of features (n) is large compared to the number of samples (N). L1 is better suited for datasets with many features.

The Stochastic Gradient Descent algorithm with L1 regularization is known as the **Least Absolute Shrinkage and Selection Operator (Lasso)** algorithm.

In both cases the hyper-parameters of the model are as follows:

- The learning rate α of the SGD algorithm
- A parameter λ to tune the amount of regularization added to the model

A third type of regularization called **ElasticNet** consists in adding both a L2 and a L1 regularization term to the model. This brings up the best of both regularization schemas at the expense of an extra hyper-parameter.

In other contexts, although experts have different opinions (`https://www.quora.com/What-is-the-difference-between-L1-and-L2-regularization`) on which type of regularization is more effective, the consensus seems to favor L2 over L1 regularization.

L2 and L1 regularization are both available in Amazon ML while ElasticNet is not. The amount of regularization available is limited to three values for λ: mild (10^{-6}), medium (10^{-4}), and aggressive (10^{-2}).

Evaluating the performance of your model

Evaluating the predictive performance of a model requires defining a measure of the quality of its predictions. There are several available metrics both for regression and classification. The metrics used in the context of Amazon ML are the following ones:

- **RMSE for regression**: The root mean squared error is defined by the square of the difference between the true outcome values and their predictions:

$$RMSE = \frac{1}{N} \sum_{j=1}^{N} (\hat{y_j} - y_j)^2$$

- **F-1 Score and ROC-AUC for classification**: Amazon ML uses logistic regression for binary classification problems. For each prediction, logistic regression returns a value between 0 and 1. This value is interpreted as a probability of the sample belonging to one of the two classes. A probability lower than 0.5 indicates belonging to the first class, while a probability higher than 0.5 indicates a belonging to the second class. The decision is therefore highly dependent on the value of the threshold. A value which we can modify.
- Denoting one class positive and the other negative, we have four possibilities depicted in the following table:

	Predicted Yes	**Predicted No**
Real value: Yes	True Positive (TP)	False Negative (FN) (or type II error)
Real value: No	False Positive (FP)	True Negative

- This matrix is called a **confusion matrix** (`https://en.wikipedia.org/wiki/Confusion_matrix`). It defines four indicators of the performance of a classification model:

  - TP: How many Yes were correctly predicted Yes
  - FP: How many No were wrongly predicted Yes
  - FN: How many Yes were wrongly predicted No
  - TN: How many No were correctly predicted No

- From these four indicators, we can define the following metrics:

  - **Recall:** This denotes the amount of predicted positives actually positive. Recall is also called **True Positive Rate** (**TPR**) or sensitivity. It is the probability of detection:

    $$Recall = (TP / TP + FN)$$

  - **Precision** as the fraction of the real positives over all the positive predicted values:

    $$Precision = (TP / TP + FP)$$

  - **False Positive Rate** is the number of falsely predicted positives over all the true negatives. It's the probability of false alarm:

    $$FPR = FP / FP + TN$$

  - Finally, the **F1-score** is defined as the weighted average of the recall and the precision, and is given by the following:

    $$F1\text{-}score = 2\ TP / (\ 2\ TP + FP + FN)$$

  - A F1 score is always between 0 and 1, with 1 the best value and 0 the worst one.

As noted previously, these scores are all dependent on the initial threshold used to interpret the result of the logistic regression in order to decide when a prediction belongs to one class or the other. We can choose to vary that threshold. This is where the ROC-AUC comes in.

If you plot the True Positive Rate (Recall) against the False Positive Rate for different values of the decision threshold, you obtain a graph like the following, called the **Receiver Operating Characteristic** or **ROC curve**:

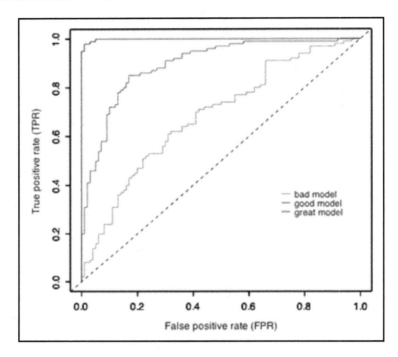

- The diagonal line indicates an equal probability of belonging to one class or another. The closer the curve is to the upper-left corner, the better your model performances are.
- The ROC curve has been widely used since WWII, when it was first invented to detect enemy planes in radar signals.
- Once you have the ROC curve, you can calculate the **Area Under the Curve** or **AUC**.
- The AUC will give you a unique score for your model taking into account all the possible values for the probability threshold from 0 to 1. The higher the AUC the better.

Summary

In this chapter, we focused on two important elements of a predictive analytics project: the data and the evaluation of the predictive power of the model. We first listed the most common problems encountered with raw data, their impact on the linear regression model, and ways to solve them. The reader should now be able to identify and deal with missing values, outliers, imbalanced datasets, and normalization.

We also introduced the two most frequent problems in predictive analytics: underfitting and overfitting. L1 and L2 regularization is an important element in the Amazon ML platform, which helps overcome overfitting and make models more robust and able to handle previously unseen data.

We are now ready to dive into the Amazon Machine Learning platform in the next chapter.

3
Overview of an Amazon Machine Learning Workflow

This chapter offers an overview of the workflow of a simple Amazon Machine Learning (Amazon ML) project, which comprises three main phases:

1. Preparing the data
2. Training and selecting the model
3. Making predictions

The reader will learn how to get started on the Amazon Machine Learning platform, how to set up an account, and how to secure it. In the second part, we go through a simple numeric prediction problem based on a classic dataset. We describe each of the three steps mentioned above, what happens, what to expect, and how to interpret the final result.

In this chapter, we will study the following:

- Opening an Amazon Web Services (AWS) account
- Setting up the account
- Overview of a standard Amazon Machine Learning workflow

Opening an Amazon Web Services Account

Signing up for an AWS account is straightforward. Go to `http://aws.amazon.com/`, and choose **Create a AWS Account**. If you don't have an AWS account yet, take advantage of the free tier access. New free-tier accounts enjoy free resources up to a certain limit for up to 12 months. These free resources are available for many AWS services, such as EC2, S3, RDS or Redshift, and so forth. Unfortunately, Amazon Machine Learning is not included in the AWS Free Tier. You will be billed for your Amazon ML usage. However, since Amazon ML requires your data to be stored on S3 or another AWS source such as RedShift, which are included in the Free Tier offer, it will still be advantageous to start with a free tier account. Follow the instructions to open a free tier account. You will be asked for your name, e-mail, address, phone number, and payment information.

If you are already an Amazon retail customer, it will be easier if you separate your AWS account from your personal retail amazon account by using a different e-mail address for your AWS account. This is especially true if you plan to recover the costs of working on Amazon ML for professional purposes. Using the same e-mail for both your personal retail account (Amazon Prime, echo, and so on) and your AWS account could become confusing.

Security

The e-mail and password you have used to open an AWS account are called your root credentials. They give you root access to every AWS service, which means unlimited access to unlimited resources. Someone obtaining your root credentials without your knowledge could rack up a heavy bill and they could carry out all types of activities through your account in your name. It is highly recommended not to use this root access in your everyday operations with AWS and to set up your account with the highest security level possible.

Fortunately, AWS offers many ways to control and compartmentalize access to your AWS account through users, groups, roles, policies, passwords, and multi-factor authentication to reduce risks of unlawful access and fraud. Configuring and managing access to your account is done via the **AWS Identity and Access Management (IAM)** service. The IAM service is free of charge.

The IAM service allows you to create and configure all the access points to the different AWS services you plan to use. Having this level of granularity is important. You can restrict access by user, by service, by role, or even enable temporary access through tokens, which are limited in time. Enabling multi-factor authentication is another strongly recommended feature you should enable in order to prevent unauthorized access to your AWS account.

In the context of this book, we will create a single user with unlimited access to only two services: Amazon ML and S3. We will extend this user's access to other AWS services as we need them in following chapters.

 We won't go through all the features offered by IAM here, but it's strongly recommended that you familiarize yourself with the IAM documentation and best practices (`http://docs.aws.amazon.com/IAM/latest/UserGuid e/best-practices.html`).

Setting up the account

When you set up your account for the first time, you are given access to your root public and secret access keys. These keys will be useful as you manage data on S3 and models in Amazon ML via the command line interface (AWS CLI). These two keys will only be available for you to view and copy at the time of creation. Once that page in your browser is closed, you can no longer access them and will need to create new ones. Creating new root keys is done by accessing **My Account | Security Credentials**. It's worth noting that no one can have access to your keys in AWS, not even the administrator of your account.

We won't go through all the possible actions you can take in IAM to configure, manage, and secure access to your account as a full presentation of IAM is beyond the scope of this book. Your access management needs and policies will depend on the size of your organization and security constraints. We assume here that you are a unique individual user of the account and that you do not need to set up password policies for other users, groups, or roles. However, we strongly recommend you familiarize yourself with IAM documentation and implement the IAM best practice (`https://aws.amazon.com/documentation/iam`).

We will create a new user whose username is `AML@Packt` and will use this access for the rest of the book. The only time when we use the root access (with the password you used to create the AWS account in the first place) is when we need to add or remove services to and from the `AML@Packt` user, for instance, when we want the user to use Amazon Athena for data processing or **Amazon Lambda** for scripting.

The IAM dashboard is available at `https://console.aws.amazon.com/iam`. It displays how many IAM assets you have created (users, roles, groups, and so on) as well as your security status as shown by this screenshot:

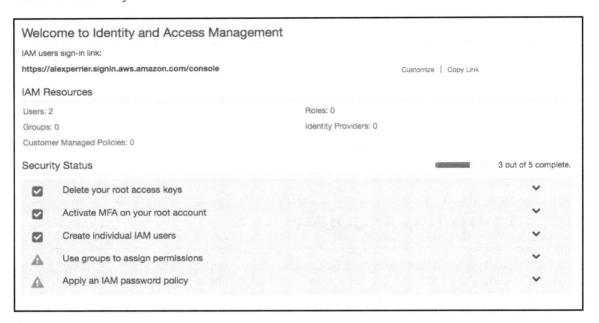

This screenshot shows that we have implemented the following three items:

- **Delete your root access keys**: These keys were given to you when you created your account. Since they provide unlimited access to your account, you should delete them and use only user-based access keys to access your account.
- **Activate Multi Factor Authentication on your root account:** After you have logged in with your login and password, Multi Factor Authentication (MFA) requires you to input a six digit code. This code can either be sent to you via text or e-mail or made available via an authenticator app installed on your mobile phone. MFA is a easy-to-implement and efficient means to secure access to your account.
- **Create individual IAM users:** By creating individual users you can restrict, manage their access level, and deactivate their account easily.

You could also create groups to assign permissions to your users and define a password policy.

Creating a user

Let's start by creating your user. Go to the IAM dashboard at `https://console.aws.amazon.com/iam/` and click on **Users** on the left sidebar. The user creation process is straightforward:

1. Click **Create New Users**.
2. Enter your user name. Keep the **Generate an access key for each user** checkbox selected.

At that point, your user is created and you can choose to view and download the user security credentials. One of these two keys, the **Secret Access Key**, will no longer be available once you move away from this page. Be sure to copy or download the two keys now. If you lose the keys, you can always recreate a pair of new keys for that user from the **IAM > Users dashboard**. This screenshot is an example of the two user keys for the `AML@Packt` user we just created. Your keys will obviously be different than these ones:

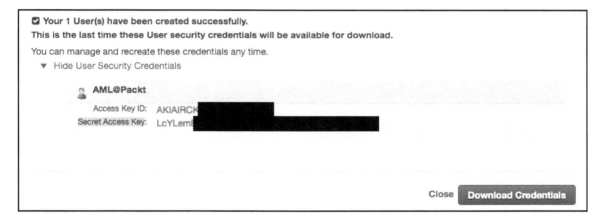

And that's it! Your AML@Packt user has been created. You can use AML@Packt's access keys to access and manage AWS services via APIs and the command line. At this point, the AML@Packt user has unlimited access to all AWS services. In order to restrict the access scope of that user, you will need to attach policies to the user.

Defining policies

Policies declare what services a user or a group can access and the level of access (read-only, full access, and so forth). You can define global policies that take care of several services at the same time and attach them to groups of users, or you can attach specific mono-service policies to your user. This is what we'll do now.

Once you have created your user and downloaded its credentials, you end up on the IAM user dashboard with a list of all your created users. Select the AML@Packt user and the permissions tab. Check all the services you know that the user will need to access. In our case, we select two services each with full access, which will be sufficient to explore the Amazon Machine Learning service:

- Amazon Machine Learning Full Access
- Amazon S3 Full Access

We will add other policies to these users to enable other services (Athena, RedShift, RDS, and so on) as needed later on.

Creating login credentials

Last but not least if we want to use the `AML@Packt` user to log in to the AWS console, we must create login credentials for that user. As shown in the next screenshot, the **Security Credentials** tab is where you manage the user access keys, sign in credentials, and SSH keys:

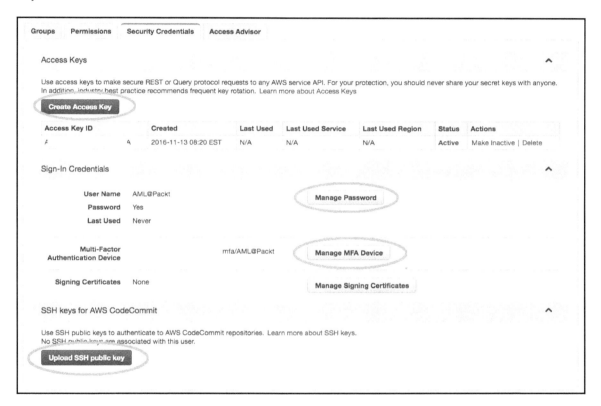

 SSH keys are not the same as access keys. SSH keys will let you SSH into certain assets, such as *EC2* servers. Many services machine learning included have no use for SSH keys. Access keys, on the other hand, are used to programmatically manage AWS services. Access keys are necessary for setting the credentials needed to use the command line interface (AWS CLI).

Click on **Manage Password** and set a password for the user. This is what the permission for user `AML@Packt` looks like:

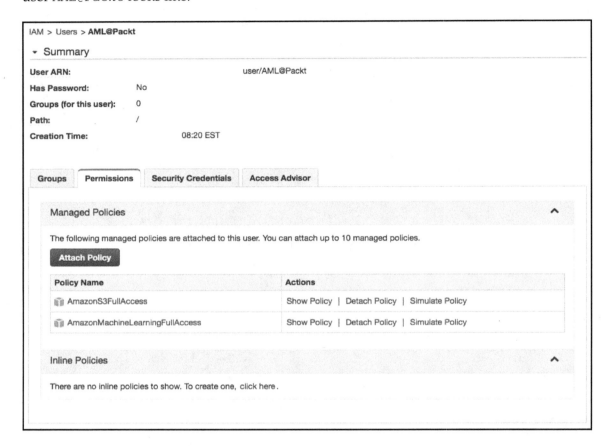

At this point, our IAM dashboard looks like this:

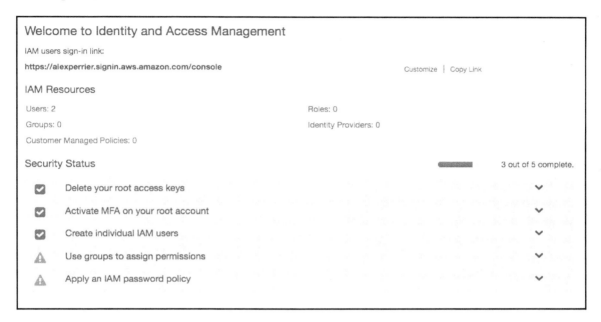

This previous screenshot shows the following:

- We have deleted the root access keys. We can no longer programmatically access all AWS services in an unlimited fashion via the command line or APIs. We can still log in as root to the AWS console to create and manage access for people, but these will depend on the policies and access level we provide them with.
- We have activated **Multi Factor Authentication (MFA)**, a simple and very efficient way to secure access to AWS Services from your root access credentials.
- We have created the AML@Packt user, which we will use to log in to AWS and when using the APIs or the command line.

We have not created groups or password policies that would further constrain the root access as we intend to only access Amazon ML through the AML@Packt user.

Here is a summary of the different ways you can access and use AWS services:

- Log in on the AWS Console with your root password and login using **Multi Factor Authentication (MFA)**.
- Log in with the `AML@Packt` user with that user's login and password using MFA. The `AML@Packt` user can only use S3 and Amazon ML services. This is quite restrictive, but just the right amount of access for that user, nothing more.
- Programmatically access S3 and Amazon ML via the S3 and Amazon ML access keys using the command line interface or AWS SDKs.

We had started with one user, the root user able to access everything AWS can offer programmatically and via the console. The new setup is much more secure and worth the time it took to set it up. Our newly gained understanding of IAM roles and policies will also be helpful later on when we start using different AWS services in tandem as the services will need to have appropriate access to one another.

Before we dive into the presentation of a standard Amazon ML workflow, we need a brief word on regions.

Choosing a region

AWS currently operates data centers in 14 regions across the globe. More regions are being frequently opened across the globe (`https://aws.amazon.com/about-aws/global-infrastructure/`). Most AWS services require you to choose a region of operation. The rule of thumb is to choose the region that is closest to you or the end-users accessing your resources.

Choosing a region may depend on other factors, which may vary across regions, including:

- Latency
- Pricing
- Security and compliance rules
- Availability of the service
- SLA–Service Level Agreements
- Use of renewable energy. At the time of writing, AWS offers two carbon neutral regions (`https://aws.amazon.com/about-aws/sustainability/`) and is actively creating others .

Amazon ML is only available in Northern Virginia and Ireland. You can check the following page for AWS availability per region: `https://aws.amazon.com/about-aws/glo bal-infrastructure/regional-product-services/`.

 GovCloud: From the AWS documentation: The AWS GovCloud (US) is an isolated AWS region designed to host sensitive data and regulated workloads in the cloud, helping customers support their US government compliance requirements. IAM is region free, with the following exception: IAM is available in the US East (N. Virginia) region and in the GovCloud region. Users and roles created in the US East region can be used in all other regions except the GovCloud region. And GovCloud IAM users cannot be used outside of the GovCloud region.

Overview of a standard Amazon Machine Learning workflow

The Amazon Machine Learning service is available at `https://console.aws.amazon.com /machinelearning/`. The Amazon ML workflow closely follows a standard Data Science workflow with steps:

1. Extract the data and clean it up. Make it available to the algorithm.
2. Split the data into a training and validation set, typically a 70/30 split with equal distribution of the predictors in each part.
3. Select the best model by training several models on the training dataset and comparing their performances on the validation dataset.
4. Use the best model for predictions on new data.

As shown in the following Amazon ML menu, the service is built around four objects:

- **Datasource**
- **ML model**
- **Evaluation**
- **Prediction**

The Datasource and Model can also be configured and set up in the same flow by creating a new **Datasource and ML model**. Let us take a closer look at each one of these steps.

The dataset

For the rest of the chapter, we will use the simple `Predicting Weight by Height and Age` dataset (from *Lewis Taylor (1967)*) with 237 samples of children's age, weight, height, and gender, which is available at `https://v8doc.sas.com/sashtml/stat/chap55/sect51.htm`.

This dataset is composed of 237 rows. Each row has the following predictors: sex (F, M), age (in *months*), height (in *inches*), and we are trying to predict the weight (in *lbs*) of these children. There are no missing values and no outliers. The variables are close enough in range and normalization is not required. In short, we do not need to carry out any preprocessing or cleaning on the original dataset. Age, height, and weight are numerical variables (real-valued), and sex is a categorical variable.

We will randomly select 20% of the rows as the held-out subset to use for prediction on previously unseen data and keep the other 80% as training and evaluation data. This data split can be done in Excel or any other spreadsheet editor:

- By creating a new column with randomly generated numbers
- Sorting the spreadsheet by that column
- Selecting 190 rows for training and 47 rows for prediction (roughly a 80/20 split)

Let us name the training set `LT67_training.csv` and the held-out set that we will use for prediction `LT67_heldout.csv`, where *LT67* stands for *Lewis and Taylor,* the creator of this dataset in 1967.

As with all datasets, scripts, and resources mentioned in this book, the training and holdout files are available in the GitHub repository at `https://github.com/alexperrier/packt-aml`.

Note that it is important for the distribution in age, sex, height, and weight to be similar in both subsets. We want the data on which we will make predictions to show patterns that are similar to the data on which we will train and optimize our model.

In the rest of this section, we will do the following:

1. Load the data on S3.
2. Let Amazon ML infer the schema and transform the data.
3. Create a model.
4. Evaluate the model's performance.
5. Make a prediction on the held-out dataset.

Loading the data on S3

Follow these stepsto load the training and held-out datasets on S3:

1. Go to your s3 console at `https://console.aws.amazon.com/s3`.
2. Create a bucket if you haven't done so already. Buckets are basically folders that are uniquely named across all S3. We created a bucket named `aml.packt`. Since that name has now been taken, you will have to choose another bucket name if you are following along with this demonstration.

3. Click on the bucket name you created and upload both the `LT67_training.csv` and `LT67_heldout.csv` files by selecting **Upload** from the **Actions** drop-down menu:

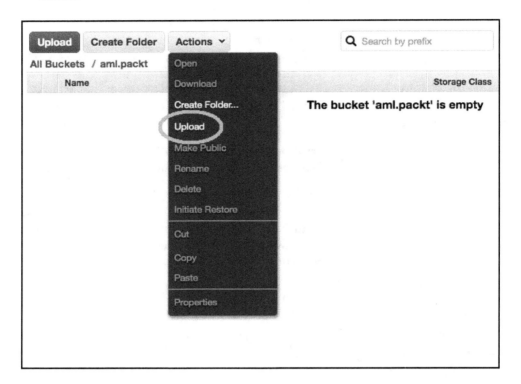

Both files are small, only a few KB, and hosting costs should remain negligible for that exercise.

Note that for each file, by selecting the **Properties** tab on the right, you can specify how your files are accessed, what user, role, group or AWS service may download, read, write, and delete the files, and whether or not they should be accessible from the Open Web. When creating the datasource in Amazon ML, you will be prompted to grant Amazon ML access to your input data. You can specify the access rules to these files now in S3 or simply grant access later on.

Our data is now in the cloud in an S3 bucket. We need to tell Amazon ML where to find that input data by creating a datasource. We will first create the datasource for the training file `ST67_training.csv`.

Declaring a datasource

Go to the Amazon ML dashboard, and click on **Create new... | Datasource and ML model**. We will use the faster flow available by default:

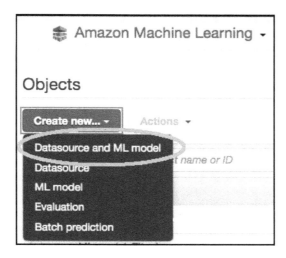

As shown in the following screenshot, you are asked to specify the path to the `LT67_training.csv` file `{S3://bucket}{path}{file}`. Note that the S3 location field automatically populates with the bucket names and file names that are available to your user:

Specifying a **Datasource name** is useful to organize your Amazon ML assets. By clicking on **Verify**, Amazon ML will make sure that it has the proper rights to access the file. In case it needs to be granted access to the file, you will be prompted to do so as shown in the following screenshot:

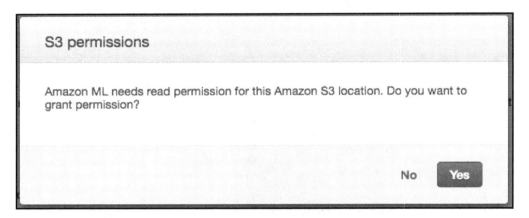

Just click on **Yes** to grant access. At this point, Amazon ML will validate the datasource and analyze its contents.

Creating the datasource

An Amazon ML datasource is composed of the following:

- The location of the data file: The data file is not duplicated or cloned in Amazon ML but accessed from S3
- The schema that contains information on the type of the variables contained in the CSV file:
  - Categorical
  - Text
  - Numeric (real-valued)
  - Binary

As we will see in Chapter 4, *Loading and Preparing the Dataset*, it is possible to supply Amazon ML with your own schema or modify the one created by Amazon ML.

At this point, Amazon ML has a pretty good idea of the type of data in your training dataset. It has identified the different types of variables and knows how many rows it has:

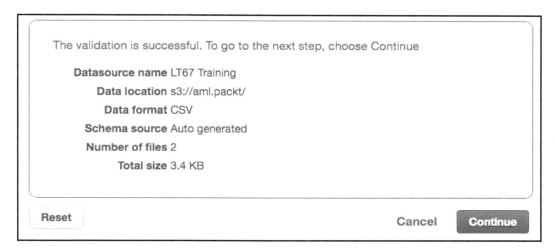

Move on to the next step by clicking on **Continue**, and see what schema Amazon ML has inferred from the dataset as shown in the next screenshot:

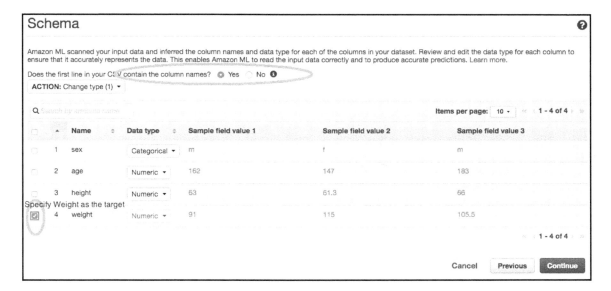

Amazon ML needs to know at that point which is the variable you are trying to predict. Be sure to tell Amazon ML the following:

- The first line in the CSV file contains te column name
- The target is the `weight`

We see here that Amazon ML has correctly inferred the following:

- `sex` is **categorical**
- `age`, `height`, and `weight` are **numeric** (continuous real values)

Since we chose a numeric variable as the target Amazon ML, will use Linear Regression as the predictive model. For binary or categorical values, we would have used Logistic Regression. This means that Amazon ML will try to find the best *a*, *b*, and *c* coefficients so that the weight predicted by the following equation is as close as possible to the observed real weight present in the data:

$$predicted\ weight = a * age + b * height + c * sex$$

Amazon ML will then ask you if your data contains a row identifier. In our present case, it does not. Row identifiers are useful when you want to understand the prediction obtained for each row or add an extra column to your dataset later on in your project. Row identifiers are for reference purposes only and are not used by the service to build the model.

You will be asked to review the datasource. You can go back to each one of the previous steps and edit the parameters for the schema, the target and the input data. Now that the data is known to Amazon ML, the next step is to set up the parameters of the algorithm that will train the model.

The model

We select the default parameters for the training and evaluation settings. Amazon ML will do the following:

- Create a recipe for data transformation based on the statistical properties it has inferred from the dataset
- Split the dataset (`ST67_training.csv`) into a training part and a validation part, with a 70/30 split. The split strategy assumes the data has already been shuffled and can be split sequentially.

In Chapter 4, *Loading and Preparing the Dataset*, we will take the longer road and work directly on the recipes, the schemas, and the validation split. On the next page, you are asked to review the model you just created.

The recipe will be used to transform the data in a similar way for the training and the validation datasets. The only transformation suggested by Amazon ML is to transform the categorical variable sex into a binary variable, where m = 0 and f = 1 for instance. No other transformation is needed.

The default advanced settings for the model are shown in the following screenshot:

```
Advanced settings

            Maximum ML model Size    100MB
        Maximum number of data p...  10
        Shuffle type for training data  Auto
                Regularization type  L2
              Regularization amount  1e-6 - Mild
```

We see that Amazon ML will pass over the data 10 times, shuffle splitting the data each time. It will use an **L2** regularization strategy based on the sum of the square of the coefficients of the regression to prevent overfitting. We will evaluate the predictive power of the model using our LT67_heldout.csv dataset later on.

Regularization comes in 3 levels with a *mild* (10^{-6}), *medium* (10^{-4}), or *aggressive* (10^{-02}) setting, each value stronger than the previous one. The default setting is mild, the lowest, with a regularization constant of *0.00001* (10^{-6}) implying that Amazon ML does not anticipate much overfitting on this dataset. This makes sense when the number of predictors, three in our case, is much smaller than the number of samples (190 for the training set).

Clicking on the **Create ML model** button will launch the model creation. This takes a few minutes to resolve, depending on the size and complexity of your dataset. You can check its status by refreshing the model page. In the meantime, the model status remains pending.

At that point, Amazon ML will split our training dataset into two subsets: a training and a validation set. It will use the training portion of the data to train several settings of the algorithm and select the best one based on its performance on the training data. It will then apply the associated model to the validation set and return an evaluation score for that model. By default, Amazon ML will sequentially take the first 70% of the samples for training and the remaining 30% for validation.

It's worth noting that Amazon ML will not create two extra files and store them on S3, but instead create two new datasources out of the initial datasource we have previously defined. Each new datasource is obtained from the original one via a `Data rearrangement` JSON recipe such as the following:

```
{
  "splitting": {
    "percentBegin": 0,
    "percentEnd": 70
  }
}
```

You can see these two new datasources in the Datasource dashboard. Three datasources are now available where there was initially only one, as shown by the following screenshot:

Validation	LT67 Training_[percentBegin=70, percentEnd=100, strateg...	Datasource	ds-Xvst5TheIjZ	Completed	Nov 13, 2016 1:53:15 PM	4 mins.
Training	LT67 Training_[percentBegin=0, percentEnd=70, strategy=...	Datasource	ds-qsQDRuCbMxn	Completed	Nov 13, 2016 1:53:15 PM	4 mins.
Original	LT67 Training	Datasource	ds-nySfodn55Qm	Completed	Nov 13, 2016 1:32:34 PM	4 mins.

While the model is being trained, Amazon ML runs the Stochastic Gradient algorithm several times on the training data with different parameters:

- Varying the learning rate in increments of powers of 10: 0.01, 0.1, 1, 10, and 100.
- Making several passes over the training data while shuffling the samples before each path.
- At each pass, calculating the prediction error, the **Root Mean Squared Error (RMSE)**, to estimate how much of an improvement over the last pass was obtained. If the decrease in RMSE is not really significant, the algorithm is considered to have converged, and no further pass shall be made.
- At the end of the passes, the setting that ends up with the lowest RMSE wins, and the associated model (the weights of the regression) is selected as the best version.

Once the model has finished training, Amazon ML evaluates its performance on the validation datasource. Once the evaluation itself is also ready, you have access to the model's evaluation.

The evaluation of the model

Amazon ML uses the standard metric RMSE for linear regression. RMSE is defined as the sum of the squares of the difference between the real values and the predicted values:

$$RMSE = \sqrt{\frac{1}{N} \sum_{i=1}^{N} (\hat{y} - y)^2}$$

Here, $\hat{y}$ is the predicted values, and y the real values we want to predict (the weight of the children in our case). The closer the predictions are to the real values, the lower the RMSE is. A lower RMSE means a better, more accurate prediction.

Comparing with a baseline

The RMSE is a relative quantity and not an absolute one. An RMSE of 100 may be good for a certain context, while a RMSE of 10 may be a sign of poor predictions in another context. It is, therefore, important to have a baseline that we can compare our model to. Each Amazon ML evaluation provides a baseline, which is calculated differently depending on the nature of the problem (regression, binary or multiclass classification). The baseline is the score we would obtain using the most simple and obvious model:

- The baseline for regression is given by a model that always predicts the mean of the target
- The baseline for binary classification is an AUC of *0.5*, which is the score for a model that randomly assigns 0 or 1
- The baseline for a multiclass classification problem is the macro average *F1* score for a model that would always predict the most common class

In our current case, when predicting the weight of students from the height, age, and sex, our training dataset has a baseline RMSE of *18.71*, while our model gives an RMSE of *14.44*. Our model does 22.8% better than simply predicting the average of the weights of all the students.

Another thing to look at in the evaluation is the distribution of the residuals, which are defined as the difference between $\hat{y}$ and y:

$$Residuals = \hat{y} - y$$

As we've seen in Chapter 1, *Introduction to Machine Learning and Predictive Analytics*, one of the conditions for a linear regression to be considered valid is that the residuals are independent, identically distributed, and their distribution follows a **Gaussian distribution** or **Bell-shaped curve**. Amazon ML shows a histogram of the residuals that can help us visually assess the Gaussian nature of the residuals distribution.

When the shape bends to the right (left), this means that more predictions are greater (lower) than their targets. In both cases, the conclusion is that there is still some signal in the data that has not been captured by the model. When the distribution of residuals is centered on 0, the linear regression is considered valid. The following diagram shows the distributions of residuals for our current regression model:

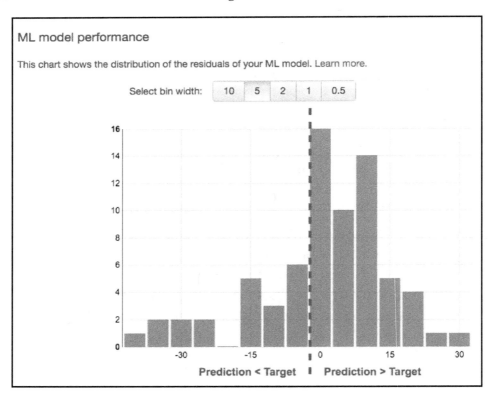

We can see that our predictions are often larger than the targets, which indicates that our model could still be improved. There is information in the data that has not been exploited by that model.

Note that it may not be possible to extract the information in these patterns with a linear regression model. Other more complex models may be more adapted to this particular dataset. Transforming the data to create new variables may also be the key to a better model. The histogram of residuals is a good, simple diagnostic with regard to the quality of our model as it shows us that it could be improved in some way.

Making batch predictions

We now have a model that has been properly trained and selected among other models. We can use it to make predictions on new data.

Remember that, at the beginning of this chapter, under the section *Loading the Data on S3*, we uploaded two datasets to S3, the training dataset and the held-out dataset. We've used the training dataset to create the best model possible. We will now apply that model on the held-out dataset.

A batch prediction consists in applying a model to a datasource in order to make predictions on that datasource. We need to tell Amazon ML which model we want to apply on which data.

Batch predictions are different from streaming predictions. With batch predictions, all the data is already made available as a datasource, while for streaming predictions, the data will be fed to the model as it becomes available. The dataset is not available beforehand in its entirety.

In the Main Menu select **Batch Predictions** to access the dashboard predictions and click on **Create a New** Prediction:

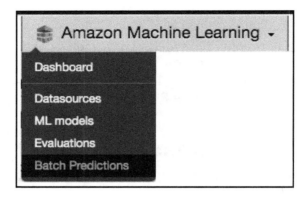

The first step is to select one of the models available in your model dashboard. You should choose the one that has the lowest RMSE:

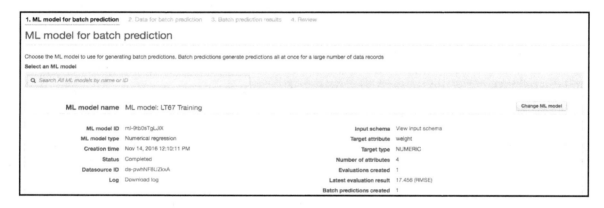

The next step is to associate a datasource to the model you just selected. We had uploaded the held-out dataset to S3 at the beginning of this chapter (under the *Loading the data on S3* section) but had not used it to create a datasource. We will do so now.

When asked for a datasource in the next screen, make sure to check **My data is in S3, and I need to create a datasource,** and then select the held-out dataset that should already be present in your S3 bucket:

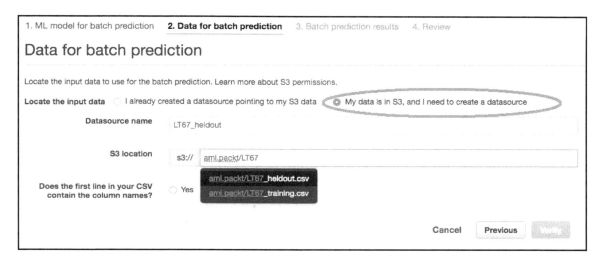

Don't forget to tell Amazon ML that the first line of the file contains columns.

 In our current project, our held-out dataset also contains the true values for the weight of the students. This would not be the case for "real" data in a real-world project where the real values are truly unknown. However, in our case, this will allow us to calculate the RMSE score of our predictions and assess the quality of these predictions.

The final step is to click on the **Verify** button and wait for a few minutes:

- Amazon ML will run the model on the new datasource and will generate predictions in the form of a CSV file.
- Contrary to the evaluation and model-building phase, we now have real predictions. We are also no longer given a score associated with these predictions.
- After a few minutes, you will notice a new batch-prediction folder in your S3 bucket. This folder contains a `manifest` file and a results folder. The manifest file is a JSON file with the path to the initial datasource and the path to the results file. The results folder contains a gzipped CSV file:

Uncompressed, the CSV file contains two columns, `trueLabel`, the initial target from the held-out set, and `score`, which corresponds to the predicted values. We can easily calculate the RMSE for those results directly in the spreadsheet through the following steps:

1. Creating a new column that holds the square of the difference of the two columns.
2. Summing all the rows.
3. Taking the square root of the result.

The following illustration shows how we create a third column C, as the squared difference between the `trueLabel` column A and the **score** (or predicted value) column B:

C2		f_x Σ =	=(B2-A2)^2
	A	B	C
1	trueLabel	score	square difference
2	95	95.2	0.023
3	91	109.1	326.941
4	115	109.0	35.808
5	105.5	122.8	299.633
6	94.5	88.4	36.615
7	171.5	137.7	1143.326
8	112	104.9	50.768

As shown in the following screenshot, averaging column C and taking the square root gives an RMSE of 11.96, which is even significantly better than the RMSE we obtained during the evaluation phase (*RMSE 14.4*):

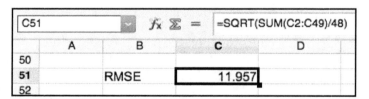

C51		f_x Σ =	=SQRT(SUM(C2:C49)/48)
	A	B	C	D
50				
51		RMSE	11.957	
52				

The fact that the RMSE on the held-out set is better than the RMSE on the validation set means that our model did not overfit the training data, since it performed even better on new data than expected. Our model is robust.

The left side of the following graph shows the True (*Triangle*) and Predicted (*Circle*) `Weight` values for all the samples in the held-out set. The right side shows the histogram of the residuals. Similar to the histogram of residuals we had observed on the validation set, we observe that the residuals are not centered on *0*. Our model has a tendency to overestimate the weight of the students:

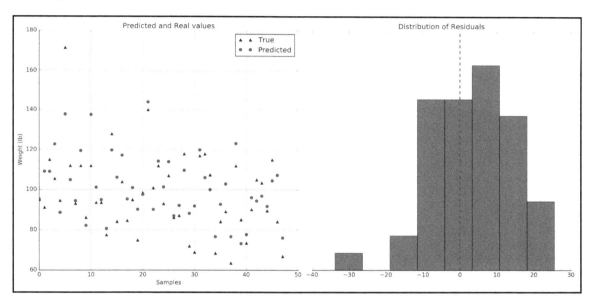

Summary

In the first part of this chapter, we went through the Amazon account creation and how to properly set up and secure access to your AWS account. Using a combination of Multi Factor Authentication and User creation, we were able to quickly reach a satisfactory level of safety. AWS is a powerful platform with powerful tools and it's important to implement the best access protection possible.

In the second part, we went through the different steps involved in a simple linear regression prediction, from loading the data into S3, making that data accessible to Amazon ML via datasources, creating models, interpreting evaluations, and making predictions on new data.

The Amazon ML flow is smooth and facilitates the inherent data science loop: data, model, evaluation, and prediction.

In the following chapter, we will dive further into data preparation and data transformation. This time we will use a classic binary classification problem, namely, *survival on the Titanic,* which is based on a very interesting dataset.

4

Loading and Preparing the Dataset

Data preparation involves data cleaning and feature engineering. It is the most time-consuming part of a machine learning project. Amazon ML offers powerful features to transform and slice the data. In this chapter, we will create the datasources that Amazon ML requires to train and select models. Creating a datasource involves three steps:

1. Making the dataset available on AWS S3.
2. Informing Amazon ML about the nature of the data using the *schema*.
3. Transforming the initial dataset with recipes for feature engineering.

In a second part, we will extend Amazon ML data modification capabilities in order to carry out powerful feature engineering and data cleansing by using Amazon SQL service Athena. Athena is a serverless SQL-based query service perfectly suited for data munging in a predictive analytics context.

Working with datasets

You cannot do predictive analytics without a dataset. Although we are surrounded by data, finding datasets that are adapted to predictive analytics is not always straightforward. In this section, we present some resources that are freely available. We then focus on the dataset we are going to work with for several chapters. The `Titanic` dataset is a classic introductory datasets for predictive analytics.

Finding open datasets

There is a multitude of dataset repositories available online, from local to global public institutions, from non-profit organizations to data-focused start-ups. Here's a small list of open dataset resources that are well suited for predictive analytics. This, by far, is not an exhaustive list:

 This thread on Quora points to many other interesting data sources: `https://www.quora.com/Where-can-I-find-large-datasets-open-to-the-public`. You can also ask for specific datasets on Reddit at `https://www.reddit.com/r/datasets/`.

- **UCI Machine Learning Repository** is a collection of datasets maintained by *UC Irvine* since 1987, hosting over 300 datasets related to classification, clustering, regression, and other ML tasks, `https://archive.ics.uci.edu/ml/`
- **The Stanford Large Network Dataset Collection** at `https://snap.stanford.edu/data/index.html` and other major universities also offer great collections of open datasets
- **Kdnuggets** has an extensive list of open datasets at `http://www.kdnuggets.com/datasets`
- `Data.gov` and other US government agencies; `data.UN.org` and other UN agencies
- **Open data websites** from governments across the world: CA: `http://open.canada.ca/`, FR: `http://www.data.gouv.fr/fr/`, JA: `http://www.data.go.jp/`, IN: `https://data.gov.in/`
- AWS offers open datasets via partners at `https://aws.amazon.com/government-education/open-data/`

The following startups are data centered and give open access to rich data repositories:

- **Quandl** and **Quantopian** for financial datasets
- `Datahub.io`, `Enigma.com`, and `Data.world` are dataset-sharing sites
- `Datamarket.com` is great for time series datasets
- `Kaggle.com`, the data science competition website, hosts over a 100 very interesting datasets

AWS public datasets: AWS hosts a variety of public datasets, such as the Million Song Dataset, the mapping of the **Human Genome**, the US Census data as well as many others in Astrology, Biology, Math, Economics, and so on. These datasets are mostly available using EBS snapshots although some are directly accessible on S3. The datasets are large, from a few gigabytes to several terabytes, and they are not meant to be downloaded on your local machine, they are only to be accessible via an EC2 instance (take a look at `http://docs.aws.amazon.com/AWSEC2/latest/UserGuide /using-public-data-sets.html` for further details). AWS public datasets are accessible at `https://aws.amazon.com/public-datasets/`.

Introducing the Titanic dataset

Throughout this present chapter and in `Chapter 5`, *Model Creation* and `Chapter 6`, *Predictions and Performances*, we will use the classic `Titanic` dataset. The data consists of demographic and traveling information for 1309 of the Titanic passengers, and the goal is to predict the survival of these passengers. The full Titanic dataset is available from the *Department of Biostatistics* at the *Vanderbilt University School of Medicine* (`http://biostat.mc .vanderbilt.edu/wiki/pub/Main/DataSets/titanic3.csv`) in several formats. The *Encyclopedia Titanica* website (`https://www.encyclopedia-titanica.org/`) is the website of reference regarding the Titanic. It contains all the facts, history, and data surrounding the Titanic, including a full list of passengers and crew members. The Titanic dataset is also the subject of the introductory competition on Kaggle (`https://www.kaggle.com/c/titanic`, requires opening an account with Kaggle). You can also find a CSV version in this book's GitHub repository at `https://github.com/alexperrier/packt-aml/blob/master/ch4`.

The Titanic data contains a mix of textual, Boolean, continuous, and categorical variables. It exhibits interesting characteristics such as missing values, outliers, and text variables ripe for text mining, a rich dataset that will allow us to demonstrate data transformations. Here's a brief summary of the 14 attributes:

- `pclass`: Passenger class (1 = 1st; 2 = 2nd; 3 = 3rd)
- `survival`: A Boolean indicating whether the passenger survived or not (0 = No; 1 = Yes); this is our target
- `name`: A field rich in information as it contains title and family names
- `sex`: Male/female
- `age`: Age, a significant portion of values are missing

- `sibsp`: Number of siblings/spouses aboard
- `parch`: Number of parents/children aboard
- `ticket`: Ticket number.
- `fare`: Passenger fare (British Pound).
- `cabin`: Cabin. Does the location of the cabin influence chances of survival?
- `embarked`: Port of embarkation (C = Cherbourg; Q = Queenstown; S = Southampton)
- `boat`: Lifeboat, many missing values
- `body`: Body Identification Number
- `home.dest`: Home/destination

Take a look at `http://campus.lakeforest.edu/frank/FILES/MLFfiles/Bio150/Titanic/TitanicMETA.pdf` for more details on these variables.

We have 1309 records and 14 attributes, three of which we will discard. The `home.dest` attribute has too few existing values, the `boat` attribute is only present for passengers who have survived, and the `body` attribute is only for passengers who have not survived. We will discard these three columns later on while using the data schema.

Preparing the data

Now that we have the initial raw dataset, we are going to shuffle it, split it into a training and a held-out subset, and load it to an S3 bucket.

Splitting the data

As we saw in `Chapter 2`, *Machine Learning Definitions and Concepts*, in order to build and select the best model, we need to split the dataset into three parts: training, validation, and test, with the usual ratios being 60%, 20%, and 20%. The training and validation sets are used to build several models and select the best one while the held-out set is used for the final performance evaluation on previously unseen data. We will use the held-out subset in `Chapter 6`, *Predictions and Performances* to simulate batch predictions with the model we build in `Chapter 5`, *Model Creation*.

Since Amazon ML does the job of splitting the dataset used for model training and model evaluation into training and validation subsets, we only need to split our initial dataset into two parts: the global training/evaluation subset (80%) for model building and selection, and the held-out subset (20%) for predictions and final model performance evaluation.

Shuffle before you split: If you download the original data from the Vanderbilt University website, you will notice that it is ordered by `pclass`, the class of the passenger, and by alphabetical order of the `name` column. The first 323 rows correspond to the first class followed by second (277) and third (709) class passengers. It is important to shuffle the data before you split it so that all the different variables have have similar distributions in each training and held-out subsets. You can shuffle the data directly in the spreadsheet by creating a new column, generating a random number for each row, and then ordering by that column.

You will find an already shuffled `titanic.csv` file for this book at `https://github.com/a lexperrier/packt-aml/blob/master/ch4/titanic.csv`. In addition to shuffling the data, we have removed punctuation in the name column: commas, quotes, and parenthesis, which can add confusion when parsing a CSV file.

We end up with two files: `titanic_train.csv` with 1047 rows and `titanic_heldout.csv` with 263 rows. The next step is to upload these files on S3 so that Amazon ML can access them.

Loading data on S3

AWS S3 is one of the main AWS services dedicated to hosting files and managing their access. Files in S3 can be public and open to the Internet or have access restricted to specific users, roles, or services. S3 is also used extensively by AWS for operations such as storing log files or results (predictions, scripts, queries, and so on).

Files in S3 are organized around the notion of buckets. Buckets are placeholders with unique names similar to domain names for websites. A file in S3 will have a unique locator URI: `s3://bucket_name/{path_of_folders}/filename`. The bucket name is unique across S3. In this section, we will create a bucket for our data, upload the titanic training file, and open its access to Amazon ML.

We will show in `Chapter 7`, *Command Line and SDK* and the files in S3 can be entirely managed via the command line. For now, we will use the S3 online interface. Go to `https ://console.aws.amazon.com/s3/home`, and open an S3 account if you don't have one yet.

 S3 pricing: S3 charges for the total volume of files you host and the volume of file transfers depends on the region where the files are hosted. At the time of writing, for less than 1TB, AWS S3 charges $0.03/GB per month in the US east region. All S3 prices are available at `https://aws.am azon.com/s3/pricing/` also `http://calculator.s3.amazonaws.com/in dex.html` for the AWS cost calculator.

Creating a bucket

Once you have created your S3 account, the next step is to create a bucket for your files. Click on the **Create bucket** button:

1. **Name and a region**: Since bucket names are unique across S3, you must choose a name for your bucket that has not been already taken. We chose the name `aml.packt` for our bucket, and we will use this bucket throughout book. Regarding the region, you should always select a region that is the closest to the person or application accessing the files in order to reduce latency and prices.
2. **Set Versioning, Logging, and Tags**: Versioning will keep a copy of every version of your files, which prevents accidental deletions. Since versioning and logging induce extra costs, we chose to disable them.
3. **Set permissions.**
4. **Review and save.**

These steps are illustrated by the following screenshots:

Loading the data

To upload the data, simply click on the upload button and select the `titanic_train.csv` file that we created earlier on. You should, at this point, have the training dataset uploaded to your AWS S3 bucket. We added a `/data` folder in our `aml.packt` bucket to compartmentalize our objects. It will be useful later on when the bucket will also contain folders created by Amazon ML.

At this point, only the owner of the bucket (that is you) is able to access and modify its contents. We need to grant the Amazon ML service permissions to read the data and add other files to the bucket. When creating the Amazon ML datasource, we will be prompted to grant these permissions via the Amazon ML console. We can also modify the bucket's policy upfront.

Granting permissions

We need to edit the policy of the `aml.packt` bucket. To do so, we have to perform the following steps:

1. Click on your bucket.
2. Select the **Permissions** tab.

3. In the dropdown, select `Bucket Policy` as shown in the following screenshot. This will open an editor:

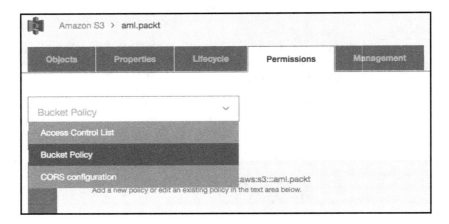

4. Paste in the following JSON file. Make sure to replace `{YOUR_BUCKET_NAME}` with the name of your bucket and save:

```
{
  "Version": "2012-10-17",
  "Statement": [
    {
      "Sid": "AmazonML_s3:ListBucket",
      "Effect": "Allow",
      "Principal": {
        "Service": "machinelearning.amazonaws.com"
      },
      "Action": "s3:ListBucket",
      "Resource": "arn:aws:s3:::{YOUR_BUCKET_NAME}",
      "Condition": {
        "StringLike": {
          "s3:prefix": "*"
        }
      }
    },
    {
      "Sid": "AmazonML_s3:GetObject",
      "Effect": "Allow",
      "Principal": {
        "Service": "machinelearning.amazonaws.com"
      },
      "Action": "s3:GetObject",
      "Resource": "arn:aws:s3:::{YOUR_BUCKET_NAME}/*"
```

```
      },
      {
        "Sid": "AmazonML_s3:PutObject",
        "Effect": "Allow",
        "Principal": {
          "Service": "machinelearning.amazonaws.com"
        },
        "Action": "s3:PutObject",
        "Resource": "arn:aws:s3:::{YOUR_BUCKET_NAME}/*"
      }
    ]
  }
```

Further details on this policy are available at `http://docs.aws.amazon.com/machine-learning/latest/dg/granting-amazon-ml-permissions-to-read-your-data-from-amazon-s3.html`. Once again, this step is optional since Amazon ML will prompt you for access to the bucket when you create the datasource.

Formatting the data

Amazon ML works on comma separated values files (`.csv`), a very simple format where each row is an observation and each column is a variable or attribute. There are, however, a few conditions that should be met:

- The data must be encoded in plain text using a character set, such as ASCII, Unicode, or EBCDIC
- All values must be separated by commas; if a value contains a comma, it should be enclosed by double quotes
- Each observation (row) must be smaller than 100k

There are also conditions regarding end of line characters that separate rows. Special care must be taken when using Excel on *OS X (Mac)*, as explained on this page: `http://docs.aws.amazon.com/machine-learning/latest/dg/understanding-the-data-format-for-amazon-ml.html`.

What about other data file formats?

Unfortunately, Amazon ML datasources are only compatible with CSV files and Redshift or RDS databases and they do not accept formats such as JSON, TSV, or XML. However, other services such as Athena, a serverless database service, do accept a wider range of formats. We will see later in this chapter how to circumvent the Amazon ML file format restrictions using Athena.

Now that the data is on S3, the next step is to tell Amazon ML its location by creating a datasource.

Creating the datasource

When working with Amazon ML, the data always resides in S3 and it is not duplicated in Amazon ML. A datasource is the metadata that indicates the location of the input data allowing Amazon ML to access it. Creating a datasource also generates descriptive statistics related to the data and a schema with information on the nature of the variables. Basically, the datasource gives Amazon ML all the information it requires to be able to train a model. The following are the steps you need to follow to create a datasource:

1. Go to Amazon Machine Learning: `https://console.aws.amazon.com/machinel earning/home`.
2. Click on getting started, you will be given a choice between accessing the **Dashboard** and **Standard setup**. This time choose the standard setup:

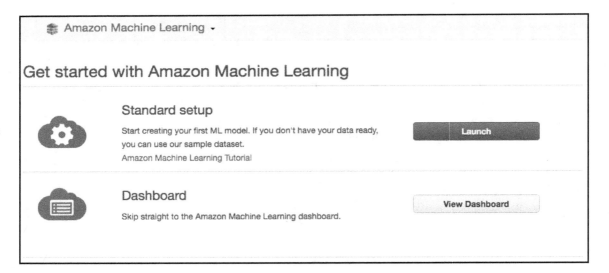

Perform the following steps, as shown in the following screenshot:

1. Choose an **S3** location.
2. Start typing the name of the bucket in the **s3 location** field, and the list folders and files should show up.
3. Select the `titanic_train.csv` file.

4. Give the datasource the name **Titanic training set**, and click on **Verify**.

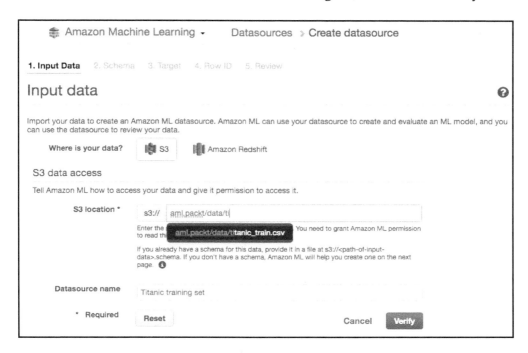

If you haven't previously set up the bucket policy, you will be asked to grant permissions to Amazon ML to read the file in S3; click on **Yes** to confirm:

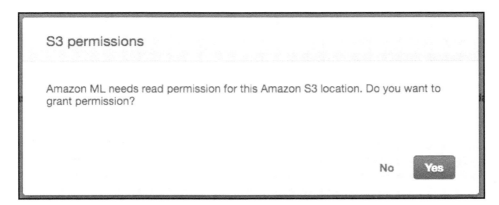

You will see a confirmation that your datasource was successfully created and is accessible by Amazon ML:

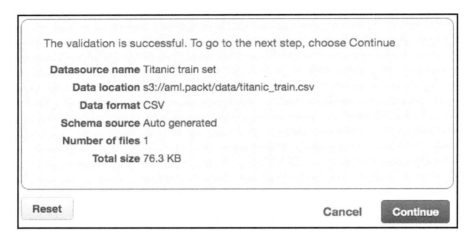

The validation is successful. To go to the next step, choose Continue

Datasource name Titanic train set

Data location s3://aml.packt/data/titanic_train.csv

Data format CSV

Schema source Auto generated

Number of files 1

Total size 76.3 KB

Reset   Cancel   Continue

Click on `Continue` in order to finalize the datasource creation. At this point, Amazon ML has scanned the `titanic_train.csv` file and inferred the data type for each column. This meta information is regrouped in the schema.

Other datasources: Amazon ML allows you to define a Redshift or RDS database as the source of your data instead of S3. Amazon Redshift is a *"fast, fully managed, petabyte-scale data warehouse solution"*. It is far less trivial to set up than S3, but it will handle much larger and more complex volumes of data. Redshift allows you to analyze your data with any SQL client using industry-standard ODBC/JDBC connections. We will come back to Redshift in `Chapter 8`, *Creating Datasources from Redshift*.

Verifying the data schema

The data schema is the meta information, the dictionary of a data file. It informs Amazon ML of the type of each variable in the dataset. Amazon ML will use that information to correctly read, interpret, analyze, and transform the data. Once created, the data schema can be saved and reused for other subsets of the same data. Although Amazon ML does a good job of guessing the nature of your dataset, it is always a good idea to double-check and sometimes make some necessary adjustments.

By default, Amazon ML assumes that the first row of your file contains an observation. In our case, the first row of the `titanic_train.csv` file contains the names of the variables. Be sure to confirm that this is the case by selecting **Yes** in that form:

```
Does the first line in your CSV contain the column names?  ● Yes  ○ No  ❶
```

Amazon ML classifies your data according to four data types:

- **Binary**: 0 or 1, Yes or No, Male or Female, False or True (`survived` in the Titanic dataset)
- **Categorical**: Variables that can take a finite number of values with numbers or characters (`pclass` or `embarked`, `sibsp`, `parch`)
- **Numeric**: A quantity with continuous values (`age` or `fare`)
- **Text**: Free text (`name`, `ticket`, `home.dest`)

Note that some variables in the `Titanic` dataset could be associated with different data types. `ticket`, `cabin`, or `home.dest`, for instance, could be interpreted as text or categorical values. The `age` attribute could be transformed from a numerical value into a categorical one by binning. The `sex` attribute could also be interpreted as being binary, categorical, or even a text type. Having the `sex` attribute as binary would require transforming its values from male/female to 0/1, so we'll keep it as categorical even though it only takes two values.

The model-building algorithm will process the variables and their values differently depending on their data type. It may be worthwhile to explore different data types for certain variables, when that makes sense, in order to improve predictions.

The following screenshot shows the schema that Amazon ML has deduced from our `titanic_train.csv` data:

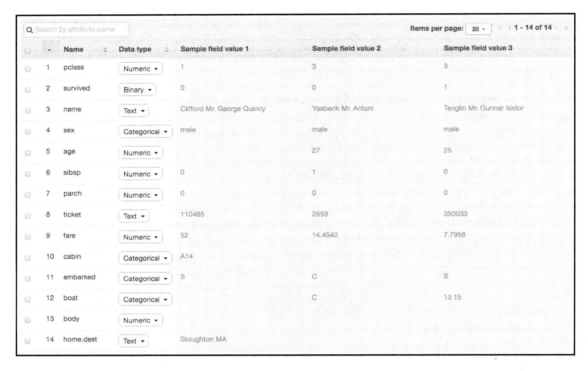

	Name	Data type	Sample field value 1	Sample field value 2	Sample field value 3
1	pclass	Numeric ▾	1	3	3
2	survived	Binary ▾	0	0	1
3	name	Text ▾	Clifford Mr. George Quincy	Yasbeck Mr. Antoni	Tenglin Mr. Gunnar Isidor
4	sex	Categorical ▾	male	male	male
5	age	Numeric ▾		27	25
6	sibsp	Numeric ▾	0	1	0
7	parch	Numeric ▾	0	0	0
8	ticket	Text ▾	110465	2659	350033
9	fare	Numeric ▾	52	14.4542	7.7958
10	cabin	Categorical ▾	A14		
11	embarked	Categorical ▾	S	C	S
12	boat	Categorical ▾		C	13 15
13	body	Numeric ▾			
14	home.dest	Text ▾	Stoughton MA		

Note that the sampled values shown here will be different on your own schema since the data has been randomized.

You can choose to keep the default choices made by Amazon ML or make some modifications. Consider the following for instance:

- `sibsp` and `parch`, respectively the number of siblings and parents, could be categorical instead of numeric if we wanted to regroup passengers with similar numbers of family members.
- `pclass` should be corrected as Categorical and not Numeric since there are only 3 possible values for `pcalss`: 1, 2, and 3.
- `cabin` could be interpreted as categorical since there are a finite number of cabins. However, the data indicates that the field could be parsed further. It has values such as C22 C26, which seems to indicate not one cabin but two. A text data type would be more appropriate.

Amazon ML needs to know what attribute we aim to predict. On the next screen, you will be asked to select the target. Confirm that **Do you plan to use this dataset to create or evaluate an ML model**, and select the `survived` attribute, as shown in the following screenshot:

Deciding between numeric and categorical: Numeric values are ordered, categorical values are not. When setting a variable to numeric, you are actually telling the model that the values are ordered. This information is useful to the algorithm when building the model. Categorical variables do not imply any order between values.

Going back to the example of the `sibsp` and `parch` attributes, these variables have a finite number of values (0 to 8 for `sibps` and 0 to 9 for `parch`) and could be categorical. However, the order of the values holds some important information. Eight siblings is more than one and indicates a big family. Therefore, it also makes sense to keep the values as numeric.

Categorical values and one-hot encoding: In the case of linear regression, categorical values are one-hot encoded. They are broken down into *N-1* binary variables when there are *N* categories. For instance, a variable with just three values *A*, *B*, and *C* is broken into two binary variables *is_it_A?* and *is_it_B?* that only take true and false values. Note that there is no need to define a third *is_it_C?* binary variable as it is directly deduced from the values of *is_it_A?* and *is_it_B?*. In the Titanic case, we have three values for the embarked variable; Amazon ML will create two binary variables equivalent to *passenger embarked at Queenstown* and *passenger embarked at Cherbourg*, with the third variable *passenger embarked at Southhampton* inferred from the values of the two first ones.

The type of the target dictates the model Amazon ML will use. Since we chose a binary target, Amazon ML will use logistic regression to train the models. A numeric target would have implied linear regression and a categorical target also logistic regression but this time for multiclass classification. Amazon ML confirms the nature of the model it will use, as shown by the following screenshot:

> You have selected a binary attribute named *survived* as the target. ML models trained on this target use logistic regression to train a binary classification model.

The final step consists of telling Amazon ML that our data does not contain a row identifier and finally reviewing our datasource. The datasource creation is now pending; depending on its size, it will take a few minutes to finish.

Reusing the schema

The schema is a JSON file, which implies that we can create one from scratch for our data or modify the one generated by Amazon ML. We will now modify the one created by Amazon ML, save it to S3, and use it to create a new datasource that does not include the `body`, `boat`, and `home.dest` variables.

Click on **View Input Schema** as shown in the next screenshot:

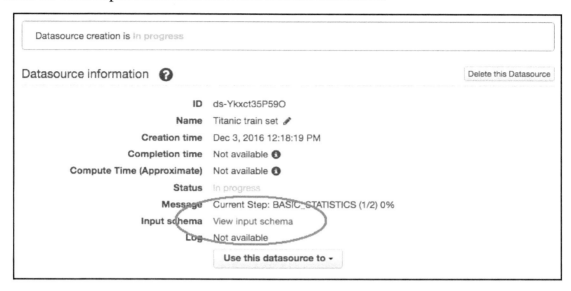

This gives us the raw schema in JSON format. Save it on your local machine with the filename `titanic_train.csv.schema`. We will load this file on S3 in the same bucket/folder where the `titanic_train.csv` file resides. By adding `.schema` to the data CSV filename, we allow Amazon ML to automatically associate the schema file to the data file and bypass the creation of its own schema.

Open the schema file with your favorite editor and edit as such:

- Add `home.dest, body, boat` in the `excludedAttributeNames` field
- Change the datatype from `CATEGORICAL` to `NUMERIC` for `sibps` and `parch`

Note that although we want to remove the fields `boat`, `body`, and `home.dest`, we still need to declare them and their data types in the schema. Your JSON file should now look as follows:

```
{
  "version" : "1.0",
  "rowId" : null,
  "rowWeight" : null,
  "targetAttributeName" : "survived",
  "dataFormat" : "CSV",
  "dataFileContainsHeader" : true,
  "attributes" : [ {
    "attributeName" : "pclass",
```

```json
      "attributeType" : "CATEGORICAL"
    }, {
      "attributeName" : "survived",
      "attributeType" : "BINARY"
    }, {
      "attributeName" : "name",
      "attributeType" : "TEXT"
    }, {
      "attributeName" : "sex",
      "attributeType" : "BINARY"
    }, {
      "attributeName" : "age",
      "attributeType" : "NUMERIC"
    }, {
      "attributeName" : "sibsp",
      "attributeType" : "NUMERIC"
    }, {
      "attributeName" : "parch",
      "attributeType" : "NUMERIC"
    }, {
      "attributeName" : "ticket",
      "attributeType" : "TEXT"
    }, {
      "attributeName" : "fare",
      "attributeType" : "NUMERIC"
    }, {
      "attributeName" : "cabin",
      "attributeType" : "TEXT"
    }, {
      "attributeName" : "embarked",
      "attributeType" : "CATEGORICAL"
    }, {
      "attributeName" : "boat",
      "attributeType" : "CATEGORICAL"
    }, {
      "attributeName" : "body",
      "attributeType" : "NUMERIC"
    }, {
      "attributeName" : "home.dest",
      "attributeType" : "TEXT"
    } ],
    "excludedAttributeNames" : ["home.dest", "body", "boat"]
  }
```

Upload that modified `titanic_train.csv.schema` file to the same S3 location as your `titanic_train.csv` data file. Your bucket/folder should now look like this:

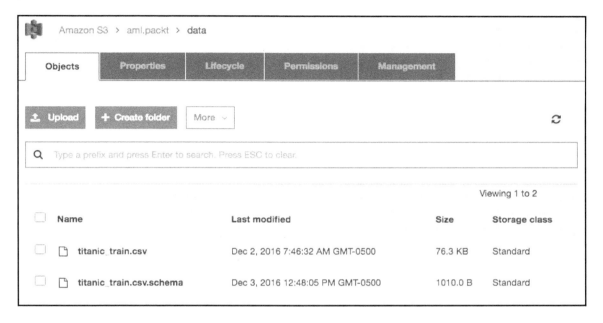

Let us now create a new datasource. Since the schema file has the same name as the data file and is contained at the same location, Amazon ML will use the schema we provided:

1. Go back to the Amazon ML dashboard and click on Create a new datasource in the main menu.
2. Indicate location and name the datasource; we named this new datasource **Titanic train set 11 variables.**

Amazon ML confirms that the schema you provided has been taken into account:

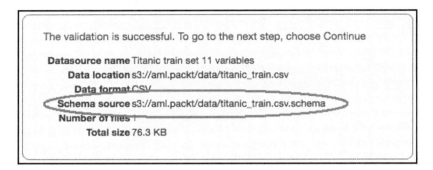

The validation is successful. To go to the next step, choose Continue

Datasource name Titanic train set 11 variables
Data location s3://aml.packt/data/titanic_train.csv
Data format CSV
Schema source s3://aml.packt/data/titanic_train.csv.schema
Number of files 1
Total size 76.3 KB

Go through the remaining datasource creation steps and notice that the data types correspond to the ones you specified in the schema file and that the three fields are no longer present.

 Schema recap: To associate a schema to a file, it suffices to name the schema with the same name as the data file and add the .schema extension. For instance, for a data file named `my_data.csv`, the schema file should be named `my_data.csv.schema` and be uploaded to the same S3 location as the data file.

Our datasource has now been created, and we can explore what type of insights into the data Amazon ML gives us.

Examining data statistics

When Amazon ML created the data source, it carried out a basic statistical analysis of the different variables. For each variable, it estimated the following information:

- Correlation of each attribute to the target
- Number of missing values
- Number of invalid values
- Distribution of numeric variables with histogram and box plot
- Range, mean, and median for numeric variables
- Most and least frequent categories for categorical variables
- Word counts for text variables
- Percentage of true values for binary variables

Go to the Datasource dashboard, and click on the new datasource you just created in order to access the data summary page. The left side menu lets you access data statistics for the target and different attributes, grouped by data types. The following screenshot shows data insights for the **Numeric** attributes. The `age` and `fare` variables are worth looking at more closely:

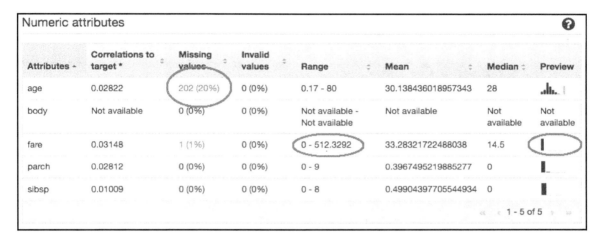

Attributes ▾	Correlations to target *	Missing values	Invalid values	Range	Mean	Median	Preview
age	0.02822	202 (20%)	0 (0%)	0.17 - 80	30.138436018957343	28	
body	Not available	0 (0%)	0 (0%)	Not available - Not available	Not available	Not available	Not available
fare	0.03148	1 (1%)	0 (0%)	0 - 512.3292	33.28321722488038	14.5	
parch	0.02812	0 (0%)	0 (0%)	0 - 9	0.3967495219885277	0	
sibsp	0.01009	0 (0%)	0 (0%)	0 - 8	0.49904397705544934	0	

1 - 5 of 5

Two things stand out:

- `age` has `20%` missing values. We should replace these missing values by the mean or the median values of the existing values of `age`.
- The mean for `fare` is 33.28, but the range is `0-512.32`, indicating a highly skewed distribution. Looking at the `fare` distribution confirms that. Click on the **Preview**.

The following screenshot shows the histogram and the associated box plot for the `fare` attribute. We can see that most of the values are below 155, with very few values above 195. This shows that the 521.32 value may well be an outlier, an invalid value caused by human error. Looking back at the original dataset, we see that four passengers from the same family with the same ticket number *(PC 17755)* paid this price for four first class cabins *(B51, B53, B55,* and *B101)*. Although that fare of 512.32 value is well above any other fare, it does look legit and not like an error of some sort. We should probably not discard or replace it. The following histogram shows the `fare` distribution:

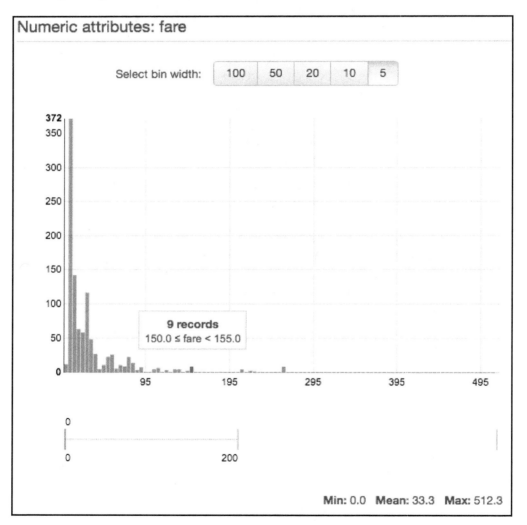

The **Text attributes** have automatically been tokenized by Amazon ML and each word has been extracted from the original attribute. Punctuation has also been removed. Amazon ML then calculates word frequency as shown in the following screenshot for the `name` attribute:

Text attributes: name

Ranking	Token	Word prominence	Count	
1	mr	0.22366	608	14.2%
2	mrs	0.11632	162	3.8%
3	miss	0.07608	200	4.7%
4	alice	0.02115	12	0.3%
5	mary	0.01706	21	0.5%
6	marie	0.01640	6	0.1%
7	bertha	0.01640	6	0.1%
8	elizabeth	0.01529	20	0.5%
9	florence	0.01376	5	0.1%
10	anne	0.01376	5	0.1%

1 - 10 of 1678 › »

Feature engineering with Athena

At this point, we have a decent set of variables that can help predict whether a passenger survived the Titanic disaster. However, that data could use a bit of cleaning up in order to handle outliers and missing values. We could also try to extract other meaningful features from existing attributes to boost our predictions. In other terms, we want to do some feature engineering. Feature engineering is the key to boosting the accuracy of your predictions.

> *Feature engineering is the process of using domain knowledge of the data to create features that make machine learning algorithms work.*

Wikipedia

ML offers what it calls data recipes to transform the data and adapt it to its linear regression and logistic regression algorithm. In Amazon ML, data recipes are part of building the predictive model, not creating the datasource. We study Amazon ML's data recipes extensively in `Chapter 5`, *Model Creation*. Amazon ML's data recipes are mostly suited to adapt the data to the algorithm and is a bit limited to correcting problems in the original data or creating new attributes from existing ones. For instance, removing outliers, extracting keywords from text, or replacing missing values are not possible with Amazon ML's recipes. We will, therefore, use SQL queries to perform some data cleaning and feature creation.

Several AWS services are based on SQL databases: Redshift, RDS, and more recently, **Athena**. SQL is not only widely used to query data but, as we will see, it is particularly well suited for data transformation and data cleaning. Many creative ideas on how to squeeze out information for the original Titanic dataset can be found online. These online sources, for instance, offer many ideas on the subject of feature engineering on the Titanic dataset:

- Analysis of the Titanic dataset for Kaggle competition on the Ultraviolet blog with code example in Python at `http://www.ultravioletanalytics.com /2014/10/30/kaggle-titanic-competition-part-i-intro/`
- Similar analysis with example in R on Trevor Stephens blog: `http://trevorstep hens.com/kaggle-titanic-tutorial/r-part-4-feature-engineering/`
- The Titanic Kaggle competition forums are ripe with ideas: `https://www.kaggle .com/c/titanic`

In our case, we will focus on the following transformations:

- Replacing the missing `age` values with the average of existing `age` values
- Instead of replacing or discarding the fare outlier values, we will create a new log (`fare`) variable with a distribution less skewed
- Extracting titles from the `name` field
- Each cabin number is referred to by three characters, where the first character is a letter relative to the deck level (A, B, C, ..., F) and the number of cabin number, on that deck; we will extract the first letter of each cabin as a new `deck` variable
- We will also combine `sibps` and `parch` to create a `family_size` variable

In the following section, we will use Athena to do these data transformations. We will first create a database and table in Athena and fill it with the Titanic data. We will then create new features using standard SQL queries on the newly created table. Finally, we will export the results to CSV in S3 and create a new datasource from it.

Introducing Athena

Athena was launched during the *AWS re:Invent* conference in *December 2016*. It complements other AWS SQL based services by offering a simple serverless service that directly interacts with S3. According to AWS, Amazon Athena is an interactive query service that makes it easy to analyze data directly from Amazon S3 using standard SQL. Several attributes of Amazon Athena make it particularly adapted for data preparation with Amazon ML:

- Athena can generate tables directly from data available in S3 in different formats (CSV, JSON, TSV, amazon logs, and others). Since datasources in Amazon ML are also S3-based, it is easy to manipulate files, perform various data transformation, and create various datasets on the fly to test your models.
- Athena is fast, simple, and can handle massive datasets.
- Athena uses `prestodb`, a distributed SQL query engine developed by Facebook that offers a very rich library of SQL functions, which are well suited to do data transformations and feature engineering.

 Amazon ML only accepts CSV files to create datasources from S3. However, since Athena can gather data from other file formats besides CSV, (JSON, TSV, ORC, and others) and export query results to a CSV file, it's possible to use Athena as a conversion tool and expand Amazon ML sourcing capabilities that way.

Presto is an open-source distributed SQL query engine optimized for low-latency, ad-hoc analysis of data. It supports the ANSI SQL standard, including complex queries, aggregations, joins, and window functions. More information can be found at `https://pre stodb.io/`.

In this section, we will perform the following:

1. Create an Athena account and a database.
2. Create and populate a table directly from the S3 Titanic CSV file.
3. Perform queries on the dataset and create new features.
4. Download the results to S3.
5. Create new training and testing datasources with the extra features in Amazon ML.

Athena is simple. Let's start with a simple overview.

A brief tour of AWS Athena

In Athena, the data is not stored in a database; it remains in S3. When you create a table in Athena, you are creating an information layer that tells Athena where to find the data, how it is structured, and what format it is in. The schema in Athena is a logical namespace of objects. Once the data structure and location are known to Athena, you can query the data via standard SQL statements.

Athena uses **Hive Data Definition Language (DDL)** to create or drop databases and tables (more information on Hive DDL can be found at `https://cwiki.apache.org/confluence /display/Hive/LanguageManual+DDL`). Athena can understand multiple formats (CSV, TSV, JSON, and so on) through the use of `serializer-deserializer` (SerDes) libraries. Athena is available either via the console (`https://console.aws.amazon.com/ath ena/`) or via JDBC connection (`http://docs.aws.amazon.com/athena/latest/ug/connect -with-jdbc.html`). We will use the console.

The **Athena** service offers four sections:

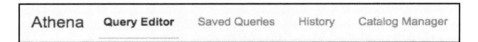

The **Query Editor:**

1. Lets you write your queries, save them, and see the results as well as navigate among your databases and tables.
2. A **Saved Queries** page listing all the queries you saved.
3. A **History** page listing all the queries you ran.
4. A **Catalog Manager** that lets you explore your stored data.

These sections are self-explanatory to use, and we will let you explore them at your leisure.

 At the time of writing, Amazon Athena does not have a **Command-Line interface (cli)**. However, Athena can be accessed via a **Java Database Connectivity (JDBC)** driver available on S3. You will find more information at `http://docs.aws.amazon.com/athena/latest/ug/connec t-with-jdbc.html`.

A few things to know:

- You can create a table by specifying the location of the data in S3 or explicitly via an SQL query.
- All tables must be created as EXTERNAL and it is not possible to **CREATE TABLE AS SELECT**. Dropping a table created with the External keyword does not delete the underlying data:

  ```
  CREATE EXTERNAL TABLE temp ();
  ```

- The presto SQL functions are available in Athena. Take a look at https://presto db.io/docs/current/functions.html for a full list.
- You can only submit one query and run five concurrent queries at the same time.

 Athena Pricing: Athena charges based on the amount of data scanned by the query with (at the time of writing) a $5 fee per TB of data scanned with a minimum of 10 MB per query. You can reduce your costs by converting your data to columnar formats or partitioning your data. Refer to https ://aws.amazon.com/athena/pricing/ for more information.

Creating a titanic database

We are going to start from scratch and go back to the original Titanic dataset available at ht tps://github.com/alexperrier/packt-aml/blob/master/ch4/original_titanic.csv . Follow these steps to prepare the CSV file:

1. Open the original_titanic.csv file.
2. Remove the header row.
3. Remove the following punctuation characters: , " ().

The file should only contain data, not column names. This is the original file with 1309 rows. These rows are ordered by pclass and alphabetical names. The resulting file is available at https://github.com/alexperrier/packt-aml/blob/master/ch4/titanic_fo r_athena.csv. Let us create a new athena_data folder in our S3 bucket and upload the titanic_for_athena.csv file. Now go to the Athena console. We will create a titanic_db database and a titanic table with the data.

Using the wizard

There are two ways to create databases and tables in Athena, via the wizard or by running queries. The wizard is accessible by clicking on the **Add table** link in the **Query Editor** page:

In four steps, the wizard allows us to create the database, the table, and load the data. Creating the columns in *step 3* involves manually typing the name of each column and specifying each column type. With 14 columns in the dataset, this manual approach is time-consuming. We will, therefore, not use the wizard and switch to creating the database and table directly in SQL:

Creating the database and table directly in SQL

To create the database, run the following query in the query editor:

```
CREATE DATABASE titanic_db;
```

Then select `titanic_db` in the database dropdown menu on the left side as follows:

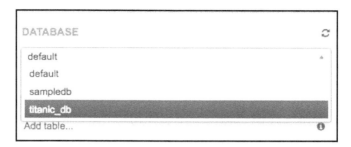

To create the table and load the data, run the following SQL query:

```
CREATE EXTERNAL TABLE IF NOT EXISTS titanic_db.titanic (
  pclass tinyint,
  survived tinyint,
  name string,
  sex string,
  age double,
  sibsp tinyint,
  parch tinyint,
  ticket string,
  fare double,
  cabin string,
  embarked string,
  boat string,
  body string,
  home_dest string
)
ROW FORMAT SERDE 'org.apache.hadoop.hive.serde2.lazy.LazySimpleSerDe' WITH
SERDEPROPERTIES (
  'serialization.format' = ',',
  'field.delim' = ','
) LOCATION 's3://aml.packt/athena_data/'
```

A few things to note about that query:

- The location `s3://aml.packt/athena_data/` points to the folder we have specially created, not to the file itself . All the files in that folder will be considered as data for that table.
- The `SERDE` corresponds to the CSV format with a comma as the field delimiter. The list of supported formats and respective SERDE is available at `https://docs.aws.amazon.com/athena/latest/ug/supported-formats.html`.
- The field types are standard SQL types (string, double, tinyint, and so on).

Once the query has finished running, the `titanic` table name appears in the left section of the page. You can click on the eye icon to select the first 10 rows of the table as follows:

Specifying the results location: Athena stores the results of your queries in a new S3 folder. You can specify what folder you want these results to be stored in by going to the settings page and specifying the desired S3 path. We have created a new folder titled `athena_query_results` in our `aml.packt` bucket and set the result location to `s3://aml.packt/athena_query_results/`.

Data munging in SQL

We will now define the SQL query that will correct the missing value and outlier problems we saw earlier and create some new variables.

Missing values

We have missing values for the `age` and `fare` variables with respective median values `28` and `14.5`. We can replace all the missing values with the median values with this statement:

```
select coalesce(age, 28) as age, coalesce(fare, 14.5) as fare from titanic;
```

We also want to keep the information that there was a missing value at least for the `age` variable. We can do that with the query that creates a new binary variable that we name: `is_age_missing`:

```
SELECT age, CASE
  WHEN age is null THEN 0
  ELSE 1
  END as is_age_missing
from titanic;
```

Handling outliers in the fare

We have seen that the `fare` had four passengers paying a much higher price than the others. There are several ways to deal with these values, one of which can be to bin the variable by defining a series of specific ranges. For instance, below 20; from 20 to 50; 50 to 100, ..., and over 200. Binning can be done with Amazon ML recipes. We could also cap the fare value at a specific threshold, such as the 95% percentile. However, we decided that these large fare values were legit and that we ought to keep them. We can still create a new variable, `log_fare`, with a more compact range and a less skewed distribution by taking the log of the `fare`:

```
select fare, log(fare +1, 2) as log_fare from titanic;
```

The `log_fare` variable has a range of *0 - 9.0*, a mean of *4.3*, and a median of *3.95*, whereas the original `fare` variable had a range of *[0, 512.3]*, mean *32.94*, and median *14.5*. The distribution of the `log_fare` is closer to a Gaussian distribution than the distribution of the original `fare` variable.

Box-Cox transformation: Because of the linear regression assumptions, it is better to have variables with Gaussian distributions. The Box-Cox transformation, also known as the power transform (see `https://en.wiki pedia.org/wiki/Power_transform`), is a common method to reshape a variable into a normally-distributed one. The Box-Cox transformation is a generalization of the log transformation we just applied to the `fare` variable.

Extracting the title from the name

If you look closely at the passenger names, you will notice that they are all in the `{family name}{title}{first names}` format. It would be interesting to extract the `title` as a new variable. The following query uses the split function, which returns an array. We need the second element of that array:

```
SELECT name, split(name, ' ')[2] as title from titanic;
```

Inferring the deck from the cabin

The cabin variable has three character values, where the first character corresponds to the Deck number (A, B, C, D, E). This is surely important information that we would like to extract. We can do so with the following query:

```
SELECT cabin, substr(cabin, 1, 1) as deck  FROM titanic;
```

Calculating family size

Finally, it makes sense to assume that the overall family size a passenger belongs to might have been a decisive factor in survival. We can aggregate the number of siblings and the number of parents and add 1 for the passenger. The following simple query will create the family size variable:

```
select sibps + parch + 1 as family_size from titanic;
```

Wrapping up

We can combine all these queries while also selecting the original attributes. Since the data is still ordered by `pclass` and passenger `name` in alphabetical order, we should also randomize the results. We end up with the following query:

```
SELECT pclass,
survived,
name,
sex,
COALESCE(age, 28) as age,
sibsp,
parch,
ticket,
COALESCE(fare, 14.5) as fare,
cabin,
embarked,
```

```
boat,
body,
home_dest,
CASE
  WHEN age is null THEN 0
  ELSE 1
  END as is_age_missing,
log(fare + 1, 2) as log_fare,
split(name, ' ')[2] as title,
substr(cabin, 1, 1) as deck,
sibsp + parch + 1 as family_size
FROM titanic
ORDER BY RAND();
```

Let us run that query. The results will be displayed in the results panel and also written in a CSV file in the query result location on S3. You can also save it on your local machine by clicking at the icon in the upper right corner of the results panel:

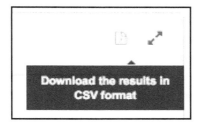

At this point, we want to split the data into a training and a testing set like we did previously and create a new Amazon ML datasource with an extended schema.

Creating an improved datasource

We need to do some manipulation on the new Titanic dataset before we upload it to S3 and create a new datasource in Amazon ML:

1. Open this new Titanic dataset in your favorite editor.
2. Select the first *1047* rows, and save them to a new CSV: ext_titanic_training.csv.
3. Select the next *263* rows and the header row, and save them to a file ext_titanic_heldout.csv.

We need to update our schema. Open the schema file `titanic_training.csv.schema`, and add the following lines to the JSON:

```
{
  "attributeName" : "is_age_missing",
  "attributeType" : "BINARY"
  }, {
  "attributeName" : "log_fare",
  "attributeType" : "NUMERIC"
  }, {
  "attributeName" : "title",
  "attributeType" : "CATEGORICAL"
  }, {
  "attributeName" : "deck",
  "attributeType" : "CATEGORICAL"
  }, {
  "attributeName" : "family_size",
  "attributeType" : "NUMERIC"
  }
```

The new schema file as well as the training and held-out sets can be found at `https://gith ub.com/alexperrier/packt-aml/tree/master/ch4`.

We then need to upload the training and the schema file to S3. These files should be in the same S3 location, `{bucket}/{folders}`.

We are now ready to create a new datasource based on this extended Titanic training set following the exact same steps as before:

1. Specify the location of the input data.
2. Review the schema.
3. Set the target as `survived`.
4. Bypass the `rowID`.
5. Review and create.

We now have 19 attributes in the schema and a brand new datasource.

Summary

In this chapter, we focused on what is commonly known as the **Extract Load Transform (ETL)** part of the data science flow with regard to the Amazon ML service. We saw that the Amazon ML datasource is a set of information comprised of location, data structure, and data analytics given to the service so that it can use that data to start training models. You should now feel comfortable creating an Amazon ML datasource from an original CSV data file made accessible via S3.

We have also explored ways to transform the data and create new features via the AWS Athena service using simple SQL queries. The ability to complement the features of Amazon ML by leveraging the AWS ecosystem is one of the main benefits of using Amazon ML.

We now have a couple of Titanic datasets, the original one and the extended one, which are split into training and held-out subsets, and we have created the associated datasources.

In Chapter 5, *Model Creation*, we will use these datasets to train models, and we will see if our new features and data cleaning result in better models.

5
Model Creation

We have now created several data sources based on the original `Titanic` dataset in S3. We are ready to train and evaluate an Amazon ML prediction model. In Amazon ML, creating a model consists of the following:

- Selecting the training datasource
- Defining a recipe for data transformation
- Setting the parameters of the learning algorithm
- Evaluating the quality of the model

In this chapter, we will start by exploring the data transformations available in Amazon ML, and we will compare different recipes for the `Titanic` dataset. Amazon ML defines recipes by default depending on the nature of the data. We will investigate and challenge these default transformations.

The model-building step is simple enough, and we will spend some time examining the available parameters. The model evaluation is where everything converges. The evaluation metrics are dependent on the type of the prediction at hand, regression, binary or multi-class classification. We will look at how these different evaluations are carried out. We will also download the model training logs to better understand what goes on under the Amazon ML hood when training the model. We will conclude the chapter by comparing the model evaluation for several data recipes and regularization strategies.

The chapter is organized as follows:

- Recipes
- Model parameters
- Evaluations
- Log analysis
- Feature engineering, recipes, and regularization

At the end of `Chapter 4`, *Loading and Preparing the Dataset,* we modified the schema to exclude three variables: `boat`, `body`, and `home.dest` from the original dataset and created a new datasource based on this schema. We will use this datasource to train the model.

Go to your Amazon ML datasource dashboard; you should see three datasources:

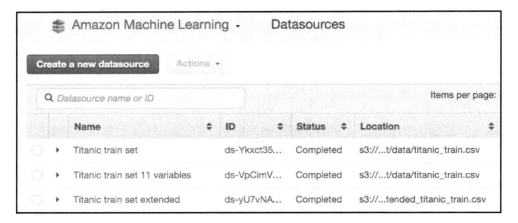

- **Titanic train set**: It is the original raw dataset with 14 variables
- **Titanic train set 11 variables**: Has 11 variables; `boat`, `body` and `home.dest` have been removed from the schema
- **Titanic train set extended**: It is the cleaned up and extended dataset we obtained through SQL-based feature engineering.

We will work with the `Titanic train set 11 variables` datasource. Before starting with the model creation, let's first review what types of data transformations are available in Amazon ML.

Transforming data with recipes

A crucial element of the data science workflow is feature engineering. Amazon ML offers certain data transformations via its data recipes. Note that although transformations are conceptually part of the ETL or data preparation phase of a predictive analytics workflow, in Amazon ML, data recipes are part of the model-building step and not of the initial datasource creation step. In this section, we start by reviewing the available data transformations in Amazon ML, and then we apply some of them to the `Titanic` dataset using the `Titanic train set 11 variables` datasource.

Managing variables

Recipes are JSON-structured scripts that contains the following three sections in the given order:

- Groups
- Assignments
- Outputs

An empty recipe instructing Amazon ML to take all the dataset variables into account for model training will be as follows:

```
{
    "groups" : {},
    "assignments" : { },
    "outputs":["ALL_INPUTS"]
}
```

The recipe does not transform the data in any way.

> The complete Amazon ML recipes documentation is available at http://d
> ocs.aws.amazon.com/machine-learning/latest/dg/recipe-format-re
> ference.html.

Grouping variables

Groups enable grouping of multiple variables to facilitate applying the same transformations to several variables. The groups section of the recipe has a naming function. Group definition follows this syntax:

```
"group_name": "group('first_variable','second_variable' )"
```

Amazon ML has defined a set of default groups based on the type of the variables: ALL_TEXT, ALL_NUMERIC, ALL_CATEGORICAL, ALL_BINARY, and the ALL_INPUTS group for all the variables at once. Let's look at a couple of examples.

Consider the following example where we want to apply the same transformation (normalization) on the `age` and `fare` variables. We can define a group and name it `TO_BE_NORMALIZED`:

```
"groups" : {
    "TO_BE_NORMALIZED" : "group('age','fare')",
},
```

Similarly, consider an e-mail spam detection context where for each e-mail, we have a header, a subject, and a body. We want to create N-grams of the e-mail title and body but not of the header; we can define a group composed of all text variables with the exception of specifically excluded ones. Here we create a group named `N_GRAM_TEXT` that combines all text variables except the header:

```
"groups" : {
    "N_GRAM_TEXT" : "group_remove(ALL_TEXT, 'header')",
},
```

Naming variables with assignments

The main purpose of assignments is naming facilitation. You can choose to name the transformed variable or group of variables in the assignments section or directly in the output section. Assignments are only for convenience and readability. Assignments follow this syntax:

```
"assignment_name": "transformation('group_name' )"
```

For instance, you could rename and normalize the numeric variables as follows:

```
"assignments": {
    "normalized_numeric": "normalize(TO_BE_NORMALIZED)",
}
```

Or rename and process the subject and body of your e-mails:

```
"assignments": {
    "bigrams": "ngram(N_GRAM_TEXT,2)",
}
```

You can also leave the assignments section empty and apply the transformations to the variables groups in the output section. In the end, it's more a question of style and readability than anything else.

Specifying outputs

The outputs section is where you explicitly list all the variables that will be used for the model training. If you have defined a group with some of the variables but you still want the original variables to be accounted for, you need to explicitly list them. The assignment section declares a list composed of the following:

- Groups
- Assignments
- Variables
- Transformation (variable)

For instance, if you wanted the original body and subject of the e-mails as well as the `bigrams` you defined in assignments, you would need to declare the outputs as follows:

```
"outputs": [
    "header",
    "subject",
    "body",
    "bigrams"
]
```

The following outputs declaration declares all the text variables and adds the bigrams assignment defined earlier on:

```
"outputs": [
    "ALL_TEXT",
    "bigrams"
    ]
```

The recipe format reference page has other examples of combining groups, assignments, and outputs to create recipes: http://docs.aws.amazon.com/machine-learning/latest /dg/recipe-format-reference.html. We will now look at the available transformations.

Data processing through seven transformations

Amazon ML offers the following seven transformations. Four transformations for text variables are as follows:

- Lowercase transformation
- Remove punctuation transformation
- N-gram transformation
- **Orthogonal sparse bigram (OSB)** transformation

Two transformations for numeric variables are as follows:

- Normalization transformation
- Quantile binning transformation

And one transformation for coupling text with categorical variables:

- Cartesian product transformation

These transformations are well explained on the Amazon ML documentation (`http://docs` `.aws.amazon.com/machine-learning/latest/dg/data-transformations-reference.ht` `ml`).

Using simple transformations

The lowercase transformation takes a text variable as input and returns the text in lowercase: `Amazon ML is great for Predictive Analytics` is returned as `amazon ml is great for predictive analytics`. Syntax for lowercase transformation is `lowercase(text_variable)` or `lowercase(group_of_text_variables)`.

The remove punctuation transformation also takes a text variable as input and removes all punctuation signs, with the exception of hyphens within words (`seat-belts` will remain as `seat-belts`). It is not possible to define your own set of punctuation signs. Syntax for the remove punctuation transformation is `no_punct(text_variable)` or `no_punct(group_of_text_variables)`.

The normalization transformation normalizes numeric variables to have a mean of zero and a variance of one. This is a useful transformation when numeric variables vary significantly in range. This transformation corresponds to the **z-score** normalization also known as standardization and not to the min-max normalization (see `Chapter 2`, *Machine Learning Definitions and Concepts*). Syntax for normalization transformation is `normalize(numeric_variable)` or `normalize(group_of_numeric_variables)`.

Text mining

The N-gram and the **orthogonal sparse bigram** (**OSB**) transformations are the main text-mining transformations available in Amazon ML.

In text mining, the classic approach is called the **bag-of-words** approach. This approach boils down to discarding the order of the word in a given text and only considering the relative frequency of the words in the documents. Although it may seem to be overly simplistic, since the order of the words is essential to understand a message, this approach has given satisfying results in all types of natural language processing problems. A key part of the bag-of-words method, is driven by the need to extract the words from a given text. However, instead of considering single words as the only elements holding information, we could extract sequences of words. These sequences are called N-grams. Sequences of two words are called bigrams, for three words trigrams, and so forth. Single words are also called unigrams. N-grams are also called tokens and the process of extracting words, and N-grams from a text is called tokenization.

For instance, consider the sentence: *The brown fox jumps over the dog*

- **Unigrams** are {*The, brown, fox, jumps, over, the, dog*}
- **Bigrams** are {*The brown, brown fox, fox jumps, jumps over, over the, the dog*}
- **Trigrams** are {*The brown fox, brown fox jumps, fox jumps over, jumps over the, over the dog*}

There is no rule or heuristic that would let you know if you need N-grams in your model or what order of N-grams would be the most beneficial for your model. It depends on the type of text you are dealing with. Only experimentation can tell.

Amazon ML offers two tokenization transformations: N-gram and OSB.

The **N-gram** transformation: Takes a text variable and an integer from 2 to 10 and returns expected N-grams. Note that all text variables are, by default, tokenized as unigrams in Amazon ML. There is no need to explicitly specify unigrams in the recipe. `ngram(text_variable, n)` will produce bigrams for *n*= 2, trigrams for *n*=3 and so forth.

The **OSB** or orthogonal sparse bigram transformation is an extension on the bigram transformation (N-*gram* with *n=2*). Given a word in a text, compose pairs of words by associating the other words separated by *1,2, …, N* words from the initial word. *N* being the size of the OSB window.
For instance, in the sentence *this is a limited time offer*, first consider the word *offer*. The OSBs for a window of four are: *time_offer, limited_<skip>_offer, a_<skip>_<skip>_offer, is_<skip>_<skip>_<skip>_offer, this_<skip>_<skip>_<skip>_<skip>_offer*. We build word pairs by skipping 1,2,..., N words each time.

The OSB transformation allows us to extract information about the context surrounding each word. For instance, the OSB *is_<skip>_<skip>_offer*, could be used to detect strings such as *is a special offer* as well as *is our best offer*. OSB extraction has been found to generally improve the performance of spam filtering algorithms. Syntax for OSB transformation is `osb(text_variable, N)`, with `N` the size of the window ranging from 2 to 10.

It's worth noting that some very standard text transformations are absent from Amazon ML recipes. Stemming and **Lemmatization** are used to regroup words with different endings to a common base form (for instance, *walking, walker* and *walked* would all be accounted for as *walk*) and are not offered in Amazon ML.

Similarly, removing very common words, known as *stopwords*, such as articles or prepositions (the, a, but, in, is, are, and so on) from a text is also a very standard text-mining transformation but is not an option in Amazon ML recipes. It is nonetheless possible that Amazon ML carries out similar transformations in the background without explicitly stating so. However, nothing in the available documentation indicates that to be the case.

Coupling variables

The Cartesian product transformation combines two categorical or text variables into one. Consider, for instance, a dataset of books and for each book, their title and genre. We could imagine that the title of a book has some correlation with its genre, and creating a new `title_genre` variable would bring forth that relation.

Consider the following four books, their titles, and genres. Coupling the words in the title with the genre of the book adds extra information to the words in the title. Information that the model could use effectively. This is illustrated in the `title_genre` column in the following table:

Title	Genre	title_genre
All the Birds in the Sky	scifi	`{all_scifi, birds_scifi, sky_scifi}`
Robots and Empire	scifi	`{robots_scifi, emprire_scifi}`
The Real Cool Killers	crime	`{real_crime, cool_crime, killers_crime}`
Bullet in the Sky	crime	`{bullet_crime, sky_crime}`

The word sky now takes a different meaning if it's in the title of a crime novel: `sky_crime` or in the title of a SciFi novel: `sky_scifi`.

In the case of the `Titanic` dataset, we could couple the `sibsp` and *parch* variables (number of siblings and number of parents) by taking their cartesian products: `sibsp*parch` and come up with a new variable that distinguishes between passengers with (without) parents and few or no siblings from those with (without) parents and many siblings. Syntax is `cartesian(var1, var2)`.

Binning numeric values

The final and most important transformation is quantile binning. The goal with quantile binning is to transform a numeric variable into a categorical one in order to better extract the relation between the variable and the prediction target. This is particularly useful in the presence of nonlinearities between a variable and the target. By splitting the original numeric variables values into *n* bins of equal size, it is possible to substitute each value by a corresponding bin. Since the number of bins is finite (from 2 to 1,000), the variable is now categorical. Syntax is `quantile_bin(var, N)` with `N` the number of bins.

There are two types of unsupervised binning, equal frequency and equal width binning. In equal frequency, each bin has the same number of samples, whereas in equal width binning, the variable range is split into N smaller ranges of equal width. Quantile binning usually refers to equal frequency binning.

Categorizing continuous data is not always a good approach as you are, by definition, throwing away information that could be useful for the model. This page lists several other problems associated with binning: `http://biostat.mc.vanderbilt.edu/wiki/Main/CatC ontinuous`. However, Amazon ML seems to be quite fond of the quantile binning technique. In fact, of all the datasets we considered, Amazon ML always applied quantile binning to all the numeric variables, in the suggested recipe and often used large, sometimes very large, number of bins. For instance, the default transformation for the `fare` variable in the `Titanic` dataset was quantile binning with 500 bins although the variable only ranged from 0 to 512. We compare the evaluations obtained by keeping the original numeric values versus applying quantile binning at the end of this chapter, *Keeping variables as numeric or applying quantile binning?* section Now that we've explored the available recipes, let's look at how Amazon ML suggests we transform our `Titanic` dataset

Creating a model

Amazon ML always suggests a recipe based on your datasource when you create a model. You can choose to use that recipe or to modify it. We will now create our first model and during that process analyze the recipe Amazon ML has generated for us.

Go to the model dashboard, and click on the **Create new...** | **ML model** button.

You will go through three screens:

1. Select the datasource, choose the `Titanic train set with 11 variables`.
2. Amazon ML will validate the datasource and present a summary.
3. Choose the default or **Custom** model creation; choose the custom path:

The next screen is split between the attributes, their type and a sample of values on the left side, and the suggested recipe on the right side, as shown in the following screenshot:

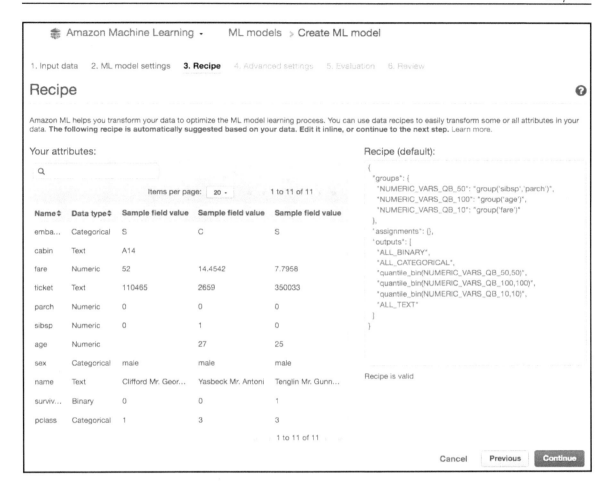

Editing the suggested recipe

This is where you can edit the recipe and replace it with a recipe of your own creation.

You can find all the JSON in this chapter in the book's GitHub repository, properly formatted and indented at `https://github.com/alexperrier/p ackt-aml/blob/master/ch5/recipes.json`.

The recipe is validated while you type. Anything not respecting the JSON format will result in the following error message: `Recipe must be valid JSON`. Some common errors include the following:

- Indentation is not respected
- The last element between braces should not be followed by a comma
- All strings must be between double quotes

 Manually formatting JSON text is not fun. This online JSON editor is very helpful: `http://www.cleancss.com/json-editor/`.

Applying recipes to the Titanic dataset

The recipe generated by Amazon ML for our dataset is as follows:

```
{
    "groups": {
        "NUMERIC_VARS_QB_50": "group('sibsp','parch')",
        "NUMERIC_VARS_QB_100": "group('age')",
        "NUMERIC_VARS_QB_10": "group('fare')"
    },
    "assignments": {},
    "outputs": [
        "ALL_BINARY",
        "ALL_CATEGORICAL",
        "quantile_bin(NUMERIC_VARS_QB_50,50)",
        "quantile_bin(NUMERIC_VARS_QB_100,100)",
        "quantile_bin(NUMERIC_VARS_QB_10,10)",
        "ALL_TEXT"
    ]
}
```

All numeric values are quantile binned. No further processing is done on the text, binary, or categorical variables. The output section of the recipe shows that the numeric variables are replaced by the binned equivalent.

Further comments can be made on this recipe:

- The `sibsp` and `parch` variables are grouped together. First of all, both `sibsp` and `parch` have similar ranges, 0 to 9 and 0 to 8 respectively. It makes sense to have the same number of bins for both variables.
- Why Amazon ML chose 50 bins for `sibsp` and `parch`, 100 bins for `age`, and 10 bins for `fare` is less clear.

We found that the number of bins was very sensitive to the data in the training set. Several versions of the initial datasets produced very different binning numbers. One constant in all our trials was that all the numeric values went through quantile binning with a rather high number of bins. In one instance, Amazon ML suggested 500 bins for the `fare` variable and 200 for the `age` variable. In both cases, we would have ended with a very small number of samples per bin since our total number of training sample consists of just 1,047 passengers. How Amazon ML calculates the optimal number of bins is not clear.

There are other transformations Amazon ML could decide to apply to our `Titanic` dataset such as the following:

- Extracting bigrams or OSBs from the passengers' titles
- Coupling `sibsp` and `parch` with cartesian product transformation

Choosing between recipes and data pre-processing.

So far we have transformed our initial dataset via scripts and Amazon ML recipes. The two techniques are complementary. Some transformation and data manipulation can only be done by preprocessing the data. We did so in `Chapter 4`, *Loading and Preparing the Dataset* with Athena and SQL. We could have achieved similar data processing with other scripting languages such as Python or R, which are most fruitful for creative feature engineering. SQL and scripts can also better deal with outliers and missing values — corrections that are not available with Amazon ML recipes.

The goal of the Amazon ML transformations is to prepare the data for consumption by the Amazon ML algorithm, whereas scripted feature engineering is about cleaning up the data and creating new variables out of the original dataset.

Although Amazon ML recipes are quite restrained, they offer an easy way to fiddle around with the dataset and quickly compare models based on different recipes. Creating a new model and associated evaluation from a given datasource and schema only takes a few clicks. And by choosing to write different recipes for each model, it becomes possible to experiment with a wide range of datasets. Recipes allow us to create a fast try-fail loop. The associated workflow becomes the following:

1. Specify the datasource.
2. Experiment with different recipes.
3. Create or remove variables.
4. Train and select the model associated to that recipe.
5. Once the best recipe is found, then start optimizing the model parameters, regularization, passes, and memory.

We can compare how we transformed the data with scripting (Athena and SQL) and with recipes:

Recipes:

- Removing features (`boat`, `body`, and `home.dest`). This can also be done via the schema or directly by removing the columns from the dataset CSV file.
- Cartesian product for an indication of family by aggregating `parch` and `sibsp`.
- Normalization of numeric values (a possibility).
- Tokenization of all text variables, names, destinations, and so on.
- Quantile binning of all numeric values; although the number of bins were large this transformation produced good results.

Scripting (SQL):

- Handling missing values for `age`: We replaced all missing values by the mean of the *age*
- Text processing: We extracted `titles` from the `name` variables
- Created a new feature, the `family_size` as the sum of `parch` and `sibsp`
- Extraction of the `deck` from the cabin number

Both approaches are very complementary.

Parametrizing the model

Now that our data has been prepared for the SGD algorithm, we are ready to set the parameters of our experiment. In a way similar to scientific experimentation, we will want to try out several sets of parameters to test several models and pick up the best one. The next screenshot shows where we actually specify our model parameters:

- Model memory
- Data passes
- Shuffling
- Regularization

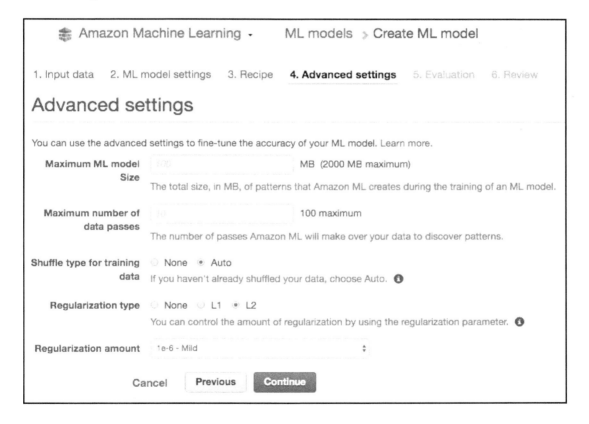

Setting model memory

Model memory is related to the memory Amazon ML must set aside to build and evaluate your model. It is set, by default, to 100Mb. In the case of the `Titanic` dataset, the model memory was always below 1Mb as shown by the logs. Model memory is also used to set aside memory when dealing with streaming data.

Setting the number of data passes

Amazon ML will use the training set of samples several times, each time shuffling it and using the new sequence to increase prediction. It's similar to squeezing a wet piece of cloth — each time you wring it, more water comes out of it. Set by default to 10 passes, it does not hurt to set it to the maximum value of a 100 at the expense of a longer training time for the model and a higher cost of operation.

Choosing regularization

As seen in `Chapter 2`, *Machine Learning Definitions and Concepts*, regularization makes your model more robust and allows it to better handle previously unseen data by reducing overfitting. The rule of thumb is to lower regularization if your evaluation score is poor (underfitting) and increase it if your model shows great performance on the training set but poor results on the evaluation set (overfitting).

Creating an evaluation

Evaluations and models are independent in Amazon ML. You can train a model and carry out several evaluations by specifying different evaluation datasets. The evaluation page, shown in the following screenshot, lets you name and specify how the model will be evaluated:

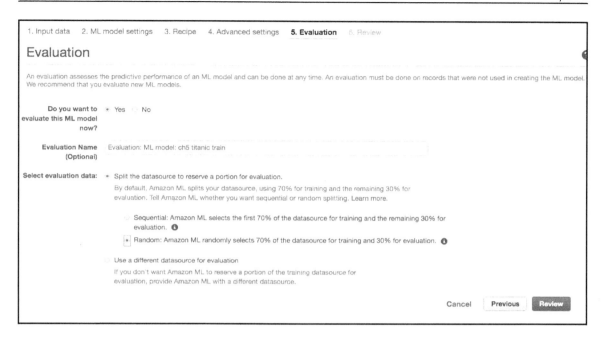

As you know by now, to evaluate a model, you need to split your dataset into two parts, the training and the evaluation sets with a 70/30 split. The training part is used to train your model, while the evaluation part is used to evaluate the model. At this point, you can let Amazon ML split the dataset into training and evaluation or specify a different datasource for evaluation.

Recall that the initial `Titanic` file was ordered by class and passenger alphabetical order. Using this ordered dataset and splitting it without shuffling, that is, taking sequentially the first 70% samples, would give the model a very different data for the training and the evaluation sets. The evaluation would not be relevant. However, if your data is not already shuffled, you can tell Amazon ML to shuffle it. It is a good practice to let Amazon ML reshuffle your data by default just in case your own randomizing left some sequential patterns in the dataset.

Amazon ML will make some verifications regarding your training and validation sets, checking that there is enough data for the validation, that the two sets follow similar distributions, and that the evaluation set has valid samples. Take a look at `http://d ocs.aws.amazon.com/machine-learning/latest/dg/evaluation-alerts.html` for more information on Evaluation Alerts.

Note that if you choose to let Amazon ML split the data, it will create two new datasources titled in a way that lets you see how the split was performed. You can reuse these new datasources if you decide to test another model with different recipes or model parameters such as regularization.

For instance:

- `Titanic.csv_[percentBegin=0, percentEnd=70, strategy=sequential]`
- `Titanic.csv_[percentBegin=70, percentEnd=100, strategy=random]`

Click on **Review**, make sure your model is as expected, and click on the final **Create ML model** button. Creating the model usually takes a few minutes.

Evaluating the model

At this point, Amazon ML will use the training set to train several models and the evaluation sets to select the best one.

Amazon ML runs several model training in parallel, each time trying new parameters and shuffling the training set at each new pass. Once the number of passes initially set has been exhausted or the algorithm has converged, whichever comes first, the model is considered trained. For each model it trains, Amazon ML uses it for prediction on the validation subset to obtain an evaluation score per model. Once all the models have been trained and evaluated this way, Amazon ML simply selects the one with the best evaluation score.

The evaluation metric depends on the type of prediction at hand. AUC and `F1` score for classification (binary and multiclass), and RMSE for regression. How the evaluation results are displayed by Amazon ML also depends on the type of prediction at hand.

We'll start with evaluation for binary classification for our Titanic prediction, followed by the regression case with a new dataset related to Air traffic delays, and finally perform multiclass classification with the classic `Iris` dataset.

Evaluating binary classification

Once your model is ready, click on the model's title from the service dashboard to access the model's result page, which contains the summary of the model, its settings and the evaluation results.

The following screenshot shows that we obtained an *AUC* score of 0.880, which is considered very good for most machine-learning applications. **AUC** stands for the **Area under the Curve** and was introduced in Chapter 2, *Machine Learning Definitions and Concepts*. It is the de-facto metric for classification problems.

The baseline for Binary classification is an AUC of 0.5, which is the score for a model that would randomly predict 0 or 1:

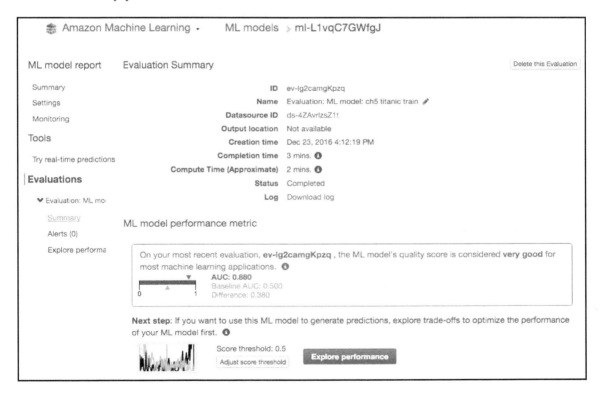

Amazon ML validates the model by checking the following conditions and raising alerts in case the conditions are not met:

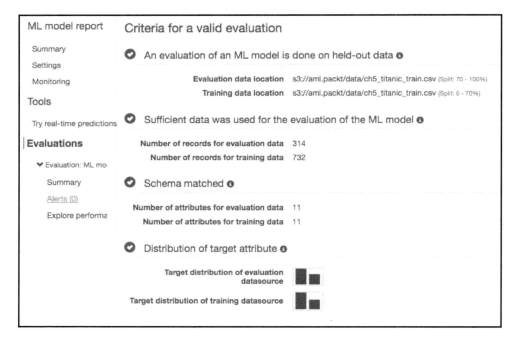

In our case, no alerts were raised:

- The training and validation datasets were separate
- The validation dataset had a sufficient number of samples
- The validation and training sets shared the same schema
- All samples of the validation set were valid and used for the evaluation, implying that the target was not missing for one or more samples
- The distribution of the target variable was similar in the training and validation sets

Most of these alerts will not happen if we let Amazon ML handle the training validation data split, but they might be more frequent if we provide the validation set ourselves.

The AUC score is not the only element Amazon ML gives us to evaluate the quality of our model. By clicking on the **Explore performance** link, we can analyze further the performance of our model.

Exploring the model performances

You may recall from `Chapter 2`: *Machine Learning Definitions and Concepts,* that in a binary classification context, a logistic regression model calculates for each sample to be predicted a probability — the probability of belonging to one class or the other. The model will not directly output the class of the sample to be predicted. The sample is assigned to one class or the other depending on whether the probability is below or above a certain threshold. By default, this threshold is set to 0.5. Although the AUC score given by the evaluation does not depend on the value of the decision threshold, other classification metrics do. We can change the value of the threshold and see how that impacts our predictions.

The **Explore performance** page of the evaluation shows several other classification metrics as well as the confusion matrix of the model. The vertical bar in the graph below is a cursor that can slide left or right. By sliding the cursor, we increase or decrease the decision threshold used to classify a prediction sample as belonging to one class or another. As we move that cursor, the following metrics vary accordingly.

- **False positive rate**
- **Precision**: proportion of predicted positives that are truly positives
- **Recall** (the proportion of positives that are correctly identified)
- **Accuracy**

For a threshold of *0.5,* we have the following sceenshot:

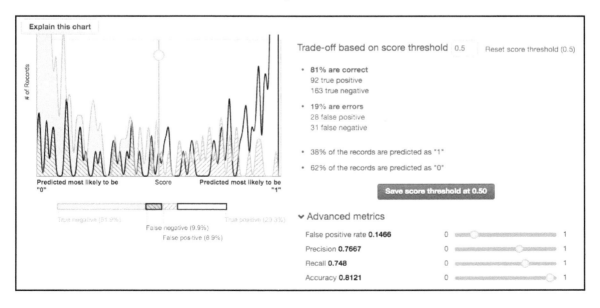

If we lower the threshold to *0.4*, accuracy decreases while recall increases, as you can see in the following screenshot:

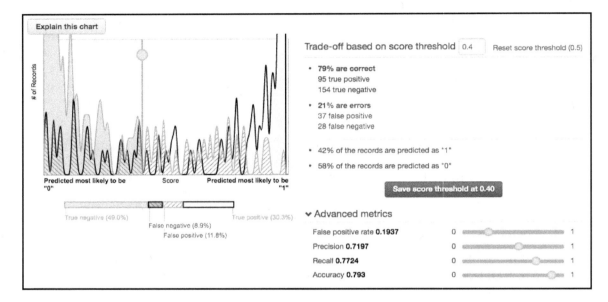

And if we raise the threshold to *0.7*, accuracy increases slightly while recall decreases:

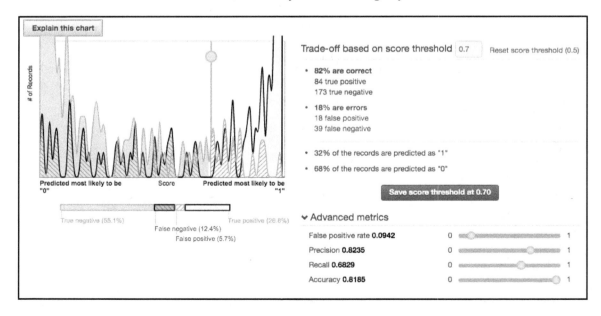

In our context, the predictions are quite clearly separated between survived and did not survive values. Slightly changing the threshold does not have a huge impact on the metrics.

Evaluating linear regression

Amazon ML uses the standard metric RMSE for linear regression. RMSE is defined as the sum of the squares of the difference between the real values and the predicted values:

$$RMSE = \sqrt{\frac{1}{N} \sum_{i=1}^{N} (\hat{y} - y)^2}$$

Where $\hat{y}$ are the predicted values and y the real values. The closer the predictions are to the real values, the lower the RMSE is; therefore, a lower RMSE is interpreted as a better predictive model.

To demonstrate the evaluation in the regression context, we will consider a simplified version of the **Airlines delay** dataset available on Kaggle at `https://www.kaggle.com/giovamata/airlinedelaycauses`. The full dataset is quite large (~250Mb). We extracted roughly *19,000* rows from the year 2008, filtering out cancelled flights. We also removed several variables that were too correlated with our target, which is the `Airdelay` variable. The resulting dataset and schema are available on GitHub at `https://github.com/alexperrier/packt-aml/tree/master/ch5`.

We upload the dataset to S3, create a datasource, train and evaluate a model and finally obtain an RMSE of **7.0557** with a baseline of **31.312**. The baseline for regression is given by a model that always predicts the average of the target:

On your most recent evaluation, **ev-W69T2ORrVmJ** , the ML model's quality score is **better** than the baseline. ❶
RMSE: 7.0557
RMSE baseline: 31.312
Difference: 24.256

Exploring further, we obtain the following histograms of residuals. As we can see in the next screenshot, the errors are roughly bell-shaped and centered around *0*, meaning that our errors are half the time overestimating/underestimating the real values. All the information available in the dataset has been consumed by the model:

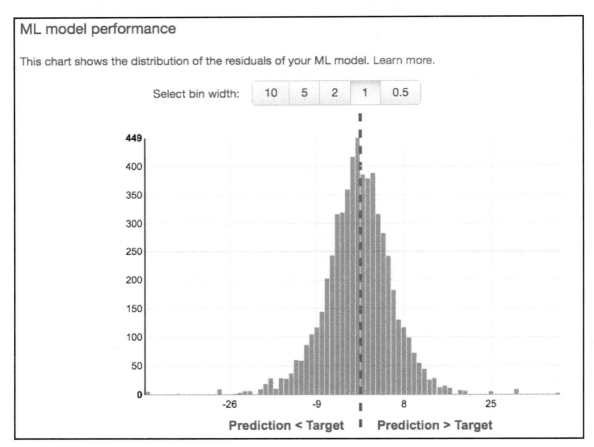

Evaluating multiclass classification

The classic dataset for multiclass classification is the `Iris` dataset composed of three types of Iris flowers. This dataset is quite simple, very popular and using it to illustrate the performance of a platform as powerful as Amazon ML seems overkill. Luckily, there are another three class datasets composed of seeds. The seeds dataset is available at `https://ar chive.ics.uci.edu/ml/datasets/seeds`and of course on the GitHub repository accompanying this book (as well as the schema).

The seed dataset has 210 samples distributed evenly among three different `seedTypes` and seven attributes. The dataset has an ID, which must be set to categorical, all attributes are NUMERIC, and the target is the `seedType`. We upload the dataset to S3, and create a datasource and a model.

The metric for multiclass classification is the *F1* score defined as the harmonic mean of precision and recall:

$$F_1 = 2 \cdot \frac{1}{\frac{1}{\text{recall}} + \frac{1}{\text{precision}}} = 2 \cdot \frac{\text{precision} \cdot \text{recall}}{\text{precision} + \text{recall}}$$

The baseline for a multiclass classification problem is the macro average *F1* score for a model that would always predict the most common class. In the case of the seed dataset, we obtain a *F1* score of **0.870** for baseline of **0.143**:

ML model performance

On your most recent evaluation, **ev-KLid4R0nNCn** , the ML model's quality score is **better** than the baseline. ⓘ

Average F1 score: 0.870
Baseline F1 score: 0.143
Difference: 0.726

0   1

Explore model performance

Performance exploration is not as developed as in the binary classification case. Amazon ML gives us the confusion matrix which shows, for each class, the ratio of correctly predicted samples over the real number of samples in that class:

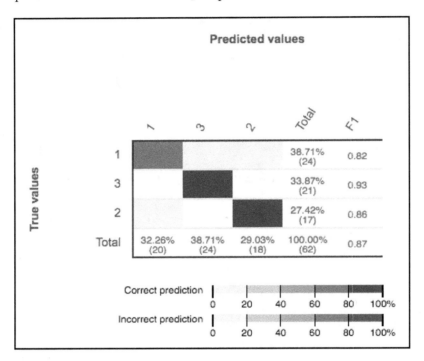

Analyzing the logs

For every operation it carries out, Amazon ML gives us access to the related logs. We can download and analyze the model training logs and infer a few things on how Amazon ML trains and selects the best model.

Go back to the last Titanic model, and in the summary part, click on the **Download Log** link. The log file is too long to be reproduced here but is available at `https://github.com` `/alexperrier/packt-aml/blob/master/ch5/titanic_training.log`:

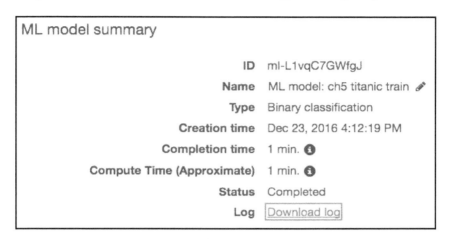

Amazon ML launches five versions of the SGD algorithm in parallel. Each version is called a learner and corresponds to a different value for the learning rate: 0.01, 0.1,1, 10, and 100. The following five metrics are calculated at each new pass of the algorithm:

- Accuracy
- Recall
- Precision
- F1-score
- AUC

The `negative-log-likelihood` is also calculated to assess whether the last iterations have brought significant improvement in reducing the residual error.

Optimizing the learning rate

If you recall from `Chapter 2`, *Machine Learning Definitions and Concepts*, under the section *Regularization on linear models*, the **Stochastic Gradient Descent (SGD)** algorithm has a parameter called the learning rate.

The SGD is based on the idea of taking each new (block of) data sample to make little corrections to the linear regression model coefficients. At each iteration, the input data samples are used either on a sample-by-sample basis or on a block-by-block basis to estimate the best correction (the so-called gradient) to make to the linear regression coefficients to further reduce the estimation error. It has been shown that the SGD algorithm converges to an optimal solution for the linear regression weights. These corrections are multiplied by a parameter called the `learning rate`, which drives the amount of correction brought to the coefficients at each iteration.

SGD calculations are low in computation costs. It's a fascinating yet simple algorithm that is used in many applications.

Imagine a marble in a bowl. Set the marble on the rim of the bowl and let it drop into the bowl with a circular movement. It will circle around the bowl while falling to the bottom. At the end of its descent, it will tend to circle around the bottom of the bowl and finally come to rest at the lowest point of the bowl. The SGD behaves similarly when you consider the marble as the prediction error at each iteration and the bottom of the bowl as the ultimate and most optimal coefficients that could be estimated. At each iteration, the prediction error becomes smaller on average. The error will not follow the most direct path to the bottom of the bowl like the marble does, nor will it reach the lowest most optimal solution, but on average, the predictions get better and the error decreases iteration after iteration. After a certain number of iterations, the error will approach its potential optimal minimum. How fast and how close it gets to the minimum error and the best coefficients depends directly on the value of the learning rate.

The learning rate controls how much the weights are corrected at each iteration. The learning rate drives the convergence of the algorithm. The larger the learning rate, the faster the convergence and potentially, the larger the residual error once converged.

Thus, choosing an optimal learning rate will be a balance between the following:

- A faster convergence and poorer estimation
- A slower convergence and more accurate estimation

However, if the learning rate is too small, the convergence can be too slow and take too long to reach an optimal solution. One standard strategy is to decrease the learning rate as the algorithm converges, thus ensuring a fast convergence at the beginning, which will slow down as the prediction error becomes slower. As the learning rate decreases, the coefficient estimation becomes more accurate. Small learning rates mean that the algorithm converges slowly, while higher values mean each new sample has a bigger impact on the correcting factor. Amazon ML does not use that strategy and keeps the learning rate constant. In Amazon ML, the learning rate is set for you. You cannot choose a value.

Visualizing convergence

By parsing the logs, we can extract the following convergence plots for our Titanic model:

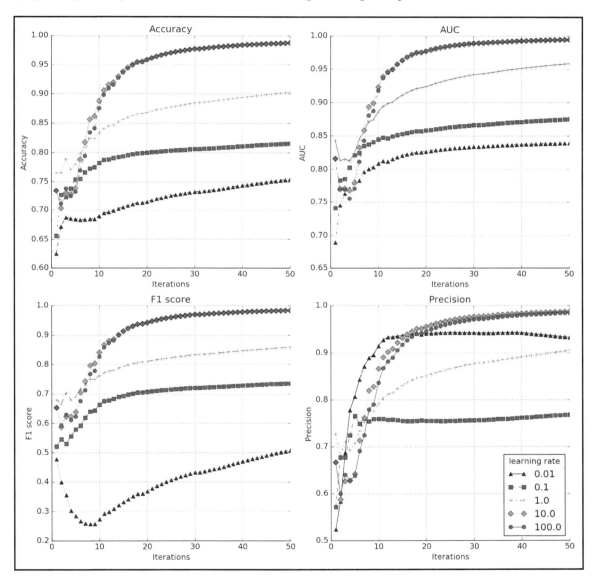

The previous screenshot of different plots shows four metrics: **Accuracy**, **AUC**, **F1 score**, and **Precision** for the five different values of the learning rate. The model was set to 50 passes with mild (10^-6) L2 regularization on the Titanic training dataset. We can see that, for all metrics, the best value for the learning rate is either 10 or 100, with a slight advantage for learning rate=100. These values converge faster and reach better scores. The smallest learning rate (0.01) converges far slower. In our context, faster convergence and large learning rate values beat smaller rate values.

The default number of passes when creating a model is *10*. We can see that 10 iterations would not have been sufficient for the score to stabilize and converge. At the 10th iteration, the curves are barely out of the chaotic initialization phase.

Looking at the negative log likelihood graph extracted from the logs, we also see that the best learner corresponds to a learning rate of 100 shown here by the curve with diamond shapes:

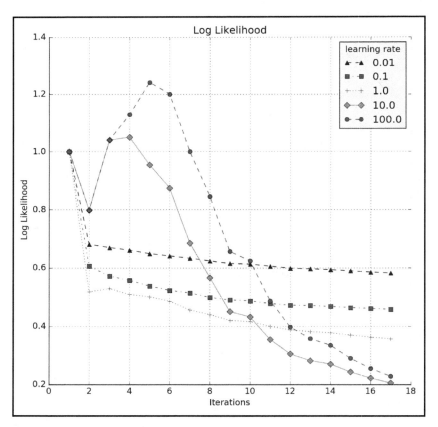

One conclusion that can be made from these graphs is that you should not limit your model to the default 10 passes.

These two convergence graphs are entirely dependent on the problem at hand. For a different dataset, we would have ended with entirely different graphs in terms of convergence rate, learning rate, and score achieved.

Impact of regularization

The following graph compares AUC for three different models:

- No regularization
- Mild regularization (10^-6)
- Aggressive regularization (10^-2)

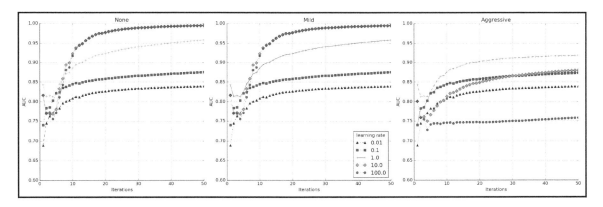

We notice that there is no significant difference between having no regularization and having mild regularization. Aggressive regularization, however, has a direct impact on the model performance. The algorithm converges to a lower AUC, and the optimal learning rate is no longer 100 but 1.

Comparing the performance graph given by Amazon ML for mild and aggressive regularization, we see that although the scores (AUC, accuracy, and so on) are very similar in both cases, the difference lies with the certainty of the predictions. In the mild regularization case (left graph), the predictions are far apart. The probabilities or predictions that a sample is zero or one are very distinct. In the aggressive regularization case (right graph), this separation is far less obvious. The probabilities for samples to belong to one class versus the other are much closer. The decision boundary is less clear:

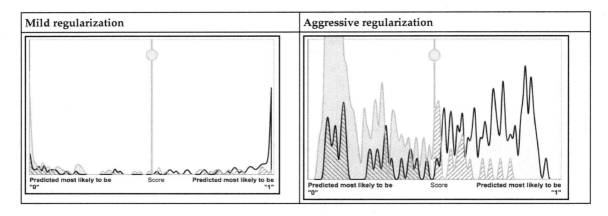

The goal of regularization being to decouple the performance of the model from the training data in order to reduce overfitting, it may well be that, on the held-out dataset on previously unseen data, heavy regularization would give better results and no regularization would perform worse than mild regularization. Less optimal performance in the training-validation phase is sometimes more robust during the real prediction phase. It's important to keep in mind that performance in the validation phase does not always translate into performance in the prediction phase.

Comparing different recipes on the Titanic dataset

In this last section, we would like to compare several recipes and see if our SQL, based feature engineering drives a better model performance. In all our experimentation, the one thing that stood out with regards to the recipes Amazon ML suggested was that all the numeric variables ended up being categorized via quantile binning. The large number of bins was also in question. We compare the following scenarios on the `Titanic` dataset:

- Suggested Amazon ML recipe
- Numeric values are kept as numeric. No quantile binning is involved in the recipe.
- The extended Titanic datasource we created in `Chapter 4`, *Loading and Preparing the Dataset* is used with the suggested Amazon ML recipe

We slightly modified the extended Titanic dataset that was used in `Chapter 4`, *Loading and Preparing the Dataset:*

- There was no need to have both `fare` and `log_fare`. We removed `fare`.
- We manually corrected some titles that were not properly extracted from the names.
- The new extended dataset is available in the GitHub repository for his chapter as `ch5_extended_titanic_training.csv`.

In all three cases, we apply L2 mild regularization.

Keeping variables as numeric or applying quantile binning?

We found that keeping all numeric variables as numeric and avoiding any quantile binning had a very direct and negative effect on the model performance. The overall score was far lower in the numeric case than in the quantile binning case: `AUC: 0.81` for all numeric versus `AUC: 0.88` for QB.

Looking at the convergence graph for the *All Numeric* model, it appears that the algorithm converged much more slowly than it had for the quantile binning model. It obviously had not converged after 50 passes, so we increased the number of passes to 100. We also noticed that in the *All Numeric* case, the best learning rate was equal to 0.01, whereas in the quantile binning model, the best learning rate was much larger (10 or 100). A smaller learning rate induces a slower convergence rate:

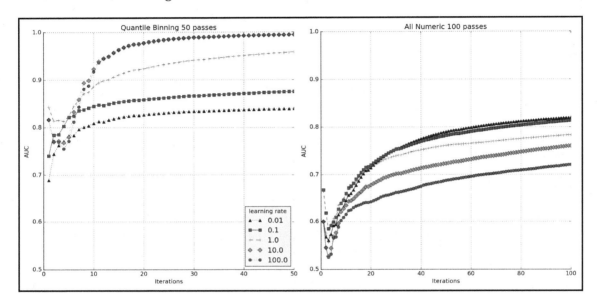

We also see on the following performance charts that the quantile binning model separates the classes much better than the All Numeric model:

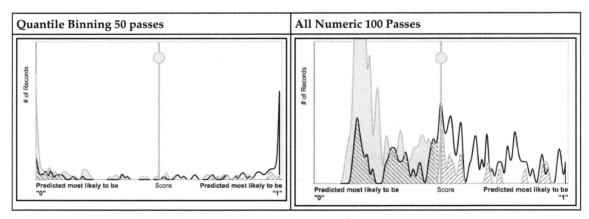

So quantile binning is definitely preferable to no quantile binning. What about our efforts to extend the initial dataset with new features? Well, somehow, our extended model did not produce better results than the initial dataset. Extracting the `title` from the `name`, replacing missing values for the `age`, and extracting the `deck` from the `cabin` did not generate an obviously better model:

- Original Titanic dataset: AUC 0.88
- Extended Titanic dataset with feature engineering: AUC 0.82

Convergence and performance charts were similar for both models and are not reproduced here. Several factors can be at play here to explain why our improved dataset did not produce a better model, and further analysis would be required to understand which feature engineering had a positive impact on the model and which one did not. However, we will see in the next chapter that this may also have been dependent on the actual samples in the evaluation set. On average, the extended dataset generates better performances but for this particular trial, the associated model performed roughly the same as the one trained on the original dataset. The conclusion being that it is worth the effort to run several trials to assess the quality and performance of a model, and not rely on a unique trial where the particularities of the evaluation set may influence the comparison between models.

Parsing the model logs

The convergence plots were obtained by parsing the Amazon ML model logs to extract the data into a CSV file that could be used later on to create plots. The process is simple and mostly based on command line scripting using the `grep` and the `sed` commands. We want to extract and parse the following lines from the log file:

```
16/12/25 13:54:03 INFO: learner-id=4202 model-performance:
        accuracy=0.6562 recall=0.5000 precision=0.5909 f1-score=0.5417
auc=0.7095
```

And convert them into a CSV format as follows:

iteration	alpha	learner	accuracy	recall	precision	f1	auc
1	0.01	1050	0.5937	0.56	0.4828	0.5185	0.6015

The first step is to extract the right lines from the log file. We notice that they all contain the string `model-performance:`. We use grep to extract all the lines containing this string into a temporary file that we name `model_performance.tmp`.

Copy-paste the log data from the Amazon ML Model page into a log file (`model.log`) and in the terminal run the following:

```
grep "model-performance:" model.log >> model_performance.tmp
```

The trick then is to replace the right sub-strings by commas using the `sed` command. The `sed` command follows this syntax:

```
sed -i.bak 's/STRING_TO_REPLACE/STRING_TO_REPLACE_IT/g' filename
```

The `-i.bak` option makes it possible to replace the string within the file itself without the need to create a temporary file.

So, for instance, replacing the string `INFO: learner-id=` by a comma in the `model_performance.tmp` file is obtained by running the following line in a terminal:

```
sed -i.bak 's/ INFO: learner-id=/,/g' model_performance.tmp
```

With the following commands, most of the original log file will have been transformed into a CSV formatted file, which you can use as a base for visualizing the convergence of the Amazon ML model. The rest of the file cleaning can be done in a spreadsheet editor:

```
sed -i.bak 's/ INFO: learner-id=/,,/g' model_performance.tmp
sed -i.bak 's/ model-performance:          accuracy=/,/g'
model_performance.tmp
sed -i.bak 's/ recall=/,/g' model_performance.tmp
sed -i.bak 's/ precision=/,/g' model_performance.tmp
sed -i.bak 's/ f1-score=/,/g' model_performance.tmp
sed -i.bak 's/ auc=/,/g' model_performance.tmp
```

A similar pattern can be used to extract the negative log likelihood data from the Amazon ML model logs:

```
sed -i.bak 's/ INFO: learner-id=/,,/g' filename
sed -i.bak 's/ model-convergence:          negative-log-likelihood=/,/g'
filename
sed -i.bak 's/ (delta=1.000000e+00) is-converged=no//g' filename
```

We end up with a CSV file with a row for each iteration and a column for the learning rate and each metric.

Summary

In this chapter, we created predictive models in Amazon ML--from selecting the datasource, applying transformations to the initial data with recipes, and analyzing the performance of the trained model. The model performance exploration depends on the type of prediction problem at hand: binary, multi-classification, or regression. We also looked at the model logs for the Titanic dataset and learned how the SGD algorithm trains and selects the best model out of several different ones with different learning rates.

Finally, we compared several data transformation strategies and their impact on the model performance and algorithm convergence in the context of the Titanic dataset. We found out that quantile binning of numeric values is a key strategy in boosting the convergence speed of the algorithm, which overall generated much better models.

So far, these models and performance evaluation are all obtained on training data. That is data that is fully available to the model from the start. The raison d'être of these models is not to run on subsets of the training data, but to make robust predictions on previously unseen data.

In the next chapter, we will apply these models on the held-out datasets we created in `Chapter 4`, *Loading and preparing the dataset*, to make real predictions.

6

Predictions and Performances

It is time to make some predictions! In `Chapter 4`, *Loading and Preparing the Dataset,* we did split the `Titanic` dataset into two subsets, the training and held-out subsets, respectively consisting of 70% and 30% of the original dataset randomly shuffled. We have used variations of the training subset extensively in `chapter 5` *Model Creation*, to train and select the best classification model. But so far, we have not used the held-out subset at all. In this chapter, we apply our models to this held-out subset to make predictions on unseen data and make a final assessment of the performance and robustness of our models.

Amazon ML offers two types of predictions: batch and streaming. Batch prediction requires a datasource. The samples you want to predict are given to the model all at once in batch mode. Streaming, also known as real-time or online predictions, requires the creation of an API endpoint and consists of submitting sequences of samples, one by one, via HTTP requests. Real-time predictions do not involve the creation of a datasource.

We will start with batch predictions on the Titanic held-out set. We will confirm that our different models perform similarly on the held-out dataset as they did on the validation subsets, assuming that all the subsets have a similar variable distribution. In `Chapter 5`, *Model Creation*, we concluded that out of our three datasources — suggested recipe with quantile binning (QB), recipe without QB, and the extended dataset — the one with extra variables (`deck`, `title`, `log_fare`, and so on) resulted in the best score on the validation subset. We will verify that this is also the case on the held-out subset.

This chapter is organized in two parts. In the first part, we look at batch predictions on the `Titanic` dataset. In the second part, we look at real-time, streaming predictions, with a new text-based quantile binning from the UCI repository. The `Spam` dataset is large enough to simulate streaming data. We will create an Amazon ML endpoint and use the Python SDK to send and retrieve classification predictions.

In this chapter, we will cover the following topics:

- Making batch predictions
- Making real-time predictions

 In real-world classification problems or regression problems, the previously unseen data you want to make predictions on will not include the target values. In our case, the held-out datasets do contain the solution, and this allows us to assess the model performance on previously unseen data. But with real-world problems, you do not have that luxury and you will have to trust your model.

Making batch predictions

Making batch predictions on Amazon ML is straightforward and follows this process:

1. From the dashboard, **create a new Batch prediction**.
2. Select the model.
3. Select the datasource on which to apply the model.
4. Set the prediction output folder and grant permissions.
5. Review and launch.

We call the `prediction` dataset or datasource, the data on which we want to make predictions. In this chapter, we are in a testing context and the `prediction` dataset is the `held-out` dataset we extracted from the whole original dataset. In a real-world context, the prediction dataset refers to entirely new data and does not include the target variable.

The prediction can only work if the distribution of the prediction dataset is similar to the distribution of the training dataset on which the model has been trained. The prediction datasource and the training datasource must also share the same schema, with one difference the prediction dataset does not need to include the target variable. Amazon ML will verify that the schema defined for your training data is relevant to your prediction data and will issue a warning if the datasets are not similar.

For the sake of convenience, we have recreated the datasets, datasources, and models for this chapter. All datasets and scripts are available in the GitHub repository at `https://github.com/alexperrier/packt-aml/tree/master/ch6`. Since we reshuffled the original Titanic data, the evaluation scores will be different from the ones obtained previously for the same dataset.

Creating the batch prediction job

To create a batch prediction, go to the Amazon ML dashboard and click on **Create new batch prediction**:

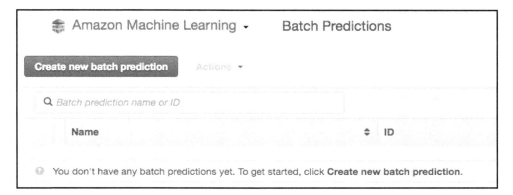

Then select the model. We choose the original model related to the `Titanic` dataset, the one using the Amazon ML suggested recipe with quantile binning:

- Quantile binning of all numeric variables
- L2 mild regularization

After the model selection comes the datasource selection. If you have not yet created a datasource for the held-out set, you can do so now. First, upload your prediction dataset to S3 and specify the S3 path for the source of the data:

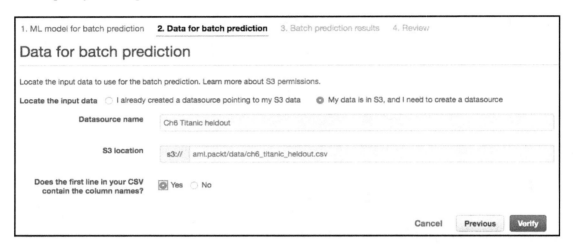

When you click on **Verify**, Amazon ML will check that the prediction dataset follows the same schema as the training dataset on which the model was trained:

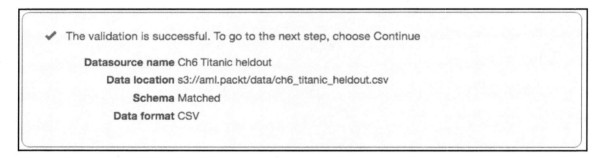

Interpreting prediction outputs

The output of the Amazon ML prediction job will consists of two files: the manifest file and the actual prediction results given in a compressed CSV file. Amazon ML will create the files on S3 in an S3 location, `s3://bucket/folder`, which you must specify. We use the same path as our data path: `s3://aml.packt/data/`. Amazon ML will create a `/batch_prediction` folder, where it will write the manifest file as well as an extra subfolder `/results`, where the CSV file with the actual predictions will be written. To recap, in our context, the manifest file will be in the `s3://aml.packt/data/batch_prediction` folder, and the compressed CSV results file will be in the `s3://aml.packt/data/batch_prediction/results/` folder. The name given to the batch prediction will dictate the naming of the manifest and results files:

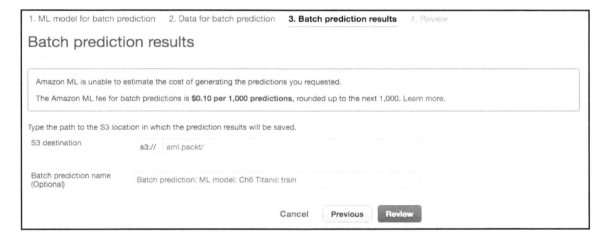

Prediction pricing: If you just created the datasource for the batch prediction, Amazon ML does not yet have access to the data statistics that it needs to calculate the prediction costs. In that case, it will simply inform you of the price, of $0.10 per 1,000 predictions. If the prediction datasource has already been validated and Amazon ML knows the number of records, the estimated price will be the number of rows times the price per prediction rounded up to the nearest cent. You are not billed for the invalid samples Amazon ML fails to predict. More information is available at `http://docs.aws.amazon.com/machine-learning/latest/dg/pricing.html`.

Review and click on the **Create batch** prediction button. The batch prediction job will take a few minutes to complete. When finished, it will have created the manifest and results files in S3 and will show up as completed in the **Batch Prediction** section of the Amazon ML dashboard.

Reading the manifest file

The manifest file contains JSON-formatted data that maps the input file to the prediction results file, as follows:

```
{S3 location of the batch prediction input file.csv : S3 location of the
prediction results file}
```

In our context, the manifest file contains the following line:

```
{"s3://aml.packt/data/ch6_titanic_heldout.csv":"s3://aml.packt/batch-
prediction/result/bp-yTDNSArMqa6-ch6_titanic_heldout.csv.gz"}
```

Multiple input files: If your input data is split into several files, all stored in the same S3 location s3://examplebucket/input/, all the input files will be considered by the batch prediction job. The manifest file will then contain the mapping from the different input files to the associated results files. For instance, if you have three input files named data1.csv, data2.csv, and data3.csv, and they are all stored in the S3 location s3://examplebucket/input/, you will see a mapping string that looks like as follows:

```
{"s3://examplebucket/input/data1.csv":"s3://examplebucket/output/batch-
prediction/result/bp-example-data1.csv.gz",
"s3://examplebucket/input/data2.csv":"
 s3://examplebucket/output/batch-prediction/result/bp-example-
data2.csv.gz", "s3://examplebucket/input/data3.csv":"
 s3://examplebucket/output/batch-prediction/result/bp-example-
data3.csv.gz"}
```

Maximum size for predictions: Amazon ML allows up to 1TB of data for prediction files. If the data on which you want to make predictions is larger, it is possible to split your data into several files, upload them to a specific S3 location, and Amazon ML will handle the different files and generate as many prediction result files as there are input files by running several batches in parallel. The manifest file will contain all the different input/output pairs, {input_file.csv : prediction_results.csv.gz} for your different batch prediction files.

Reading the results file

The output results file is compressed with gzip, originates from the UNIX world, and offers better compression than the more common zip compression. A simple click should be sufficient to open and decompress the gzipped results file into a readable CSV file. Alternatively, a call to the gunzip command from the command line should work. Take a look at http://www.gzip.org/ for installation on different systems.

For binary classification, the decompressed results file contains two or three columns, depending on whether the initial input file contained the target or not. In our case of binary classification, the result file has the following columns: trueLabel, bestAnswer, and score, where trueLabel is the initial survived column. If your initial batch prediction dataset did not include the target values, the results file will only have the bestAnswer and score columns:

- trueLabel is the original target value contained in the input file
- bestAnswer is the classification result: 0 or 1
- Score is the probability for that classification written in scientific notation

The classification cutoff threshold for the score probability is 0.5 by default, or set to the threshold value you chose while evaluating the model.

For multiclass classification with *N* potential target classes, the results file will have *N+1* or *N+2* columns. The trueLabel, bestAnswer, and N columns each with the probability scores for each one of the N classes. The chosen class will be the one that bears the highest probability score.

For a regression model, the results file will only contain one/two score columns with the predicted value, and possibly the trueLabel column.

Assessing our predictions

Since we know the real class of our held-out samples, we can calculate the **ROC-AUC** score and other metrics to see how close our prediction and validation scores are. Assuming that our data subsets have very similar distributions, both scores should end up very close. The difference only comes from randomness in the samples for the validation and held-out sets.

The following Python script uses the `scikit-learn` library (http://scikit-learn.org/) as well as the pandas library. It takes a few lines of Python to calculate the AUC score of the model on that prediction dataset. First, download the gzipped file from S3 and then, in a Python Notebook or console, run the following:

```python
import pandas as pd
from sklearn import metrics

# open file the csv file on your local
df = pd.read_csv(path/location_of_the_unzipped_results_csv_file)

# calculate the true and false positive rate
fpr, tpr, threshold = metrics.roc_curve(df.trueLabel, df.score)
roc_auc = metrics.auc(fpr, tpr)
```

 Python environment: All the Python code in this book is for Python 3.5 or above. For more information on the Anaconda library, take a look at https://www.continuum.io/downloads. Anaconda is an amazingly powerful open source data science platform in Python. It contains the most important libraries (numpy, pandas, scikit-learn, matplotlib, and many others) as well as the Jupyter Notebooks environment. We use the IPython console for its simplicity of use and many magic commands (http://ipython.readthedocs.io/en/stable/interactive/magics.html).

Running the previous Python script on the predictions results, we obtain an AUC of 0.84 on our held-out dataset, which is very close to the AUC (0.85) we obtained on the validation set in Chapter 5, *Model Creation*. We can conclude that our model is pretty stable and robust when facing new, previously unforeseen data.

The following plot shows both the ROC curves for the validation (dotted line) and held-out (solid-line) sets for the chosen model. The validation set is slightly better for higher values of the threshold. This difference is a reflection of the different data distributions in the two datasets:

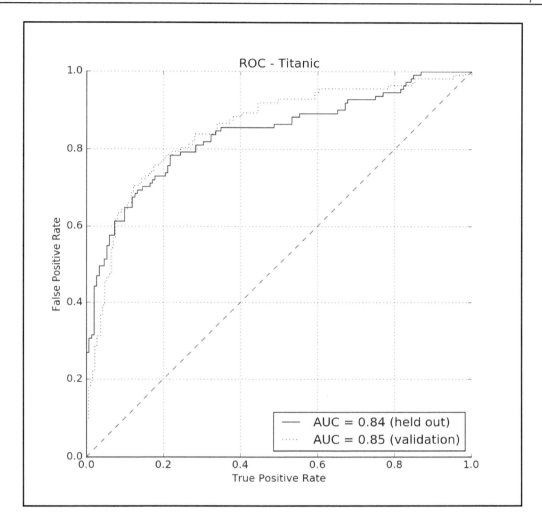

Evaluating the held-out dataset

In Chapter 5, *Model Creation*, we evaluated the performance of our different models on a slice of the training datasource. We obtained for each model an AUC score, and selected the AUC with the best AUC score. We relied on Amazon ML to create the validation set, by splitting the training dataset into two, with 70% for training and 30% of the data for validation. We could have done that split ourselves, created the validation datasource, and specified which datasource to use for the evaluation of the model.

In fact, nothing prevents us from running a model evaluation on the held-out dataset. If you go to the model summary page, you will notice a **Perform another Evaluation** button in the Evaluation section:

Click on it. You are asked to select the datasource for the evaluation. Select the held-out dataset; Amazon ML will verify that the data follows the same schema and is similar to the training data. You end up with two evaluations on the model:

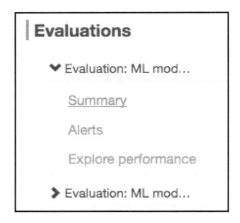

And as expected, the evaluation AUC for the held-out dataset is equal to the AUC we obtained by downloading the results and calculating the AUC in Python:

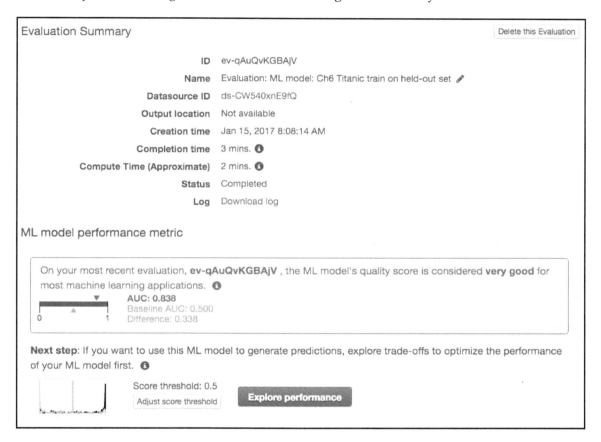

Finding out who will survive

The true value of predictions, however, is not about validating the robustness of our model; it's about making predictions on our prediction dataset, in our context, getting survival predictions on this `new` list of passengers contained in the held-out dataset.

The rows in the results file follow the exact same order as the rows in the prediction file. We can put side by side the first rows of the held-out file and the first rows of the results file, and see that the `survived` and the `trueLabel` columns are identical:

A	B	C	D	E
survived	name	trueLabel	bestAnswer	score
0	Palsson Miss. Torborg Danira	0	0	3.234488E-1
0	Sweet Mr. George Frederick	0	0	3.030103E-1
0	Thomas Mr. Tannous	0	0	2.173607E-1
1	Kantor Mrs. Sinai Miriam Sternin	1	1	5.255009E-1
0	Keeping Mr. Edwin	0	1	5.790327E-1
1	Andersen-Jensen Miss. Carla Christine Nielsine	1	0	3.982854E-1
1	Hart Miss. Eva Miriam	1	1	5.504293E-1
1	Abrahim Mrs. Joseph Sophie Halaut Easu	1	1	5.119896E-1
1	Hocking Miss. Ellen Nellie	1	0	4.442134E-1
0	Paulner Mr. Uscher	0	0	2.229598E-1

Multiplying trials

The evaluation scores on the various models and dataset version are, to a certain extent, dependent on the samples contained in the evaluation sets. If we run the following experiment several times on the three datasets, we see certain variations in the scores:

- Shuffle and split the dataset into three -- training, validation, and held-out and create the respective datasources
- Train a model on the training dataset, keeping the default Amazon ML settings (mild L2 regularization)
- Evaluate the model on the evaluation and held-out datasets

The following plot shows the respective performances of the three models for several trials. The average AUC is written on the graph. We see that on average, the extended dataset performs better (*AUC = 0.87*) than the original dataset with the default recipe (*AUC = 0.84*) and the original dataset without quantile binning (*AUC = 0.83*). We also notice that in some trials, the extended dataset performs worse than the original one. For trial 3, the default recipe is even slightly less performant than the no quantile binning one:

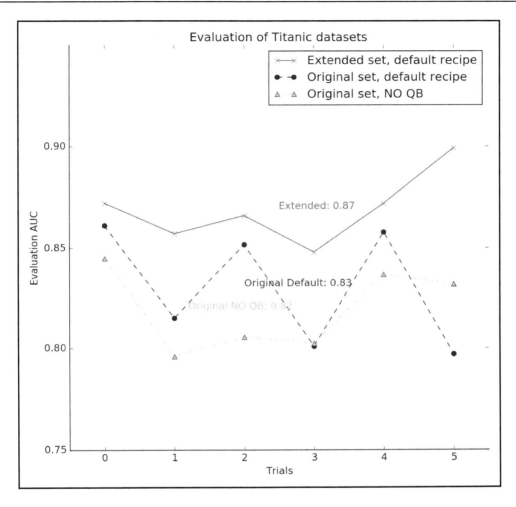

This shows the importance of inner data distribution variability. When trying out several variants of your datasets with different features and processing, it's important to base your conclusions on several runs of your models. A single evaluation may lead to missing the best model.

Making real-time predictions

With batch predictions, you submit all the samples you want the model to predict at once to Amazon ML by creating a datasource. With real-time predictions, also called streaming or online predictions, the idea is to send one sample at a time to an API endpoint, a URL, via HTTP queries, and receive back predictions and information for each one of the samples.

Setting up real-time predictions on a model consists of knowing the prediction API endpoint URL and writing a script that can read your data, send each new sample to that API URL, and retrieve the predicted class or value. We will present a Python-based example in the following section.

Amazon ML also offers a way to make predictions on data you create on the fly on the prediction page. We can input the profile of a would-be passenger on the `Titanic` and see whether that profile would have survived or not. It is a great way to explore the influence of the dataset variables on the outcome.

Before setting up API for streaming, let's see what we can gather from submitting several single passenger profiles. We can even try to answer the question – *Would you have survived on the Titanic?*

Manually exploring variable influence

Go to the model summary page and click on the **Try real-time predictions** link on the left side of the page. The following page shows a form where you can fill out values for the variables in our dataset except for the target.

Let's see if Alex Mr. Perrier, a first-class passenger who embarked at Southhampton with his family (3 sibsp and 2 parch) and who paid a fare of 100 pounds, would have survived. Well, in that case, the model gives a very low probability of survival (0.001), meaning that the model predicts with confidence that this passenger would not have survived. His 12 year old daughter would have had better chances of surviving (*probability 0.56*), though the model is less sure of it. However, if that same girl was traveling alone (*sibsp = parch = 0*), her chance of survival would surge to 0.98 under the condition that she traveled in 1st class. In 3rd class, she would have been less fortunate (*probability: 0.28*):

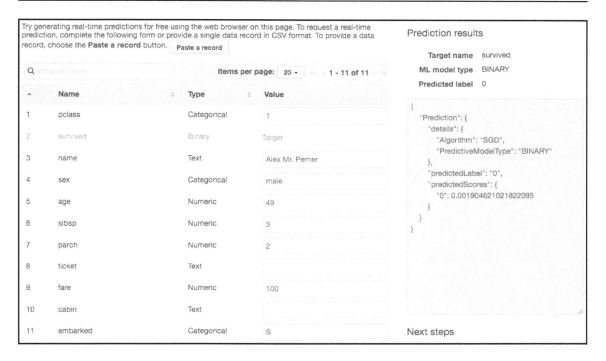

So, by changing one variable at a time in the data, we can have a better understanding of the impact of each variable on the outcome.

Setting up real-time predictions

To demonstrate real-time predictions, we will use the `Spam` dataset from the UCI repository. This dataset is composed of 5,574 SMS messages annotated spam or ham (non-spam). There are no missing values and only two variables: the nature of the SMS (ham or spam) and the text message of the SMS, nothing else. The `Spam` dataset is available at `https://archive.i cs.uci.edu/ml/datasets/SMS+Spam+Collection` in its raw form, and in the book's GitHub repository at `https://github.com/alexperrier/packt-aml/tree/master/ch6`. We have simply transformed the target from categorical: `spam` and `ham` values to binary: 1 (for spam) and 0 (for ham) so that Amazon ML understands the prediction to be of the binary-classification type.

AWS SDK

AWS offers several APIs and **Software Development Kits (SDKs)** to its many services. You can programmatically manage your files on S3, set up EC2 instances, and create datasources, models, and evaluations on Amazon ML without using the web-based user interface. The AWS APIs are low-level endpoints. In general, it is simpler and more efficient to use the SDKs, which are wrappers around the APIs and are available for several languages (Python, Ruby, Java, C++, and so on). In this book, we will use the Python SDK based on the Boto3 library. We explore in detail the use of the Python SDK in Chapter 7, *Command Line and SDK*. For now, we will only use the predict() method necessary for real-time predictions. But first, we need to enable access to AWS by setting up AWS credentials on our local machine.

Setting up AWS credentials

In order to access AWS programmatically, we first need to access AWS via the command line. This requires the following:

- Creating access keys on AWS IAM for your user
- Installing the AWS-CLI command-line interface on local
- Configuring AWS-CLI with the AWS access keys

AWS access keys

If you recall from Chapter 3, *Overview of an Amazon Machine Learning Workflow*, we had created access keys for our AML@Packt user. Access keys are user-based and composed of two parts: the **Access Key ID**, which is always available in the user security credentials tab in IAM, and the **Secret Access Key**, which is only shown at creation time. When creating these access keys, you are given the possibility of downloading them. If you did not do so at that time, you can recreate access keys for your user now. Go to the IAM console at https ://console.aws.amazon.com/iam, click on your user profile, select the **Security Credentials** tab, and click on the **Create Access Key** button. This time make sure you download the keys on your local machine or copy them somewhere. Note that there's a limit of two sets of access keys per user. You will have to delete existing keys before creating new ones if you already have two keys associated to your user:

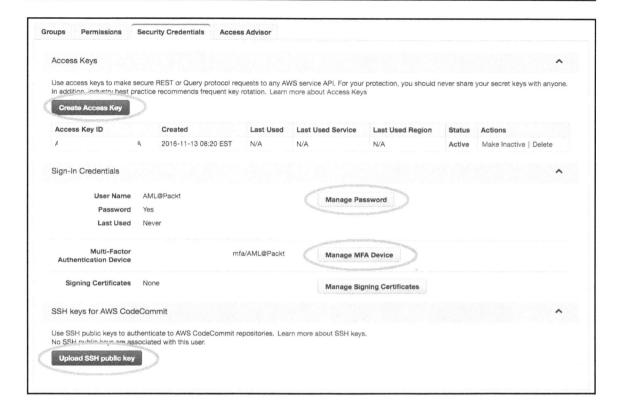

Setting up AWS CLI

So far, we have only worked with the AWS web interface, clicking from page to page on the AWS website. Another way to interact with AWS services is via the command line in a terminal window, using the `aws cli` library. CLI stands for Command Line Interface.

To install the `aws cli` library, open a terminal window. For a Python-based environment (Python 2 version 2.6.5+ or Python 3 version 3.3+), installing `aws cli` consists of running the following command in a terminal:

```
pip install awscli
```

Full instructions for installation in other environments are available at http://docs.aws.amazon.com/cli/latest/userguide/installing.html. Once AWS-CLI is installed, run the following command to configure it:

```
aws configure
```

You will be asked for your access keys, the default region, and format. See `http://docs.aw` `s.amazon.com/cli/latest/userguide/cli-chap-getting-started.html#cli-quick-co` `nfiguration`for more in-depth explanations.

In short, AWS-CLI commands follow this syntax:

```
aws {service name} {command} {parameters}
```

Test your setup by running the following:

```
aws s3 ls aml.packt
```

You should see a list of your buckets, folders, and files in your s3 account. This is what my output looks like when I list the file and folders in the `aml.packt` bucket:

```
[@:~/apps/packt(master)]$ aws s3 ls aml.packt
                           PRE athena_data/
                           PRE athena_query_results/
                           PRE batch-prediction/
                           PRE data/
                           PRE data2/
2017-01-09 17:28:37          0 .writePermissionCheck.tmp
2016-11-13 12:22:45        728 LT67_heldout.csv
2016-11-13 12:22:45       2782 LT67_training.csv
```

We will explore in detail how to run your Amazon ML projects using CLI in Chapter 7, *Command Line and SDK*.

Python SDK

We will not use the AWS-CLI any further in this chapter, but instead switch to the Python SDK. We needed to setup the credentials for the AWS CLI in order for our SDKs scripts to be able to access our AWS account. To use the Python SDK, we need to install the Boto3 library, which comes bundled in the Anaconda distribution. If you use Anaconda as your Python environment, you should already have the boto3 package installed. If not, you can install it using pip with the following:

```
pip install boto3
```

Boto3 will use the credentials we configured for the AWS CLI. There's no need for a specific setup. Boto3 is available for most AWS services. The full documentation is available at `http s://boto3.readthedocs.io/`. Our minimal use of `Boto3` only requires to specify the service we want, Machine Learning, and then use the `predict()` method to send the proper data to the model. In return, we obtain the predictions we wanted. The following Python code initiates a client to access the machine learning service.

```
import boto3
client = boto3.client('machinelearning')
```

The `predict()` method requires the following parameters:

- `MLModelId`: The ID of the model your want to use to predict
- `PredictEndpoint`: The URL of the Amazon ML endpoint for your model
- `Record`: A JSON-formatted version of the sample

The `MLModelId` and `PredictEndpoint` URL can be obtained from the model summary page. The `Record` is a JSON-formatted string. We will simulate a streaming application by opening a held-out set of samples, looping through each sample and sending it via the `predict()` method.

We have split the initial dataset into a training set of 4,400 samples and a held-out set of 1,174 samples. These subsets are available at the GitHub repository. We create a datasource for the training subset, and create a model and its evaluation with default settings (mild L2 regularization). We keep the inferred schema (binary and text), the suggested recipe (no transformation besides tokenization of the text variable), and use the default model parameters (10 passes and mild L2 regularization). The training dataset is further split by Amazon ML into a smaller training dataset and a validation dataset, respectively 70% and 30% of the initial *4,400* samples. The AUC score obtained on the validation set is very high at *0.98*:

On your most recent evaluation, **ev-JwhaNd3opip** , the ML model's quality score is considered **extremely good** for most machine learning applications. ❶

AUC: 0.983
Baseline AUC: 0.500
Difference: 0.483

0   1

To get the `ModelID` and the `endpoint` URL, go to your summary page for the model. Copy the `ModelID` from the top of the page. Then scroll down to get to the prediction section and click on the **Create endpoint** button:

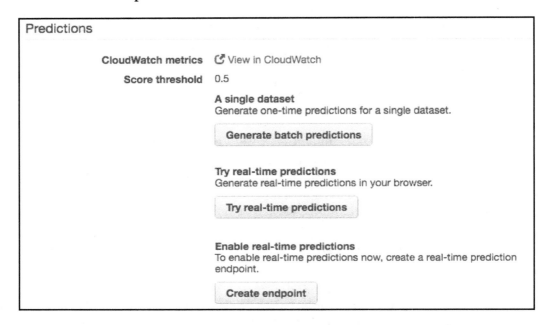

At that point, you will be given an estimate of the real-time prediction pricing for your model and asked to confirm the creation of the endpoint.

The size of your model is 502.1 KB. You will incur the reserved capacity charge of $0.001 for every hour your endpoint is active. The prediction charge for real-time predictions is $0.0001 per prediction, rounded up to the nearest penny.

After a few minutes, the endpoint will be created and you will have the endpoint URL:

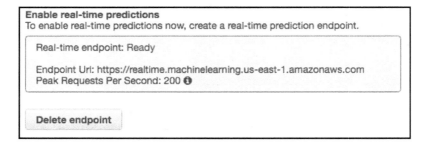

Now that we know the endpoint URL, we can write a simple Python code that sends an SMS message, a simple text, to our prediction model and see whether this message is predicted to be spam or ham. We send the text Hello world, my name is Alex to be classified as ham, while the text Call now to get dating contacts for free, no cash no credit card should probably be detected as spam due to the presence of the words *free*, *cash*, *dating*, and so forth.

The initialization/declaration part of the code is as follows:

```
import boto3
import json  # for parsing the returned predictions

# Initialize the client
client = boto3.client('machinelearning')

# The endpoint url is obtained from the model summary
endpoint_url = "https://realtime.machinelearning.us-east-1.amazonaws.com/"

# replace with your own model ID
model_id = "ml-kJmiRxxxxxx"

# The actual sample to be predicted. JSON formatted
record = { "nature": "Hello world, my name is Alex" }
```

We now use the predict() function of the machine learning service SDK:

```
response = client.predict(
    MLModelId         = model_id,
    Record            = record,
    PredictEndpoint   = endpoint_url
)
```

Finally, pretty print the response:

```
print(json.dumps(response, indent=4))
```

This returns the following JSON-formatted string:

```
{
    "ResponseMetadata": {
        "RetryAttempts": 0,
        "HTTPHeaders": {
            "content-type": "application/x-amz-json-1.1",
            "content-length": "143",
            "date": "Tue, 10 Jan 2017 16:20:49 GMT",
            "x-amzn-requestid": "bfab2af0-d750-11e6-b8c2-45ac3ab2f186"
        },
```

```
        "HTTPStatusCode": 200,
        "RequestId": "bfab2af0-d750-11e6-b8c2-45ac3ab2f186"
    },
    "Prediction": {
        "predictedScores": {
            "0": 0.001197131467051804
        },
        "predictedLabel": "0",
        "details": {
            "PredictiveModelType": "BINARY",
            "Algorithm": "SGD"
        }
    }
}
```

The JSON response is composed of two parts: the first part is related to the request itself, `ResponseMetadata`, and the second is related to the `Prediction`. The `HTTPStatusCode` in the *ResponseMetadata* part tells us that our query was successful (`"HTTPStatusCode": 200`).

The interpretation of the Prediction part is straightforward. The SMS was predicted to be spam with a very low probability of 0.12%, hence it was classified as ham, which is what we expected for the text `Hello world, my name is Alex`.

We expect the text `Call now to get dating contacts for free, no cash no credit card` to be classified as spam, the words `free`, `call`, and `dating` usually being strong indicators of spam messages. We get the following in return:

```
{
    "predictedScores": { "1": 0.810875654220581 },
    "predictedLabel": "1",
}
```

The text is classified as spam, which is what we expected. As far as we can tell from these two simple examples, our model seems to be working fine. Once we can obtain prediction via API calls on a sample-by-sample basis, it becomes feasible to hook an incoming stream of data into the endpoint and obtain real-time predictions.

To simulate that pipeline, we can use Python to read a whole file of new samples, send each one to the model, and capture the results. Let's do that with the held-out set of Spam samples.

The following Python code reads the file, loads it into a panda dataframe, and loops over each row of the dataframe. We use `iterrows()` to loop over each row of the dataframe. This method is slower than `itertuples()`, but has better code readability. The following code is not optimized:

```python
import boto3
import json
import pandas as pd

# Initialize the Service, the Model ID and the endpoint url
client = boto3.client('machinelearning')
# replace with your own endpoint url and model ID
endpoint_url = "https://realtime.machinelearning.us-east-1.amazonaws.com"
model_id = "ml-kJmiRHyn1UM"

# Memorize which class is spam and which is ham
spam_label = {'0': 'ham', '1':'spam'}

# Load the held out dataset into a panda DataFrame
df = pd.read_csv('held-out.csv')

# Loop over each DataFrame rows
for index, row in df.iterrows():
    # The record
    record = { "body": row['sms'] }
    response = client.predict(
        MLModelId      = model_id,
        Record         = record,
        PredictEndpoint = endpoint_url
    )

    # get the label and score from the response
    predicted_label = response['Prediction']['predictedLabel']
    predicted_score =
response['Prediction']['predictedScores'][predicted_label]
    print("[%s] %s (%0.2f):t %s "% (spam_label[str(row['nature'])],
                          spam_label[predicted_label],
                          predicted_score,
                          row['sms'] )
    )
```

The responses from Amazon ML are blazingly fast. Thousands of samples are processed in a few seconds. This is an extract of the results we get:

```
[ham]  ham  (0.00):      if you text on your way to cup stop that should work. And that should be BUS
[Spam] ham  (0.00):      Money i have won wining number 946 wot do i do next
[ham]  ham  (0.00):      Wewa is 130. Iriver 255. All 128 mb.
[Spam] spam (1.00):      PRIVATE! Your 2003 Account Statement for shows 800 un-redeemed S. I. M. points.
48922 Expires 21/11/04
[ham]  ham  (0.00):      I accidentally brought em home in the box
[Spam] spam (1.00):      Urgent! Please call 09061213237 from landline. £5000 cash or a luxury 4* Canary
T&Cs SAE PO Box 177. M227XY. 150ppm. 16+
```

Here, each line is formatted as follows:

```
[Predicted class] trueLabel (spam probability):        SMS message
```

Notice that, out of the three SMS detected as spam, only two were actually spam SMS. The text "*Money i have won wining number 946 wot do i do next*" was probably detected as spam due to the presence of the words "Money" or "wining" but was in fact a ham message.

Overall, across the whole predictions, the probabilities are very close to either 0 or 1, indicating that the model is very decisive in its classification. No hesitation. The ROC curve for the held-out dataset shows that high level of accuracy:

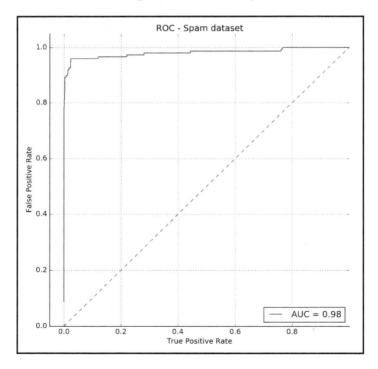

Summary

In this chapter, we explored the final step in the Amazon ML workflow, the predictions. Amazon ML offers several ways to apply your models to new datasets in order to make predictions. Batch mode involves submitting all the new data at once to the model and returning the actual predictions in a csv file on S3. Real-time predictions, on the other hand, are based on sending samples one by one to an API and getting prediction results in return. We looked at how to create an API on the Amazon ML platform. We also started using the command line and the Python SDK to interact with the Amazon ML service -- something we will explore in more depth in `Chapter 7`, *Command Line and SDK*.

As explained in the previous chapters, the Amazon ML service is built around the Stochastic Gradient Descent (SGD) algorithm. This algorithm has been around for many years and is used in many different domains and applications, from signal processing and adaptive filtering to predictive analysis or deep learning.

In the next chapter, we will present the algorithm and some if its versions, and bring to light its behavior when dealing with different types of data and prediction problems. We will explain why quantile binning of numeric values, which is often frowned upon, is such a performance and stability booster in our case.

Command Line and SDK

7

Using the AWS web interface to manage and run your projects is time-consuming. In this chapter, we move away from the web interface and start running our projects via the command line with the **AWS Command Line Interface** (**AWS CLI**) and the Python SDK with the `Boto3` library.

The first step will be to drive a whole project via the AWS CLI, uploading files to S3, creating datasources, models, evaluations, and predictions. As you will see, scripting will greatly facilitate using Amazon ML. We will use these new abilities to expand our Data Science powers by carrying out cross-validation and feature selection.

So far we have split our original dataset into three data chunks: training, validation, and testing. However, we have seen that the model selection can be strongly dependent on the data split. Shuffle the data — a different model might come as being the best one. Cross-validation is a technique that reduces this dependency by averaging the model performance on several data splits. Cross-validation involves creating many datasources for training, validation, and testing, and would be time-consuming using the web interface. The AWS CLI will allow us to quickly spin new datasources and models and carry out cross-validation effectively.

Another important technique in data science is feature elimination. Having a large number of features in your dataset either as the results of intensive feature engineering or because they are present in the original dataset can impact the model's performance. It's possible to significantly improve the model prediction capabilities by selecting and retaining only the best and most meaningful features while rejecting less important ones. There are many feature selection methods. We will implement a simple and efficient one, called recursive feature selection. The AWS Python SDK accessible via the Boto3 library will allow us to build the code wrapping around Amazon ML required for recursive feature selection.

In this chapter, you will learn the following:

- How to handle a whole project workflow through the AWS command line and the AWS Python SDK:
  - Managing data uploads to S3
  - Creating and evaluating models
  - Making and exporting the predictions
- How to implement cross-validation with the AWS CLI
- How to implement Recursive Feature Selection with AWS the Python SDK

Getting started and setting up

Creating a performing predictive model from raw data requires many trials and errors, much back and forth. Creating new features, cleaning up data, and trying out new parameters for the model are needed to ensure the robustness of the model. There is a constant back and forth between the data, the models, and the evaluations. Scripting this workflow either via the AWS CLI or with the `Boto3` Python library, will give us the ability to speed up the create, test, select loop.

Using the CLI versus SDK

AWS offers several ways besides the UI to interact with its services, the CLI, APIs, and SDKs in several languages. Though the AWS CLI and SDKs do not include all AWS services. Athena SQL, for instance, being a new service, is not yet included in the AWS CLI module or in any of AWS SDK at the time of writing.

The AWS Command Line Interface or CLI is a command-line shell program that allows you to manage your AWS services from your shell terminal. Once installed and set up with proper permissions, you can write commands to manage your S3 files, AWS EC2 instances, Amazon ML models, and most AWS services.

Generally speaking, a software development kit, or SDK for short, is a set of tools that can be used to develop software applications targeting a specific platform. In short, the SDK is a wrapper around an API. Where an API holds the core interaction methods, the SDK includes debugging support, documentation, and higher-level functions and methods. The API can be seen as the lowest common denominator that AWS supports and the SDK as a higher-level implementation of the API.

AWS SDKs are available in 12 different languages including PHP, Java, Ruby, and .NET. In this chapter, we will use the Python SDK.

Using the AWS CLI or SDK requires setting up our credentials, which we'll do in the following section

Installing AWS CLI

In order to set up your CLI credentials, you need your access key ID and your secret access key. You have most probably downloaded and saved them in a previous chapter. If that's not the case, you should simply create new ones from the **IAM** console (https://console.aws.amazon.com/iam).

Navigate to Users, select your IAM user name and click on the **Security credentials** tab. Choose **Create Access Key** and download the CSV file. Store the keys in a secure location. We will need the key in a few minutes to set up AWS CLI. But first, we need to install AWS CLI.

 Docker environment – This tutorial will help you use the AWS CLI within a docker container: https://blog.flowlog-stats.com/2016/05/03/aws-cli-in-a-docker-container/. A docker image for running the AWS CLI is available at https://hub.docker.com/r/fstab/aws-cli/.

There is no need to rewrite the AWS documentation on how to install the AWS CLI. It is complete and up to date, and available at http://docs.aws.amazon.com/cli/latest/userguide/installing.html. In a nutshell, installing the CLI requires you to have Python and pip already installed.

Then, run the following:

```
$ pip install --upgrade --user awscli
```

Add AWS to your $PATH:

```
$ export PATH=~/.local/bin:$PATH
```

Reload the bash configuration file (this is for OSX):

```
$ source ~/.bash_profile
```

Check that everything works with the following command:

```
$ aws --version
```

You should see something similar to the following output:

```
$ aws-cli/1.11.47 Python/3.5.2 Darwin/15.6.0 botocore/1.5.10
```

Once installed, we need to configure the AWS CLI type:

```
$ aws configure
```

Now input the access keys you just created:

```
$ aws configure

AWS Access Key ID [None]: ABCDEF_THISISANEXAMPLE
AWS Secret Access Key [None]: abcdefghijk_THISISANEXAMPLE
Default region name [None]: us-west-2
Default output format [None]: json
```

Choose the region that is closest to you and the format you prefer (JSON, text, or table). JSON is the default format.

The AWS configure command creates two files: a config file and a credential file. On OSX, the files are ~/.aws/config and ~/.aws/credentials. You can directly edit these files to change your access or configuration. You will need to create different profiles if you need to access multiple AWS accounts. You can do so via the AWS configure command:

```
$ aws configure --profile user2
```

You can also do so directly in the config and credential files:

```
~/.aws/config

[default]
output = json
region = us-east-1

[profile user2]
output = text
region = us-west-2
```

You can edit `Credential` file as follows:

~/.aws/credentials

```
[default]
aws_secret_access_key = ABCDEF_THISISANEXAMPLE
aws_access_key_id = abcdefghijk_THISISANEXAMPLE

[user2]
aws_access_key_id = ABCDEF_ANOTHERKEY
aws_secret_access_key = abcdefghijk_ANOTHERKEY
```

Refer to the AWS CLI setup page for more in-depth information:
http://docs.aws.amazon.com/cli/latest/userguide/cli-chap-getting-started.htm
l

Picking up CLI syntax

The overall format of any AWS CLI command is as follows:

```
$ aws <service> [options] <command> <subcommand> [parameters]
```

Here the terms are stated as:

- `<service>`: Is the name of the service you are managing: S3, machine learning, and EC2
- `[options]` : Allows you to set the region, the profile, and the output of the command
- `<command> <subcommand>`: Is the actual command you want to execute
- `[parameters]` : Are the parameters for these commands

A simple example will help you understand the syntax better. To list the content of an S3 bucket named `aml.packt`, the command is as follows:

```
$ aws s3 ls aml.packt
```

Here, `s3` is the service, `ls` is the command, and `aml.packt` is the parameter. The `aws help` command will output a list of all available services.
To get help on a particular service and its commands, write the following:

```
$ aws <service> help
```

For instance, `aws s3 help` will inform you that the available `s3` commands on single objects are ls, mv, and rm for list, move, and remove, and that the basic `aws s3` command follows the following format:

```
$ aws s3 <command> sourceURI destinationURI  [parameters]
```

Here, `sourceURI` or `destinationURI` can be a file (or multiple files) on your local machine and a file on S3 or both files on S3. Take the following, for instance:

```
$ aws s3 cp /tmp/foo/ s3://The_Bucket/ --recursive --exclude "*" --include
"*.jpg"
```

This will copy all (thanks to the parameter — recursive) JPG files (and only `*.jpg` files) in the `/tmp/foo` folder on your local machine to the S3 bucket named `The_Bucket`.

There are many more examples and explanations on the AWS documentation available at `http://docs.aws.amazon.com/cli/latest/userguide/cli-chap-using.html`.

Passing parameters using JSON files

For some services and commands, the list of parameters can become long and difficult to check and maintain.

For instance, in order to create an Amazon ML model via the CLI, you need to specify at least seven different elements: the Model ID, name, type, the model's parameters, the ID of the training data source, and the recipe name and URI (`aws machinelearning create-ml-model help`).

When possible, we will use the CLI ability to read parameters from a JSON file instead of specifying them in the command line. AWS CLI also offers a way to generate a JSON template, which you can then use with the right parameters. To generate that JSON parameter file model (the JSON skeleton), simply add `--generate-cli-skeleton` after the command name. For instance, to generate the JSON skeleton for the create model command of the machine learning service, write the following:

```
$ aws machinelearning create-ml-model --generate-cli-skeleton
```

This will give the following output:

```
{
    "MLModelId": "",
    "MLModelName": "",
    "MLModelType": "",
    "Parameters": {
        "KeyName": ""
    },
    "TrainingDataSourceId": "",
    "Recipe": "",
    "RecipeUri": ""
}
```

You can then configure this to your liking.

To have the skeleton command generate a JSON file and not simply output the skeleton in the terminal, add > filename.json:

```
$ aws machinelearning create-ml-model --generate-cli-skeleton >
filename.json
```

This will create a filename.json file with the JSON template. Once all the required parameters are specified, you create the model with the command (assuming the filename.json is in the current folder):

```
$ aws machinelearning create-ml-model file://filename.json
```

Before we dive further into the machine learning workflow via the CLI, we need to introduce the dataset we will be using in this chapter.

Introducing the Ames Housing dataset

In this chapter, we will use the Ames Housing dataset that was compiled by *Dean De Cock* for use in data science education. It is a great alternative to the popular but older Boston Housing dataset. The Ames Housing dataset is used in the Advanced Regression Techniques challenge on the Kaggle website: https://www.kaggle.com/c/house-prices-advanced-regression-techniques/. The original version of the dataset is available: http://www.amstat.org/publications/jse/v19n3/decock/AmesHousing.xlsand in the GitHub repository for this chapter.

The `Ames Housing` dataset contains 79 explanatory variables describing (almost) every aspect of residential homes in Ames, Iowa with the goal of predicting the selling price of each home. The dataset has 2930 rows. The high number of variables makes this dataset a good candidate for Feature Selection.

For more information on the genesis of this dataset and an in-depth explanation of the different variables, read the paper by *Dean De Cock* available in PDF at `https://ww2.amstat.org/publications/jse/v19n3/decock.pdf`.

As usual, we will start by splitting the dataset into a train and a validate set and build a model on the train set. Both train and validate sets are available in the GitHub repository as `ames_housing_training.csv` and `ames_housing_validate.csv`. The entire dataset is in the `ames_housing.csv` file.

Splitting the dataset with shell commands

The command line is an often forgotten but powerful ally to the data scientist. Many very powerful operations on the data can be achieved with the right shell commands and executed blazingly fast. To illustrate this, we will use shell commands to shuffle, split, and create training and validation subsets of the `Ames Housing` dataset:

1. First, extract the first line into a separate file, `ames_housing_header.csv` and remove it from the original file:

   ```
   $ head -n 1 ames_housing.csv > ames_housing_header.csv
   ```

2. We just tail all the lines after the first one into the same file:

   ```
   $ tail -n +2 ames_housing.csv > ames_housing_nohead.csv
   ```

3. Then randomly sort the rows into a temporary file. (`gshuf` is the OSX equivalent of the Linux **shuf shell** command. It can be installed via `brew install coreutils`):

   ```
   $ gshuf ames_housing_nohead.csv -o ames_housing_nohead.csv
   ```

4. Extract the first 2,050 rows as the training file and the last 880 rows as the validation file:

   ```
   $ head -n 2050 ames_housing_nohead.csv > ames_housing_training.csv
   $ tail -n 880 ames_housing_nohead.csv > ames_housing_validate.csv
   ```

5. Finally, add back the header into both training and validation files:

```
$ cat ames_housing_header.csv ames_housing_training.csv > tmp.csv
$ mv tmp.csv ames_housing_training.csv

$ cat ames_housing_header.csv ames_housing_validate.csv > tmp.csv
$ mv tmp.csv ames_housing_validate.csv
```

A simple project using the CLI

We are now ready to execute a simple Amazon ML workflow using the CLI. This includes the following:

- Uploading files on S3
- Creating a datasource and the recipe
- Creating a model
- Creating an evaluation
- Prediction batch and real time

Let's start by uploading the training and validation files to S3. In the following lines, replace the bucket name `aml.packt` with your own bucket name.

To upload the files to the S3 location `s3://aml.packt/data/ch8/`, run the following command lines:

```
$ aws s3 cp ./ames_housing_training.csv s3://aml.packt/data/ch8/
upload: ./ames_housing_training.csv to
s3://aml.packt/data/ch8/ames_housing_training.csv

$ aws s3 cp ./ames_housing_validate.csv s3://aml.packt/data/ch8/
upload: ./ames_housing_validate.csv to
s3://aml.packt/data/ch8/ames_housing_validate.csv
```

An overview of Amazon ML CLI commands

That's it for the S3 part. Now let's explore the CLI for Amazon's machine learning service. All Amazon ML CLI commands are available at http://docs.aws.amazon.com/cli/latest/reference/machinelearning/. There are 30 commands, which can be grouped by object and action.

You can perform the following:

- `create` : creates the object
- `describe`: searches objects given some parameters (location, dates, names, and so on)
- `get`: given an object ID, returns information
- `update`: given an object ID, updates the object
- `delete`: deletes an object

These can be performed on the following elements:

- datasource
  - `create-data-source-from-rds`
  - `create-data-source-from-redshift`
  - `create-data-source-from-s3`
  - `describe-data-sources`
  - `delete-data-source`
  - `get-data-source`
  - `update-data-source`
- ml-model
  - `create-ml-model`
  - `describe-ml-models`
  - `get-ml-model`
  - `delete-ml-model`
  - `update-ml-model`
- evaluation
  - `create-evaluation`
  - `describe-evaluations`
  - `get-evaluation`
  - `delete-evaluation`
  - `update-evaluation`

- batch prediction
  - `create-batch-prediction`
  - `describe-batch-predictions`
  - `get-batch-prediction`
  - `delete-batch-prediction`
  - `update-batch-prediction`
- real-time end point
  - `create-realtime-endpoint`
  - `delete-realtime-endpoint`
  - `predict`

You can also handle tags and set waiting times.

Note that the AWS CLI gives you the ability to create datasources from S3, Redshift, and RDS, while the web interface only allowed datasources from S3 and Redshift.

Creating the datasource

We will start by creating the datasource. Let's first see what parameters are needed by generating the following skeleton:

```
$ aws machinelearning create-data-source-from-s3 --generate-cli-skeleton
```

This generates the following JSON object:

```
{
    "DataSourceId": "",
    "DataSourceName": "",
    "DataSpec": {
        "DataLocationS3": "",
        "DataRearrangement": "",
        "DataSchema": "",
        "DataSchemaLocationS3": ""
    },
    "ComputeStatistics": true
}
```

The different parameters are mostly self-explanatory and further information can be found on the AWS documentation at `http://docs.aws.amazon.com/cli/latest/reference/machinelearning/create-data-source-from-s3.html`.

A word on the schema: when creating a datasource from the web interface, you have the possibility to use a wizard, to be guided through the creation of the schema. As you may recall, you are guided through several screens where you can specify the type of all the columns, and the existence of a target variable and an index column. The wizard facilitates the process by guessing the type of the variables, thus making available a default schema that you can modify.

There is no default schema available via the AWS CLI. You have to define the entire schema yourself, either in a JSON format in the `DataSchema` field or by uploading a schema file to S3 and specifying its location, in the `DataSchemaLocationS3` field.

Since our dataset has many variables (79), we cheated and used the wizard to create a default schema that we uploaded to S3. Throughout the rest of the chapter, we will specify the schema location not its JSON definition.

In this example, we will create the following datasource parameter file, `dsrc_ames_housing_001.json`:

```
{
    "DataSourceId": "ch8_ames_housing_001",
    "DataSourceName": "[DS] Ames Housing 001",
    "DataSpec": {
        "DataLocationS3":
          "s3://aml.packt/data/ch8/ames_housing_training.csv",
        "DataSchemaLocationS3":
          "s3://aml.packt/data/ch8/ames_housing.csv.schema"
    },
    "ComputeStatistics": true
}
```

For the validation subset (save to `dsrc_ames_housing_002.json`):

```
{
    "DataSourceId": "ch8_ames_housing_002",
    "DataSourceName": "[DS] Ames Housing 002",
    "DataSpec": {
        "DataLocationS3":
          "s3://aml.packt/data/ch8/ames_housing_validate.csv",
        "DataSchemaLocationS3":
          "s3://aml.packt/data/ch8/ames_housing.csv.schema"
    },
    "ComputeStatistics": true
}
```

Since we have already split our data into a training and a validation set, there's no need to specify the data `DataRearrangement` field.

Alternatively, we could also have avoided splitting our dataset and specified the following `DataRearrangement` on the original dataset, assuming it had been already shuffled: (save to `dsrc_ames_housing_003.json`):

```
{
    "DataSourceId": "ch8_ames_housing_003",
    "DataSourceName": "[DS] Ames Housing training 003",
    "DataSpec": {
        "DataLocationS3":
          "s3://aml.packt/data/ch8/ames_housing_shuffled.csv",
        "DataRearrangement":
          "{"splitting":{"percentBegin":0,"percentEnd":70}}",
        "DataSchemaLocationS3":
          "s3://aml.packt/data/ch8/ames_housing.csv.schema"
    },
    "ComputeStatistics": true
}
```

For the validation set (save to `dsrc_ames_housing_004.json`):

```
{
    "DataSourceId": "ch8_ames_housing_004",
    "DataSourceName": "[DS] Ames Housing validation 004",
    "DataSpec": {
        "DataLocationS3":
          "s3://aml.packt/data/ch8/ames_housing_shuffled.csv",
        "DataRearrangement":
          "{"splitting":{"percentBegin":70,"percentEnd":100}}",
    },
    "ComputeStatistics": true
}
```

Here, the `ames_housing.csv` file has previously been shuffled using the `gshuf` command line and uploaded to S3:

```
$ gshuf ames_housing_nohead.csv -o ames_housing_nohead.csv
$ cat ames_housing_header.csv ames_housing_nohead.csv > tmp.csv
$ mv tmp.csv ames_housing_shuffled.csv
$ aws s3 cp ./ames_housing_shuffled.csv s3://aml.packt/data/ch8/
```

Note that we don't need to create these four datasources; these are just examples of alternative ways to create datasources.

We then create these datasources by running the following:

```
$ aws machinelearning create-data-source-from-s3 --cli-input-json
file://dsrc_ames_housing_001.json
```

We can check whether the datasource creation is pending:

[DS] Ames Housing 001	Datasource	ch8_ames_housing_001	In progress

In return, we get the datasoure ID we had specified:

```
{
    "DataSourceId": "ch8_ames_housing_001"
}
```

We can then obtain information on that datasource with the following:

```
$ aws machinelearning  get-data-source --data-source-id
ch8_ames_housing_001
```

This returns the following:

```
{
    "Status": "COMPLETED",
    "NumberOfFiles": 1,
    "CreatedByIamUser": "arn:aws:iam::178277xxxxxxx:user/alexperrier",
    "LastUpdatedAt": 1486834110.483,
    "DataLocationS3": "s3://aml.packt/data/ch8/ames_housing_training.csv",
    "ComputeStatistics": true,
    "StartedAt": 1486833867.707,
    "LogUri":
"https://eml-prod-emr.s3.amazonaws.com/178277513911-ds-ch8_ames_housing_001
/.....",
    "DataSourceId": "ch8_ames_housing_001",
    "CreatedAt": 1486030865.965,
    "ComputeTime": 880000,
    "DataSizeInBytes": 648150,
    "FinishedAt": 1486834110.483,
    "Name": "[DS] Ames Housing 001"
}
```

Note that we have access to the operation log URI, which could be useful to analyze the model training later on.

Creating the model

Creating the model with the `create-ml-model` command follows the same steps:

1. Generate the skeleton with the following:

   ```
   $ aws machinelearning create-ml-model --generate-cli-skeleton >
   mdl_ames_housing_001.json
   ```

2. Write the configuration file:

   ```
   {
       "MLModelId": "ch8_ames_housing_001",
       "MLModelName": "[MDL] Ames Housing 001",
       "MLModelType": "REGRESSION",
       "Parameters": {
           "sgd.shuffleType": "auto",
           "sgd.l2RegularizationAmount": "1.0E-06",
           "sgd.maxPasses": "100"
       },
       "TrainingDataSourceId": "ch8_ames_housing_001",
       "RecipeUri": "s3://aml.packt/data/ch8
         /recipe_ames_housing_001.json"
   }
   ```

   Note the parameters of the algorithm. Here, we used mild L2 regularization and 100 passes.

3. Launch the model creation with the following:

   ```
   $ aws machinelearning create-ml-model --cli-input-json
   file://mdl_ames_housing_001.json
   ```

4. The model ID is returned:

   ```
   {
       "MLModelId": "ch8_ames_housing_001"
   }
   ```

5. This `get-ml-model` command gives you a status update on the operation as well as the URL to the log.

   ```
   $ aws machinelearning get-ml-model --ml-model-id
   ch8_ames_housing_001
   ```

6. The `watch` command allows you to repeat a shell command every *n* seconds. To get the status of the model creation every *10s*, just write the following:

```
$ watch -n 10 aws machinelearning get-ml-model --ml-model-id
ch8_ames_housing_001
```

The output of the `get-ml-model` will be refreshed every 10s until you kill it.

> It is not possible to create the default recipe via the AWS CLI commands. You can always define a blank recipe that would not carry out any transformation on the data. However, the default recipe has been shown to be positively impacting the model performance. To obtain this default recipe, we created it via the web interface, copied it into a file that we uploaded to S3. The resulting file `recipe_ames_housing_001.json` is available in our GitHub repository. Its content is quite long as the dataset has 79 variables and is not reproduced here for brevity purposes.

Evaluating our model with create-evaluation

Our model is now trained and we would like to evaluate it on the evaluation subset. For that, we will use the `create-evaluation` CLI command:

1. Generate the skeleton:

```
$ aws machinelearning create-evaluation --generate-cli-skeleton >
eval_ames_housing_001.json
```

2. Configure the parameter file:

```
{
    "EvaluationId": "ch8_ames_housing_001",
    "EvaluationName": "[EVL] Ames Housing 001",
    "MLModelId": "ch8_ames_housing_001",
    "EvaluationDataSourceId": "ch8_ames_housing_002"
}
```

3. Launch the evaluation creation:

```
$ aws machinelearning create-evaluation --cli-input-json
file://eval_ames_housing_001.json
```

4. Get the evaluation information:

```
$ aws machinelearning get-evaluation --evaluation-id
ch8_ames_housing_001
```

5. From that output, we get the performance of the model in the form of the RMSE:

```
"PerformanceMetrics": {
    "Properties": {
        "RegressionRMSE": "29853.250469108018"
    }
}
```

The value may seem big, but it is relative to the range of the `salePrice` variable for the houses, which has a mean of 181300.0 and std of 79886.7. So an RMSE of 29853.2 is a decent score.

 You don't have to wait for the datasource creation to be completed in order to launch the model training. Amazon ML will simply wait for the parent operation to conclude before launching the dependent one. This makes chaining operations possible.

The next step would be to make batch predictions or create a real-time endpoint. These would follow the exact same steps of model creation and evaluation, and are not presented here.

At this point, we have a trained and evaluated model. We chose a certain set of parameters and carried out a certain preprocessing of the data via the default recipe. We now would like to know whether we can improve on that model and feature set by trying new parameters for the algorithm and doing some creative feature engineering. We will then train our new models and evaluate them on the validation subset. As we've seen before, the problem with that approach is that our evaluation score can be highly dependent on the evaluation subset. Shuffling the data to generate new training and validation sets may result in different model performance and make us choose the wrong model. Even though we have shuffled the data to avoid sequential patterns, there is no way to be sure that our split is truly neutral and that both subsets show similar data distribution. One of the subsets could present anomalies such as outliers, or missing data that the other does not have. To solve this problem, we turn to cross-validation.

What is cross-validation?

To lower the dependence on the data distribution in each split, the idea is to run many trials in parallel, each with a different data split, and average the results. This is called cross-validation.

The idea is simply to average the model performance across K trials, where each trial is built on a different split of the original dataset. There are many strategies to split the dataset. The most common one is called **k-fold cross-validation** and consists of splitting the dataset into **K chunks**, and for each trial using *K-1* chunks aggregated to train the model and the remaining chunk to evaluate it. Another strategy, called **leave-one-out (LOO)**, comes from taking this idea to its extreme with *K* as the number of samples. You train your model on all the samples except one and estimate the error on the remaining sample. LOO is obviously more resource intensive.

The strategy we will implement is called **Monte Carlo cross-validation**, where the initial dataset is randomly split into a training and validation set in each trial. The advantage of that method over k-fold cross validation is that the proportion of the training/validation split is not dependent on the number of iterations (*K*). Its disadvantage is that some samples may never be selected in the validation subset, whereas others may be selected more than once. Validation subsets may overlap.

Let's look at an example with k =5 trials. We will repeat these steps five times to evaluate one model (for instance, L2 mild regularization):

1. Shuffle the Ames Housing dataset.
2. Split the dataset into training and validation subsets.
3. Train the model on the training set.
4. Evaluate the model on the validation set.

At this point, we have five measures of the model performance; we average it to get a measure of overall model performance. We repeat the aforementioned five steps to evaluate another model (for instance, L1 medium regularization). Once we have tested all our models, we select the one that gives the best average performance on the trials.

This is why scripting becomes a necessity. To test one model setup, a cross-validation with *K trials* (K fold or Monte Carlo) requires 2*K datasources, K models, and K evaluations. This will surely be too time-consuming when done via the web interface alone. This is where scripting the whole process becomes extremely useful and much more efficient.

There are many ways to actually create the different subset files for cross-validation. The simplest way might be to use a spreadsheet editor with random sorting, and some cutting and pasting. R and Python libraries, such as the popular `scikit-learn` library or the Caret package, have rich methods that can be used out of the box. However, since this chapter is about the AWS command line interface, we will use shell commands to generate the files. We will also write shell scripts to generate the sequence of AWS CLI commands in order to avoid manually editing the same commands for the different data files and models.

Implementing Monte Carlo cross-validation

We will now implement a Monte Carlo cross-validation strategy with five trials using shell commands and AWS CLI. And we will use this evaluation method to compare two models, one with L2 mild regularization and the second with L1 heavy regularization on the Ames Housing dataset. Cross-validation will allow us to conclude with some level of confidence which model performs better.

Generating the shuffled datasets

We will use the datasource creation `DataRearrangement` field to split the data into a training and a validation subset. So, we only need to create five files of shuffled data in the first place.

The following shell script will create five shuffled versions of the `Ames Housing` dataset and upload the files to S3. You can either save that code in a file with the `.sh` extension (`datasets_creation.sh`) or run it with `sh ./datasets_creation.sh`:

```
#!/bin/bash
for k in 1 2 3 4 5
do
    filename="data/ames_housing_shuffled_$k.csv"
    gshuf data/ames_housing_nohead.csv -o data/ames_housing_nohead.csv
    cat data/ames_housing_header.csv data/ames_housing_nohead.csv >
tmp.csv;
    mv tmp.csv $filename
    aws s3 cp ./$filename s3://aml.packt/data/ch8/
done
```

Note that in this chapter, the code is organized around the following folder structure. All the command lines are run from the root folder, for instance, to run a Python script: `python py/the_script.py`, to list the data files `ls data/` and to run shell scripts: `sh ./shell/the_script.sh`.

```
.
├── data
├── images
├── py
└── shell
```

All the shell scripts and command are based on bash shell and should probably require adaptation to other shells such as zsh.

Our datasets have been created and uploaded to S3. The general strategy is now to create templates for each of the parameter JSON files required for the Amazon ML CLI commands: create datasources, models, and evaluations. We will create the template files for the following:

- Training datasource
- Evaluation datasource
- L2 model
- L1 model
- L2 evaluation
- L1 evaluation

In all these template files, we will index the filenames with `{k}` and use the `sed` shell command to replace `{k}` with the proper index (1 to 5). Once we have the template files, we can use a simple shell script to generate the actual JSON parameter files for the datasources, models, and evaluations. We will end up with the following:

- 10 datasource configuration files (five for training and five for evaluation)
- 10 model configuration files (five for L2 and five for L1)
- 10 evaluation configuration files (one for each of the models)

In the end, we will obtain five RMSE results for the L2 model and five RMSE results for the L1 model, whose average will tell us which model is the best, which type of regularization should be selected to make sales price predictions on the Ames Housing dataset.

Let's start by writing the configuration files.

Generating the datasources template

The template for the training files is as follows:

```
{
    "DataSourceId": "CH8_AH_training_00{k}",
    "DataSourceName": "[DS AH] training 00{k}",
    "DataSpec": {
        "DataLocationS3": "s3://aml.packt/data/ch8/shuffled_{k}.csv",
        "DataSchemaLocationS3":"s3://aml.packt/data/ch8
         /ames_housing.csv.schema",
        "DataRearrangement": "{"splitting":
        {"percentBegin":0,"percentEnd":70}}"
    },
    "ComputeStatistics": true
}
```

And the template for for validation datasources is as follows:

```
{
    "DataSourceId": "CH8_AH_evaluate_00{k}",
    "DataSourceName": "[DS AH] evaluate 00{k}",
    "DataSpec": {
        "DataLocationS3": "s3://aml.packt/data/ch8/shuffled_{k}.csv",
        "DataSchemaLocationS3":"s3://aml.packt/data/ch8
        /ames_housing.csv.schema",
        "DataRearrangement": "{"splitting":
        {"percentBegin":70,"percentEnd":100}}"
    },
    "ComputeStatistics": true
}
```

The only different between the training and the validation templates are the names/IDs and the splitting ratio in the `DataRearrangement` field. We save these files to `dsrc_training_template.json` and `dsrc_validate_template.json` respectively.

Generating the models template

In the case of a model with L2 regularization, the model template is as follows:

```
{
    "MLModelId": "CH8_AH_L2_00{k}",
    "MLModelName": "[MDL AH L2] 00{k}",
    "MLModelType": "REGRESSION",
    "Parameters": {
        "sgd.shuffleType": "auto",
        "sgd.l1RegularizationAmount": "0.0",
```

```
        "sgd.l2RegularizationAmount": "1.0E-06",
        "sgd.maxPasses": "100"
    },
    "TrainingDataSourceId": "CH8_AH_training_00{k}",
    "RecipeUri": "s3://aml.packt/data/ch8/recipe_ames_housing_001.json"
}
```

And for a model with L1 regularization, the model template is as follows:

```
{
    "MLModelId": "CH8_AH_L1_00{k}",
    "MLModelName": "[MDL AH L1] 00{k}",
    "MLModelType": "REGRESSION",
    "Parameters": {
        "sgd.shuffleType": "auto",
        "sgd.l1RegularizationAmount": "1.0E-04",
        "sgd.l2RegularizationAmount": "0.0",
        "sgd.maxPasses": "100"
    },
    "TrainingDataSourceId": "CH8_AH_training_00{k}",
    "RecipeUri": "s3://aml.packt/data/ch8/recipe_ames_housing_001.json"
}
```

Note that the same recipe is used for both models. If we wanted to compare the performance of data preprocessing strategies, we could modify the recipes used in both models. The template files are very similar. The only difference is in the model name and ID and in the values for the `l1RegularizationAmount` and `l2RegularizationAmount`. We save these files to `mdl_l2_template.json` and `mdl_l1_template.json` respectively.

Generating the evaluations template

In the case of a model with L2 regularization, the evaluation template is as follows:

```
{
    "EvaluationId": "CH8_AH_L2_00{k}",
    "EvaluationName": "[EVL AH L2] 00{k}",
    "MLModelId": "CH8_AH_L2_00{k}",
    "EvaluationDataSourceId": "CH8_AH_evaluate_00{k}"
}
```

And for a model with L1 regularization, the evaluation template is as follows:

```
{
    "EvaluationId": "CH8_AH_L1_00{k}",
    "EvaluationName": "[EVL AH L1] 00{k}",
    "MLModelId": "CH8_AH_L1_00{k}",
    "EvaluationDataSourceId": "CH8_AH_evaluate_00{k}"
}
```

Save these files to `eval_l2_template.json` and `eval_l1_template.json` espectively.

We will now use these template files to generate the different configuration files for the datasources, models, and evaluations. To keep things separate, all the generated files are in a subfolder `cfg/`.

The following shell script generates the actual configuration files that we will feed to the AWS CLI Machine Learning commands. It uses the `sed` command to find and replace the instances of `{k}` with the numbers 1 to 5. The output is written to the configuration file. Since there will be many configuration files generated, the files are written in a `/cfg` subfolder under `/data`. The folder structure is now as follows:

```
.
├──── data
│     └──── cfg
│     └──── templates
├──── images
├──── py
└──── shell

#!/bin/bash

for k in 1 2 3 4 5
do
    # training datasource
    sed 's/{k}/1/g' data/templates/dsrc_training_template.json > data/cfg
    /dsrc_training_00$k.json

    # evaluation datasource
    sed 's/{k}/1/g' data/templates/dsrc_validate_template.json > data/cfg
    /dsrc_validate_00$k.json

    # L2 model
    sed 's/{k}/1/g' data/templates/mdl_l2_template.json > data/cfg
    /mdl_l2_00$k.json

    # L2 evaluation
    sed 's/{k}/1/g' data/templates/eval_l2_template.json > data/cfg
```

```
/eval_12_00$k.json

# L1 model
sed 's/{k}/1/g' data/templates/mdl_l1_template.json > data/cfg
/mdl_l1_00$k.json

# L1 evaluation
sed 's/{k}/1/g' data/templates/eval_l1_template.json > data/cfg
/eval_l1_00$k.json

done
```

The last remaining step is to execute the AWS commands that will create the objects in Amazon ML. We also use a shell loop to execute the AWS CLI commands.

Create datasources for training and evaluation:

```
#!/bin/bash
for k in 1 2 3 4 5
do
    aws machinelearning create-data-source-from-s3 --cli-input-json
    file://data/cfg/dsrc_kfold_training_00$k.json
    aws machinelearning create-data-source-from-s3 --cli-input-json
    file://data/cfg/dsrc_kfold_validate_00$k.json
done
```

Train models with L2 and L1 regularization:

```
#!/bin/bash
for k in 1 2 3 4 5
    aws machinelearning create-ml-model --cli-input-json file://data
    /cfg/mdl_12_00$k.json
    aws machinelearning create-ml-model --cli-input-json file://data
    /cfg/mdl_l1_00$k.json
done
```

Evaluate trained models:

```
#!/bin/bash
for k in 1 2 3 4 5
    aws machinelearning create-evaluation --cli-input-json file://cfg
    /eval_12_00$k.json
    aws machinelearning create-evaluation --cli-input-json file://cfg
    /eval_l1_00$k.json
done
```

You can check the status of the different jobs with the `get-data-source`, `get-ml-model` and `get-evaluation` CLI commands or on the Amazon ML dashboard. Once all the evaluation is finished, you capture the RMSE for each model by first creating a couple of files to receive the RMSE score and then running the following, final shell loop:

```
#!/bin/bash
for k in 1 2 3 4 5
    aws machinelearning get-evaluation --evaluation-id CH8_AH_L2_00$k |
    grep RegressionRMSE >> l2_model_rmse.log
    aws machinelearning get-evaluation --evaluation-id CH8_AH_L1_00$k |
    grep RegressionRMSE >> l1_model_rmse.log
done
```

The `get-evaluation` command, given the ID of the evaluation, returns a JSON-formatted string that is fed to a grepping command and added to the `l1/l2_model_rmse.log` files.

The results

We end up with the following results for the two models:

```
l1 | 26570.0 | 28880.4 | 27287.8 | 29815.7 | 27822.0]

L2 | 36670.9 | 25804.3 | 28127.2 | 30539.0 | 24740.4
```

On average, L1 gives an RMSE of 28075.2 (std: 1151), while L2 gives an RMSE of 29176.4 (std: 4246.7). Not only is the L1 model better performing, but it is also more robust when it comes to handling data variations since its std is lower.

Conclusion

Cross-validation may be too time-consuming to implement via shell only. There are many files to create and coordinate. There are simpler ways to implement cross-validation with libraries such as `scikit-learn` for Python or Caret for R, where the whole model training and evaluation loop over several training and validation sets only requires a few lines of code. However, we showed that it was possible to implement cross-validation with Amazon ML. Cross-validation is a key component of the data-science workflow. Not being able to do cross validation with Amazon ML would have been a significant flaw in the service. In the end, the AWS CLI for machine learning is a very powerful and useful tool to conduct sequences of trials and compare results across different models, datasets, recipes, and features.

Boto3, the Python SDK

Another tool to interact with the Amazon ML service outside of the web interface is an SDK. Simply put, an SDK is a wrapper around an API that makes working with the service much simpler and more efficient, as many details of the interactions are taken care of. AWS offers SDKs in the most widespread languages such as PHP, Java, Ruby, .Net, and of course, Python. In this chapter, we will focus on working with the Amazon ML service through the Python SDK. The Python SDK requires the Boto3 module.

Installation of the Boto3 module is done via pip. Refer to the quickstart guide available at `ht tp://boto3.readthedocs.io/en/latest/guide/quickstart.html`if you need more information and troubleshooting:

```
pip install boto3
```

Boto3 is available for most AWS services. The complete list can be found at `http://boto3.readthedocs.io/en/latest/reference/services/index.html`. We will focus on Boto3 for S3 and Amazon ML.

Setting up permissions for SDK access can be done via the `aws configure` command that we followed at the beginning of this chapter, or directly by adding your access keys to the `~/.aws/credentials` file.

Overall, the `Boto3` logic is very similar to the AWS CLI logic and follows similar steps: declaring the service to be used and running commands with the appropriate set of parameters. Let's start with a simple example around S3 with the following Python script, which will list all the buckets in your account:

```python
import boto3
# Initialize the S3 client
s3 = boto3.resource('s3')
# List all the buckets in out account
for bucket in s3.buckets.all():
    print(bucket.name)
```

Uploading a local file to a bucket would be achieved by the following:

```python
# load the file
data = open('data/ames_housing_nohead.csv', 'rb')
s3.Object('aml.packt', 'data/ames_housing_nohead.csv').put(Body=data)
```

The put command returns a JSON string, with an HTTPStatusCode field with a 200 value, indicating that the upload was successful.

Working with the Python SDK for Amazon Machine Learning

The list of available methods can be found at http://boto3.readthedocs.io/en/latest/reference/services/machinelearning.html and closely follows the list of available commands for the AWS CLI for the Machine Learning service organized around the main objects: datasource, model, evaluation, batch prediction, and real-time endpoints. For each object, the methods are: create, update, describe, get, and delete.

We will now implement the standard Amazon ML workflow. But first, let's define a naming method for the objects we will create. An important part of the workflow revolves around naming convention for object names and IDs. When working with the CLI, we created the names and IDs on the fly. This time we will use the following function to name our objects:

```python
def name_id_generation(prefix, mode, trial):
    Id = '_'.join([prefix, mode, "%02d"%int(trial)])
    name = "[%s] %s %02d"% (prefix, mode, int(trial) )
    return {'Name':name, 'Id':Id}
```

This function takes in two strings and one integer as arguments, a prefix for the type of the object (datasource, model, and so on), a mode to specify training versus validation datasource, and a trial value to easily increment our experiments. The function returns a dictionary.

Let's now define a few variables that we will use later on in the script:

```python
# The iteration number of our experiements
trial = 5
# The S3 location of schemas and files
data_s3   = 's3://aml.packt/data/ch8/ames_housing_shuffled.csv'
schema_s3 = 's3://aml.packt/data/ch8/ames_housing.csv.schema'
recipe_s3 = 's3://aml.packt/data/ch8/recipe_ames_housing_001.json'

# And the parameters for the SGD algrithm
sgd_params = {
  "sgd.shuffleType": "auto",
  "sgd.l1RegularizationAmount": "1.0E-04",
  "sgd.maxPasses": "100"
}
```

We need to import the following libraries:

```python
import boto3
import time
import json
```

Declare that we want to interact with the Machine Learning service:

```
client = boto3.client('machinelearning')
```

We are now all set to create our training and validation datasources with the following:

```
# Create datasource for training
resource = name_id_generation('DS', 'training', trial)
print("Creating datasources for training (%s)"% resource['Name'] )
response = client.create_data_source_from_s3(
  DataSourceId = resource['Id'] ,
  DataSourceName = resource['Name'],
  DataSpec = {
    'DataLocationS3' : data_s3,
    'DataSchemaLocationS3' : schema_s3,
    'DataRearrangement':'{"splitting":{"percentBegin":0,"percentEnd":70}}'
  },
   ComputeStatistics = True
)

# Create datasource for validation
resource = name_id_generation('DS', 'validation', trial)
print("Creating datasources for validation (%s)"% resource['Name'] )
response = client.create_data_source_from_s3(
  DataSourceId = resource['Id'] ,
  DataSourceName = resource['Name'],
  DataSpec = {
    'DataLocationS3': data_s3,
    'DataSchemaLocationS3': schema_s3,
    'DataRearrangement':'{"splitting":{"percentBegin":0,"percentEnd":70}}'
  },
  ComputeStatistics = True
)
```

In both cases, we call on the naming function we defined earlier to generate the Name and ID of the datasource and use that dictionary when calling the create_data_source_from_s3 Boto3 method.

We launch the training of the model with the following:

```
# Train model with existing recipe
resource = name_id_generation('MDL', '', trial)
print("Training model (%s) with params:n%s"%
              (resource['Name'], json.dumps(sgd_params, indent=4)) )
response = client.create_ml_model(
  MLModelId = resource['Id'],
  MLModelName = resource['Name'],
  MLModelType = 'REGRESSION',
```

```
    Parameters = sgd_params,
    TrainingDataSourceId= name_id_generation('DS', 'training', trial)['Id'],
    RecipeUri = recipe_s3
)
```

And create the evaluation:

```
resource = name_id_generation('EVAL', '', trial)
print("Launching evaluation (%s) "% resource['Name'] )
response = client.create_evaluation(
    EvaluationId = resource['Id'],
    EvaluationName = resource['Name'],
    MLModelId = name_id_generation('MDL', '', trial)['Id'],
    EvaluationDataSourceId = name_id_generation('DS', 'validation', trial)
    ['Id']
)
```

You can now go to the Amazon ML dashboard and verify that you have two datasources, one model, and one evaluation in the **In progress** or **Pending** status:

▸	[EVAL] 04	Evaluation	EVAL__04	Pending
▸	[MDL] 04	ML model	MDL__04	Pending
▸	[DS] validation 04	Datasource	DS_validation_04	In progress
▸	[DS] training 04	Datasource	DS_training_04	In progress

Waiting on operation completion

All these object, creation operations are, by default, chained by Amazon ML. This means that Amazon ML will wait on the datasources to be ready before launching the model training, and will also wait for the model training to be completed before trying to run the evaluation. However, at this point, we still need to wait for the evaluation to be complete before we can access its results. Similarly, we need to wait for the different objects to have been utilized by the next operation before deleting them.

This is where the waiter methods become useful. Waiters are methods that simply wait for an AWS operation to be completed, to have status *Completed*. Waiters exists for all AWS operations and services. Amazon ML offers four waiters for models, datasources, evaluations, and batch predictions:

- `MachineLearning.Waiter.BatchPredictionAvailable`
- `MachineLearning.Waiter.DataSourceAvailable`
- `MachineLearning.Waiter.EvaluationAvailable`
- `MachineLearning.Waiter.MLModelAvailable`

A Machine Learning waiter follows the syntax – first, declare the object the waiter has to monitor, for instance an evaluation:

```
waiter = client.get_waiter('evaluation_available')
```

Then call the `wait` method on the waiter you just declared:

```
waiter.wait(FilterVariable='Name', EQ='the name of the evaluation')
```

Once the wait method is called, the Python scripts hangs until the operation reaches a status of `Completed`. The wait function takes the following:

- A filter value: `FilterVariable = CreatedAt, LastUpdatedAt, Status, Name, IAMUser, MLModelId, DataSourceId, DataURI`
- An operator: EQ, GT, LT, GE, LE, NE
- Other parameters that depend on the nature of the object

With that parameter structure, you can make your script wait on a specific object completion, or wait on all the objects based on a datasource, a model, or even a user name. If we were to launch several evaluations for different models based on the same validation datasource, we would simply call a waiter for each model as such:

```
waiter.wait(FilterVariable='DataSourceId', EQ='the DatasourceId')
```

Wrapping up the Python-based workflow

Now that we know how to wait for all our evaluation to finish, we still need to get the evaluation result and delete the models and datasources we have created. As in the case of the `get-evaluation` AWS CLI command, the Boto3 `get_evaluation` method returns a JSON string with the model performance measure, the RMSE in the case of regression. The following script wraps up our trial:

```
t0 = time.time()
# declare the waiter and call the wait method on the evaluation
waiter = client.get_waiter('evaluation_available')
print("Waiting on evaluation to finish ")
waiter.wait(FilterVariable='Name', EQ=name_id_generation('EVAL', '',
trial)['Name'])
t = time.time() - t0
print("Evaluation has finished after %sm %ss"% (int(t/60), t%60) )
# get the evaluation results
response = client.get_evaluation(
  EvaluationId=name_id_generation('EVAL', '', trial)['Id']
)
RMSE =float(response['PerformanceMetrics']['Properties']['RegressionRMSE'])
print("[trial %0.2f] RMSE %0.2f"% (trial, RMSE) )
# and delete the resources
print("Deleting datasources and model")
response = client.delete_data_source(
  DataSourceId=name_id_generation('DS', 'training', trial)['Id']
)
response = client.delete_data_source(
  DataSourceId=name_id_generation('DS', 'validation', trial)['Id']
)
response = client.delete_ml_model(
  MLModelId=name_id_generation('MDL', '', trial)['Id']
)
```

Putting all the code blocks together returns the following output:

```
Creating datasources for training ([DS] training 04)
Creating datasources for validation ([DS] validation 04)
Training model ([MDL] 04) with params:
{
  "sgd.shuffleType": "auto",
  "sgd.l1RegularizationAmount": "1.0E-04",
  "sgd.maxPasses": "100"
}
Launching evaluation ([EVAL] 04)
Waiting on evaluation to finish
Evaluation has finished after 11m 43.78s
[trial 4] RMSE 22437.33
Deleting datasources and model
```

Implementing recursive feature selection with Boto3

In many real-world cases, the original dataset could have a very large number of variables. As dimensionality increases, so does the need for a larger sample set. This is called the *curse of dimensionality*, a classic predictive analytics problem. Simply put, if there is not enough diversity to infer a representative distribution for some variables, the algorithm will be unable to extract relevant information from the said variables. These low-signal variables drag down the algorithm's performance without adding any data fuel by adding useless complexity to the model. One strategy is to reduce the number of variables on which to train the model. However, that implies identifying which features can be dropped without significant loss of information.

There are many techniques to reduce the number of features:

- **Wrapper** techniques: These use rules and criteria to select the best and most impacting features.
- **Filter** techniques: These use statistical tests to measure the importance of each feature. Measuring the correlation with the target could be a simple way to remove non-significant variables.
- **Embedded** methods: For certain models, such as random forests, iteratively train the model on subsets of features, it is possible to evaluate the impact of the features that are left out during each iteration and thus infer the importance of each feature.

The method most adapted to the Amazon Machine Learning context is the recursive evaluation of each feature's importance, filtering out the least important ones by measuring when performance drops significantly with the discarding of a certain feature. It is a brute force version of Recursive Feature Elimination.

It follows these steps:

1. Build an initial model with all N features.
2. Then identify and remove the least important features by:
   - Building N subsets, removing a different feature in each subset
   - Building a model for each subset and evaluating its performance
   - Identifying the features for which the model's performance was least impacted

3. You now have *N-1* features. Reiterate steps 1 to 3 to identify and remove the next least important feature.

4. Stop when you notice a significant drop in the model's performance compared to the initial N-feature model.

The inverse version of this algorithm starts with *N* models, each built with just one feature, with a new feature added at each iteration. Choose the new feature as the new feature that generates the best increase in performance. Stop when adding new features does not lead to a significant increase in the model's performance.

In the rest of the chapter, we will show how to implement this feature selection strategy in Python.

Managing schema and recipe

Removing or adding features to a dataset directly impacts the schema and the recipe. The schema is used when creating the datasources, while the recipe is needed to train the model, as it specifies which data transformation will be performed prior to the model training.

Modifying the schema to remove features from the dataset can be done by simply adding the names of the variable to the `excludedAttributeNames` field. We can take the initial schema, and each time we remove a feature from the initial feature list, we add it to the excludedAttributeNames list. The steps are as follows:

1. Open the JSON formatted schema into a schema dict
2. Append the feature name to schema `['excludedAttributeNames']`
3. Save the schema to a properly indented JSON file
4. Upload the file to S3

When creating the datasource, we will point to the S3 location of the schema we just updated.

The initial recipe generated by default by Amazon ML for the Ames Housing dataset applies different quantile binning transformations on certain numerical features. The groups section of the recipe is as follows:

```
"groups": {
  "NUMERIC_VARS_QB_50":
"group('LotFrontage','KitchenAbvGr','BsmtFinSF1','GarageCars','1stFlrSF','S
creenPorch','LowQualFinSF','LotArea','OverallCond','2ndFlrSF','GarageArea',
'EnclosedPorch','HalfBath')",
  "NUMERIC_VARS_QB_100":
```

```
"group('BsmtFinSF2','WoodDeckSF','BsmtHalfBath','MiscVal','GrLivArea','Fire
places')",
  "NUMERIC_VARS_QB_500": "group('OverallQual')",
  "NUMERIC_VARS_QB_20": "group('TotalBsmtSF')",
  "NUMERIC_VARS_QB_200":
"group('MSSubClass','OpenPorchSF','YearRemod/Add','BsmtFullBath','MasVnrAre
a')",
  "NUMERIC_VARS_QB_10":
"group('PoolArea','BedroomAbvGr','TotRmsAbvGrd','YearBuilt','MoSold','YrSol
d','GarageYrBlt','FullBath','BsmtUnfSF','3SsnPorch')"
  }
```

Adding or removing variable names from that structure requires a more complex script than just adding an element in a list. Since such a script would not add much educational value to the book, we decided to use a default simple recipe that does not perform any transformation on the dataset. As long as we have a baseline RMSE with all the features available, the recursive feature elimination strategy is still valid. The only difference is that the overall RMSE scores will probably be made higher by not applying any quantile binning to our numerical data. The recipe we use is defined by the following:

```
{
"groups" : {},
"assignments" : { },
"outputs" : [ "ALL_INPUTS" ]
}
```

This is available in our examples at the S3 location s3://aml.packt/data/ch8/recipe_ames_housing_default.json. Using that recipe to evaluate our baseline model gives a baseline RMSE of *61507.35*. We will use that baseline RMSE to see whether removing a feature improved (lower) or degraded (higher) the model performance.

The following script is broken into three parts:

- Initialization and functions
- Launching the Amazon ML workflow
- Getting the evaluation results and deleting the resources

The script is available in our GitHub repo in its entirety. We use the same strategy to have a function to generate the names and IDs. We start with the following script to initialize the variable and declare the function:

```
import pandas as pd
import boto3
import json
```

```python
# Local schema with all the features
original_schema_filename = 'data/ames_housing.csv.schema'
# Initialize boto3 objects
s3 = boto3.resource('s3')
client = boto3.client('machinelearning')

# load dataset and feature_ names
df = pd.read_csv('data/ames_housing.csv')
original_features = df.columns.difference(['SalePrice', 'Order'])

# load original schema with all the features
schema = json.load( open(original_schema_filename) )

# SGD parameters: L1 heavy regularization
sgd_parameters = {
  "sgd.shuffleType": "auto",
  "sgd.l1RegularizationAmount": "1.0E-04",
  "sgd.maxPasses": "100"
}

# memorize all object Ids for future deletion
baseline_rmse = 61507.35
datasource_ids = []
model_ids = []
evaluation_ids = []
features_rmse = {}

def generate_trial(n):
  n = "X" + str(n).zfill(3)
  return {
    'schema_filename': "rfs_ames_housing_%s.schema"% n,
    'recipe_s3': 's3://aml.packt/RFS/recipe_ames_housing_default.json',
    'data_s3': 's3://aml.packt/RFS/ames_housing_shuffled.csv',
    'datasource_training_id': "rfs_training_%s"% n,
    'datasource_training_name': "[DS RFS] training %s"% n,
    'datasource_validation_id': "rfs_validation_%s"% n,
    'datasource_validation_name': "[DS RFS] validation %s"% n,
    'model_id': "rfs_%s"% n,
    'model_name': "[MDL RFS] %s"% n,
    'evaluation_id': "rfs_%s"% n,
    'evaluation_name': "[EVAL RFS] %s"% n,
  }
```

We now launch the datasource, model, and evaluation creation. The script only looks at the first 10 features, and not the entire set of 79 features, to save on resources.

> You will notice that we added a prefix "X" to the numbering of the Amazon ML objects. We found that sometimes, Amazon ML cannot create an object if the IDs and names have been used on previous objects that have now been deleted. That problem may disappear after some time. In any case, making sure that all new datasources, models, evaluations, and batch predictions have names and IDs that have never been used previously removes any naming issue.

The second part launches the creation of the datasources, models, and evaluations:

```
for k in range(10):
 print("="* 10 + " feature: %s"% original_features[k])
 trial = generate_trial(k)

 # remove feature[k] from schema and upload to S3
 schema['excludedAttributeNames'] = [original_features[k]]
 with open("data/%s"%trial['schema_filename'], 'w') as fp:
 json.dump(schema, fp, indent=4)
 s3.Object('aml.packt', "RFS/%s"%
trial['schema_filename']).put(Body=open("data/%s"%trial['schema_filename'],
'rb'))

 # create datasource
 print("Datasource %s"% trial['datasource_training_name'])
 datasource_ids.append( trial['datasource_training_id'] )
 response = client.create_data_source_from_s3(
   DataSourceId = trial['datasource_training_id'] ,
   DataSourceName= trial['datasource_training_name'] ,
   DataSpec={
     'DataLocationS3': trial['data_s3'],
     'DataRearrangement': '{"splitting":
     {"percentBegin":0,"percentEnd":70}}',
     'DataSchemaLocationS3': "s3://aml.packt/RFS/%s"%
     trial['schema_filename']
   },
   ComputeStatistics=True
 )

 # Create datasource for validation
 print("Datasource %s"% trial['datasource_validation_name'])
 datasource_ids.append( trial['datasource_validation_id'] )
 response = client.create_data_source_from_s3(
 DataSourceId = trial['datasource_validation_id'] ,
 DataSourceName= trial['datasource_validation_name'] ,
```

```
DataSpec={
'DataLocationS3': trial['data_s3'],
'DataRearrangement': '{"splitting":{"percentBegin":70,"percentEnd":100}}',
'DataSchemaLocationS3': "s3://aml.packt/RFS/%s"% trial['schema_filename']
},
ComputeStatistics=True
)

# Train model with existing recipe
print("Model %s"% trial['model_name'])
model_ids.append(trial['model_id'] )
response = client.create_ml_model(
MLModelId = trial['model_id'],
MLModelName = trial['model_name'],
MLModelType = 'REGRESSION',
Parameters = sgd_parameters,
TrainingDataSourceId = trial['datasource_training_id'] ,
RecipeUri = trial['recipe_s3']
)

print("Evaluation %s"% trial['evaluation_name'])
evaluation_ids.append(trial['evaluation_id'])
response = client.create_evaluation(
EvaluationId = trial['evaluation_id'],
EvaluationName = trial['evaluation_name'],
MLModelId = trial['model_id'],
EvaluationDataSourceId= trial['datasource_validation_id']
)
```

Finally, the third part waits for the evaluation to be complete, records the RMSE for each removed feature, and deletes the datasources and models (we kept the evaluations to avoid having to rerun the whole script to get the results):

```
for k in range(10):
trial = generate_trial(k)
waiter = client.get_waiter('evaluation_available')
print("Waiting on evaluation %s to finish "% trial['evaluation_name'])
waiter.wait(FilterVariable='Name', EQ=trial['evaluation_name'])
print("Evaluation has finished ")

response = client.get_evaluation( EvaluationId=trial['evaluation_id'] )
features_rmse[original_features[k]] =
float(response['PerformanceMetrics']['Properties']['RegressionRMSE'])
print("[%s] RMSE %0.2f"% (original_features[k],
float(response['PerformanceMetrics']['Properties']['RegressionRMSE'])) )
# Now delete the resources
print("Deleting datasources and model")
response = client.delete_data_source(
```

```
DataSourceId = trial['datasource_training_id']
)
response = client.delete_data_source(
DataSourceId = trial['datasource_validation_id']
)
response = client.delete_ml_model(
MLModelId = trial['model_id']
)

print("removing the feature increased the RMSE by ")
for k,v in features_rmse.items():
 print("%s t%0.2f %% "% (k, (baseline_rmse - v)/ baseline_rmse *100.0 ) )
```

In the end, we get the following RMSE variations for the first 10 features:

- `1stFlrSF 0.07%`
- `2ndFlrSF -18.28%`
- `BedroomAbvGr -0.02 %`
- `BsmtExposure -0.56 %`
- `BsmtFinSF2 -0.50 %`
- `BsmtCond 0.00 %`
- `BsmtFinSF1 -2.56 %`
- `Alley 0.00 %`
- `3SsnPorch -4.60 %`
- `BldgType -0.00 %`

For instance, removing the `2ndFlrSF` feature increased the RMSE by nearly 20%. This feature is definitely very important to predict salesPrice. Similarly, features `3SsnPorch` and `BsmtFinSF1` are also important to the model, since removing them increases the RMSE. On the other hand, removing `1stFlrSF`, `Alley`, `BedroomAbvGr` or `BldgType` only modified the RMSE by less than 0.10%. We can probably remove these feature without too much impact on the model performance.

Summary

In this chapter, we have moved away from the Amazon ML web interface and learned how to work with the service through the AWS CLI and the Python SDK. The commands and methods for both types of interaction are very similar. The functions and commands perform a standard set of operations from creation to deletion of Amazon ML objects: datasources, models, evaluation, and batch predictions. The fact that Amazon ML chains the sequence of dependent object creation allows you to create all the objects at once without having to wait for one upstream to finish (datasource or model) before creating the downstream one (model or evaluation). The waiter methods make it possible to wait for all evaluations to be completed before retrieving the results and making the necessary object deletion.

We showed how scripting Amazon ML allowed us to implement Machine Learning methods such as cross-validation and Recursive Feature Selection, both very useful methods in predictive analytics. Although we end up having to create many datasources and objects to conduct cross-validation and feature selection, the overall costs remain under control.

In the next chapter, we will start using other AWS services to expand the capabilities of Amazon ML. We will look at other datasources beyond S3, such as Redshift and RDS, and how to use Amazon Lambda for machine learning.

8
Creating Datasources from Redshift

In this chapter, we will use the power of SQL queries to address non-linear datasets. Creating datasources in Redshift or RDS gives us the potential for upstream SQL-based feature engineering prior to the datasource creation. We implemented a similar approach in `Chapter 4`, *Loading and Preparing the Dataset*, by leveraging the new AWS Athena service to apply preliminary transformations on the data before creating the datasource.

This enabled us to expand the `Titanic` dataset by creating new features, such as the `Deck` number, replacing the `Fare` with its log or replacing missing values for the `Age` variable. The SQL transformations were simple, but allowed us to expand the original dataset in a very flexible way. The **AWS Athena** service is S3 based. It allows us to run SQL queries on datasets hosted on S3 and dump the results in S3 buckets. We were still creating Amazon ML datasources from S3, but simply adding an extra data preprocessing layer to massage the dataset.

AWS offers two other SQL services from which it is possible to create datasources: RDS and Redshift. Datasource creation is very similar for both RDS and Redshift, and we will focus on creating datasources in Redshift via the Python SDK `Boto3`. The key point for us is that RDS/Redshift-based datasources are created directly via SQL queries, thus giving us the opportunity for further feature engineering. Redshift also integrates seamlessly with AWS Kinesis, a service we'll explore for streaming data in `Chapter 9`, *Building a Streaming Data Analysis Pipeline*.

Amazon Machine Learning is built on intrinsically linear models leveraging with good results quantile binning data transformation as a method to handle non-linearities in the dataset. Polynomial regression is another important machine learning method used to deal with non-linear datasets. We will use our new SQL powers to implement polynomial regression using Amazon ML.

In this chapter, you will learn the following:

- Choosing between RDS and Redshift
- How to create a Redshift database with PostgreSQL
- How to load your S3 data into Redshift
- How to create a datasource from Redshift
- What is polynomial regression
- How to use polynomial regression with Amazon ML

Choosing between RDS and Redshift

AWS offers no less than six different cloud database and SQL/NoSQL services: RDS, Aurora, DynamoDB, Redshift, Athena, and AWS Database Migration Service! Out of all these services, only two are compatible with Amazon Machine Learning: RDS and Redshift. You can store data in either service and create datasources from these sources. The datasource creation methods for the two services have similar parameters, but differ quite significantly when it comes to the underlying AWS service communication.

RDS and Redshift are very different services. Redshift is a data warehouse used to answer a few complex and long running queries on large datasets, while RDS is made for frequent, small, and fast queries. Redshift is more suited for massive parallel processing to perform operations on millions of rows of data with minimal latency, while RDS offers a server instance that runs a given database. RDS offers several different database types – MySQL, PostgreSQL, MariaDB, Oracle, SQL Server, and Amazon Aurora, while Redshift is Amazon's own analytics database offering based on the **ParAccel** technology and running a fork of PostgreSQL. You connect to Redshift using standard ODBC and JDBC connections. Amazon Redshift and PostgreSQL have a number of very important differences that you must be aware of as you build your database in Redshift. Many functions, data types, and PostgreSQL features are not supported in Amazon Redshift. More info is available at `http://docs.aws.amazon.com/redshift/latest/dg/c_redshift-and-postgres-sql.html`.

 A more in-depth explanation of the difference between RDS and Redshift can be found on this thread: `https://www.quora.com/What-is-the-difference-between-redshift-and-RDS`

In the context of Amazon ML, an important difference between the two services is that the Amazon ML web console only allows for datasource creation from S3 and Redshift, but not from RDS, as shown in this screenshot:

Input data

Import your data to create an Amazon ML datasource. Amazon ML can use your datasource

Where is your data?   S3    Amazon Redshift

The Python SDK and the AWS CLI, however, both allow datasource creation from RDS and Redshift.

SDK:

- `create_data_source_from_rds()`: http://boto3.readthed ocs.io/en/latest/reference/services/machinelearning.h tml#MachineLearning.Client.create_data_source_from_rd s

- `create_data_source_from_redshift()`: http://boto3.rea dthedocs.io/en/latest/reference/service/machinelearni ng.html#MachineLearning.Client.create_data_source_fro m_redshift

CLI:

- `create-data-source-from-rds`: http://docs.aws.amazon. com/cli/latest/reference/machinelearning/create-data- source-from-rds.html

- `create-data-source-from-redshift`: http://docs.aws.am azon.com/cli/latest/reference/machinelearning/create- data-source-from-redshift.html

We now compare the parameters required by the Python SDK to connect to either services:

- Redshift parameters:

```
{
    "DatabaseInformation": {
      "DatabaseName": "string",
      "ClusterIdentifier": "string"
    },
    "SelectSqlQuery": "string",
    "DatabaseCredentials": {
      "Username": "string",
      "Password": "string"
    },
    "S3StagingLocation": "string",
    "DataRearrangement": "string",
    "DataSchema": "string",
    "DataSchemaUri": "string"
}
```

- RDS parameters:

```
{
    "DatabaseInformation": {
      "DatabaseName": "string"
      "InstanceIdentifier": "string",
    },
    "SelectSqlQuery": "string",
    "DatabaseCredentials": {
      "Username": "string",
      "Password": "string"
    },
    "S3StagingLocation": "string",
    "DataRearrangement": "string",
    "DataSchema": "string",
    "DataSchemaUri": "string",
    "ResourceRole": "string",
    "ServiceRole": "string",
    "SubnetId": "string",
    "SecurityGroupIds": ["string", ...]
}
```

The difference between the two sets of parameters lies in the way we allow access to the data store. Both sets include `DatabaseInformation`, `DatabaseCredentials`, `SelectSqlQuery`, `DataSchema`, and `DataRearrangement`. RDS also requires manually setting up two roles with the right policies: `ResourceRole: DataPipelineDefaultRole` and `ServiceRole:DataPipelineDefaultResourceRole`.

RDS is more adapted to our volume of data than Redshift, and we should use RDS instead of Redshift for our machine learning project. However, we previously found that manually creating the roles and policies for RDS required an in-depth knowledge of AWS inner permissions workings, which was too complex for this book. Although the parameters and concepts are very similar for creating datasources from RDS and Redshift, in the background, they differ quite a lot. RDS datasource creation involves the creation of AWS data pipelines, another AWS service that allows you to process and move data between different AWS computeing and storage services. Having to set up data pipelines adds a non-trivial layer of complexity to the whole project.

Redshift, on the other hand, does not require building a data pipeline and setting permissions, roles, and policies to create datasources. In the end, this extra simplicity made Redshift more adapted to this book, as we wanted to keep the focus on the machine learning side of things and not delve into the intricacies of AWS access roles and policies, although RDS would have been more suited for our low volume of data.

> **Redshift**: Presenting Redshift in depth far exceeds the scope of this book. We recommend the *Getting Started with Amazon Redshift* book by *Stefan Bauer, Packt* (`https://www.packtpub.com/big-data-and-business-inte lligence/getting-started-amazon-redshift`), the AWS documentation (`https://aws.amazon.com/redshift/getting-started /`) and this blog post for a good introduction to Cluster Configuration (`htt ps://www.periscopedata.com/amazon-redshift-guide/cluster-confi guration`).

Let's start with Redshift, using the AWS Redshift console to create a PostgreSQL-based instance and load the `Titanic` dataset we already have available in our S3 bucket.

Creating a Redshift instance

Log in to your AWS account, and go to the Redshift dashboard at `https://console.aws.am`
`azon.com/redshift/`.

Creating a database in Redshift is quite simple and well handled by the AWS Redshift
wizard. First, click on the **Launch Cluster** button. In the first screen, we define the **Cluster
identifier*** as `amlpackt`, the **Database name** as `amlpacktdb`, and the **Master user name** as
shown in the following screenshot:

Cluster identifier*	amlpackt
Database name	amlpacktdb
Database port*	5439
Master user name*	alexperrier
Master user password*	··········
Confirm password*	··········

In the next screen, we choose the default parameters to configure the node, as shown in the following screenshot:

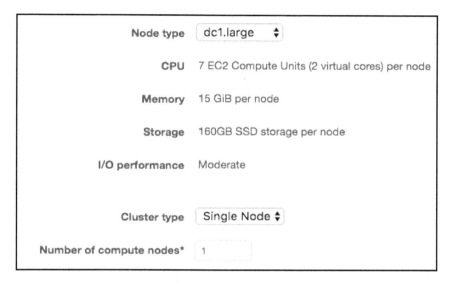

Choose the default settings for the next configuration screen, but make sure that the cluster is publicly accessible. You do not need a public IP:

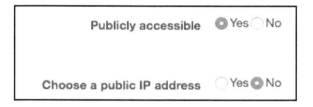

Choose the Machine Learning/RDS VPC security group:

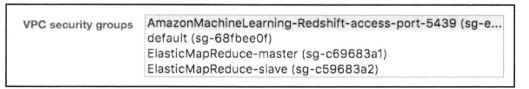

The final validation screen prior to launching the cluster will inform you about the associated costs as shown here:

⚠ Unless you are eligible for the free trial, you will start accruing charges as soon as your cluster is active.

Applicable charges:
The on-demand hourly rate for this cluster will be **$0.25** , or **$0.25** /node.If you have purchased reserved nodes in this region for this node type that are active, your costs will be discounted. Additional nodes will be billed at the on-demand rate.

If you are eligible for a free trial, you will receive 750 hours of free usage for each month of the trial, applied across all running dc1.large nodes across all regions. Regardless of when you start your trial, you will receive two full months of free usage. Once your trial expires or your usage exceeds 750 hours/month, you can shut down your cluster, avoiding any charges, or keep it running at our standard On-demand rate.

For more information, see Amazon Redshift Free Trial FAQ, Amazon Redshift Pricing, and Reserved Nodes Documentation.

It will take a few minutes once you click on the final **Launch Cluster** button for the cluster to be ready. We will connect to the newly created database using Psql. Other external connection types are available through JDBC and ODBC. The cluster information page shows the **Endpoint** URL that you need to connect to the newly created database:

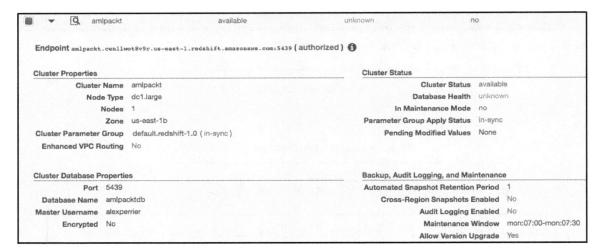

Connecting through the command line

Psql is a command line program that acts as the primary front-end to a Postgresql database. It provides a number of shell commands (pg_dump to dump the content of a database, createdb to create a database, and many others). It also has a number of meta commands to list elements and display information (see the **Psql cheatsheet** information box).

Psql cheatsheet:
q: Quit/Exit
d __table__: Show table definition, including triggers
dt : List tables
df: List functions
dv: List views
x: Pretty-format query results instead of the not-so-useful ASCII tables
connect __database__: Connect to a database
l: List databases
Adding a + on a d command will show more results: compare, for instance, d titanic with d+ titanic
see http://postgresguide.com/utilities/psql.html for more info on Psql

You can now connect from the terminal to your database using **Psql** with the following command, using the endpoint URL (amlpackt.cenllwot8v9r.us-east-1.redshift.amazonaws.com) for the host:

```
$ psql --host=amlpackt.cenllwot8v9r.us-east-1.redshift.amazonaws.com --port=5439 --username=alexperrier --password --dbname=amlpacktdb
```

The amlpacktdb database is, of course, empty:

```
alexperrier@amlpacktdb=> dt
 No relations found.
```

There are many ways we can import data into a Redshift database. To keep things simple, we will upload a CSV file available on S3 to a Redshift table with the copy command, as follows:

```
alexperrier@amlpacktdb=> copy <table name> from '<s3 path to csv file>'
CREDENTIALS 'aws_access_key_id=<aws access key
id>;aws_secret_access_key=<aws secret access key>' CSV;
```

When using the copy command, Redshift needs to authenticate with the S3 service. Authentication between AWS services can be implemented in two ways:

- **User-based**: authentication is granted by passing the user access keys. It is a simpler mean of granting access between AWS services but it is not always available.
- **Role-based**: authentication requires creating roles with the right policies and permissions. It is a preferred andmore secure mean of authentication than user-based authentication. However, it requires extra roles and policies creation steps and is less straightforward to setup.

More info on user versus role based authentication for AWS services is available at `http://docs.aws.amazon.com/redshift/latest/mgmt/redshift-iam-authentication-access-control.html`. In our copy example, we plan to use the aws access keys of our main AWS user. But before we can copy data into the table, we first need to create it with an SQL query. For the `Titanic` CSV file we have been working on, the table creation query is as follows:

```
CREATE TABLE IF NOT EXISTS titanic (
   id integer primary key,
   pclass integer,
   survived boolean,
   name varchar(255),
   sex varchar(255),
   age real,
   sibsp integer,
   parch integer,
   ticket varchar(255),
   fare real,
   cabin varchar(255),
   embarked char(1),
   boat varchar(8),
    body varchar(8),
   home_dest varchar(255)
);
```

The table now exists in our Redshift database, as shown by the `dt` command:

```
alexperrier@amlpacktdb=> dt
 List of relations
 Schema | Name | Type | Owner
 --------+---------+-------+-------------
 public | titanic | table | alexperrier
 (1 row)
```

The table structure is as expected, as shown by the d+ command:

```
alexperrier@amlpacktdb=> d+ titanic
  Table "public.titanic"
  Column | Type | Modifiers | Storage | Stats target | Description
  -----------+--------------------+-----------------------------------
  ----------------+----------+-------------+-------------
  id | integer | not null default nextval('titanic_id_seq'::regclass) |
  plain | | pclass | integer | | plain | |
  survived | boolean | | plain | |
  name | character varying(255) | | extended | |
  sex | character varying(255) | | extended | |
  age | real | | plain | |
  sibsp | integer | | plain | |
  parch | integer | | plain | |
  ticket | character varying(255) | | extended | |
  fare | real | | plain | |
  cabin | character varying(255) | | extended | |
  embarked | character(1) | | extended | |
  boat | character varying(8) | | extended | |
  body | character varying(8) | | extended | |
  home_dest | character varying(255) | | extended | |
  Indexes:
  "titanic_pkey" PRIMARY KEY, btree (id)
```

We can now upload the CSV file to S3 and fill in our table by running the following commands from your terminal:

```
# Load file on S3
$ aws s3 cp data/titanic.csv s3://aml.packt/data/ch9/
# connect to database via psql
$ psql --host=amlpackt.cenllwot8v9r.us-east-1.redshift.amazonaws.com --
port=5439 --username=alexperrier --password --dbname=amlpacktdb
# upload data from your S3 location into the titanic table
$ copy titanic from 's3://aml.packt/data/ch9/titanic.csv' CREDENTIALS
'aws_access_key_id=<access key id>;aws_secret_access_key=<access secret
key>' CSV;
```

Note that the CSV file should not include the CSV headers. To verify that the copy command worked, we can count the number of records in the Titanic table by running the following query:

```
alexperrier@amlpacktdb=> select count(*) from titanic;
  -[ RECORD 1 ]
  count | 1309
```

The result shows we now have 1309 records in the titanic table.

Executing Redshift queries using Psql

We've seen that we can connect to our database with the following `Psql` command:

```
$ psql -h amlpackt.cenllwot8v9r.us-east-1.redshift.amazonaws.com -p 5439 -U
alexperrier --password -d amlpacktdb
```

We then need to type in our password. To shorten the line and avoid having to type the password each time, we can set both the connection string and the password as shell environment variables. In your terminal, execute the following command to create a global `REDSHIFT_CONNECT` shell variable:

```
$ export REDSHIFT_CONNECT='-h amlpackt.cenllwot8v9r.us-
east-1.redshift.amazonaws.com -p 5439 -U alexperrier -d amlpacktdb'
```

Similarly for the password, execute the command:

```
$ export PGPASSWORD=your_password
```

From now on, you can connect to the database with the simple command:

```
$ psql $REDSHIFT_CONNECT
```

Note that `REDSHIFT_CONNECT` is a variable name we chose, while `PGPASSWORD` is a predefined shell variable name that is recognized by Psql.

We now have a choice in the way we can run queries on our Redshift database. We can perform either of the following steps:

- `Psql` into the database shell and type some SQL queries:

   ```
   $ psql $REDSHIFT_CONNECT
   alexperrier@amlpacktdb=> select count(*) from titanic;
   ```

- Write the SQL query into a file (for instance, `my_file.sql`) and, from the terminal, run the command:

   ```
   $ psql $REDSHIFT_CONNECT -f my_file.sql
   ```

- Run the query directly with the `Psql` command:

   ```
   $ psql $REDSHIFT_CONNECT -c 'SELECT count(*) FROM my_table'
   ```

We are now ready to work on our dataset. Since we have already worked extensively on the Titanic dataset, we will use another dataset for the rest of the chapter. Let's create an artificial dataset that exhibits strong non-linear patterns.

Creating our own non-linear dataset

A good way to create a non-linear dataset is to mix sines with different phases. The dataset we will work with in this chapter is created with the following Python script and exported to a CSV file:

```
import numpy as np
n_samples = 1000
de_linearize = lambda X: np.cos(1.5 * np.pi * X) + np.cos( 5 * np.pi * X )
X = np.sort(np.random.rand(n_samples)) * 2
y = de_linearize(X) + np.random.randn(n_samples) * 0.1
```

As usual, X is the predictor, and y the outcome. You can use variations on that script to easily generate other non-linear datasets. Note that we have used a `lambda` function, which is a Pythonic way of declaring a function on the spot when needed. Then we shuffle the dataset by sorting randomly (`np.random.rand(n_samples)`). We then save the data to a CSV file (`nonlinear.csv`) using the **Pandas** dataframe:

```
import pandas as pd
df = pd.DataFrame( {'X':X, 'y': y} )
df = df.sample(frac=1) # shuffles the entire dataframe
df.to_csv('data/nonlinear.csv', index = False)
```

Plotting the data gives the following graph:

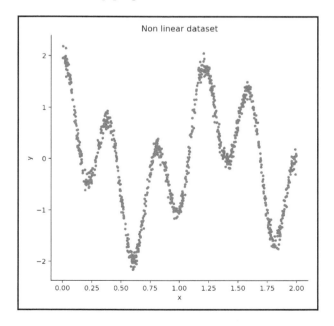

It is obviously not linear. A line has no hope of approximating, let alone predicting the outcome y from the predictor X. Now that we have a highly non-linear dataset available, we need to upload it to Redshift.

Uploading the nonlinear data to Redshift

We first need to create the table that will host the data. We will call that table `nonlinear`. It only has three columns: an index, the predictor X, and the outcome y:

```
CREATE TABLE IF NOT EXISTS nonlinear (
  id integer primary key,
  x1 real,
  y real
);
```

Once the table is created, we can upload the CSV file to S3, connect to the database, and import the data in the non-linear table with the command:

```
copy nonlinear from 's3://aml.packt/data/ch9/nonlinear.csv' CREDENTIALS
'aws_access_key_id=<access key id>;aws_secret_access_key=<access secret
key>' CSV;
```

We can verify that the `nonlinear` table now has a thousand rows with the query:

```
$ psql $REDSHIFT_CONNECT -c "select count(*) from nonlinear"
 > count
> 1000
 >(1 row)
```

Our data has been uploaded to Redshift. We are ready to create datasources and train and evaluate models! But before we dive into model building on this dataset, let's introduce the polynomial regression method, which will allow us to deal with this highly non-linear dataset.

Introducing polynomial regression

In two dimensions, where we have a predictor and an outcome, linear modeling is all about finding the best line that approximates your data. In three dimensions (two predictors and one outcome), the idea is then to find the best plane, or the best flat surface, that approximates your data. In the N dimension, the surface becomes an hyperplane, but the goal is always the same – to find the hyperplane of dimension *N-1* that gives the best approximation for regression or that separates the classes the best for classification. That hyperplane is always flat.

Coming back to the very non-linear two-dimensional dataset we created, it is obvious that no line can properly approximate the relation between the predictor and the outcome. There are many different methods to model non-linear data, including polynomial regression, step functions, splines, and **Generalized additive models** (GAM). See *Chapter 7* of *An Introduction to Statistical Learning* by *James, Witten, Hastie* and *Tibshirani Springer, 2013* for a great introduction to these methods. The book is available in PDF at http://www-bcf.usc.edu/~gareth/ISL/. We will apply the polynomial regression method.

Polynomial regression consists in replacing the standard linear model:

$$\hat{y} = w_0 + w_1 x$$

Here, $\hat{y}$ is the predicted outcome, x the predictor, (w_0, w_1) the linear model coefficients. By a polynomial function of order k:

$$y = w_0 + w_1 x + \hat{w}_2 x^2 + .. + + w_k x^k$$

The power of the polynomial regression approach is that we can use the same linear modeling method as with the linear model, and we can therefore still use Amazon ML SGD to find the coefficients $\{w_k\}$ of the polynomial regression equation. In the next section, we will train successive models by increasing the degree of the polynomial.

Establishing a baseline

We first need to establish a baseline. Amazon ML quantile binning transformation is Amazon Machine Learning preferred method of dealing with non-linearities in a dataset. Let's establish how a simple linear model performs with Amazon's default recipe. We will create a baseline score using the usual AWS console tools. This time, we choose to create a data source from Redshift and not from S3. Fill the information as shown in the next screenshot, and click on **Test access** to check your access, and at the same time, make Amazon ML create the necessary IAM role. Finally, click on **Verify** once you're done:

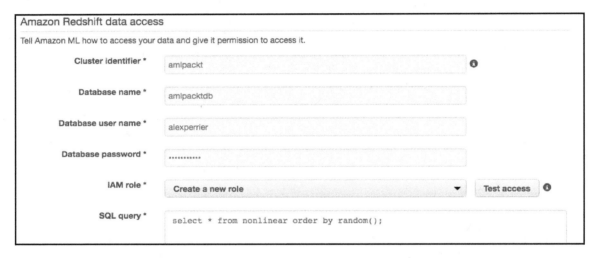

Amazon ML handles all the role and policy creation in the background by creating the following resources:

- A new role: **AmazonMLRedshift_us-east-1_amlpackt**. We will use the **arn** related to this role when creating datsources using the Python SDK.
- Two new policies attached to this role:
    - AmazonMLS3LocationAccess_aml.packt
    - AmazonMLRedshiftAccess_us-east-1_amlpackt
- AWS also sets up the Trust Relationship so that roleAmazonMLRedshift_us-east-1_amlpackt is able assume a machinelearning service role.

Creating these roles and policies manually requires a solid understanding of access permissions between services in AWS. Creating them using the console is a significant time-saver. The next steps are standard schema and target definition, and data source creation. The default schema generated by Amazon ML is as follows:

```
{
  "version" : "1.0",
  "rowId" : null,
  "rowWeight" : null,
  "targetAttributeName" : "y",
  "dataFormat" : "CSV",
  "dataFileContainsHeader" : false,
  "attributes" : [ {
    "attributeName" : "x",
    "attributeType" : "NUMERIC"
  }, {
    "attributeName" : "y",
    "attributeType" : "NUMERIC"
  } ],
  "excludedAttributeNames" : [ ]
}
```

We reuse that schema later on by saving the JSON string into the `data/nonlinear.schema` file and uploading it to S3 with `aws s3 cp data/nonlinear.schema s3://aml.packt/data/ch9/`.

Once the datasource is available, we can create and evaluate a model via the console. The recipe generated by Amazon ML during the model creation uses the quantile binning transformation on the predictor with 500 bins, which may seem like a large value since we only have 700 samples in the training dataset. The auto-generated Amazon ML recipe is as follows:

```
{
  "groups": {
    "NUMERIC_VARS_QB_500": "group('x')"
  },
  "assignments": {},
  "outputs": [
    "ALL_CATEGORICAL",
    "quantile_bin(NUMERIC_VARS_QB_500,500)"
  ]
}
```

We train a model with L2 mild regularization and 100 passes, and evaluate that model on 30% of our dataset. We obtain the following results:

- With quantile binning
  - RMSE: 0.1540
  - Baseline RMSE: 1.034
- Without quantile binning
  - RMSE: 1.0207
  - Baseline RMSE: 1.025

Quantile binning correctly handles the non-linearities and results in a pretty good score, while a raw linear model does not fare much better than the baseline. In the case of linear regression, Amazon ML baseline is simply the mean of the outcome in the training dataset.

Let's see if we can beat these results with polynomial regression.

Polynomial regression in Amazon ML

We will use `Boto3` and Python SDK and follow the same method of generating the parameters for datasources that we used in Chapter 7, *Command Line and SDK*, to do the **Monte Carlo** validation: we will generate features corresponding to power 2 of x to power P of x and run N Monte Carlo cross-validation. The pseudo-code is as follows:

```
for each power from 2 to P:
    write sql that extracts power 1 to P from the nonlinear table
    do N times
        Create training and evaluation datasource
        Create model
        Evaluate model
        Get evaluation result
        Delete datasource and model
    Average results
```

In this exercise, we will go from *2 to 5* powers of x and do 5 trials for each model. The Python code to create a datasource from Redshift using `create_data_source_from_rds()` is as follows:

```
response = client.create_data_source_from_redshift(
    DataSourceId='string',
    DataSourceName='string',
    DataSpec={
        'DatabaseInformation': {
```

```
            'InstanceIdentifier': 'amlpackt',
            'DatabaseName': 'amlpacktdb'
        },
        'SelectSqlQuery': 'select x, y from nonlinear order by random()',
        'DatabaseCredentials': {
            'Username': 'alexperrier',
            'Password': 'my_password'
        },
    'S3StagingLocation': 's3://aml.packt/data/ch9/',
    'DataRearrangement': '{"splitting":{"percentBegin":0,"percentEnd":70 }
  }',
    'DataSchemaUri': 's3://aml.packt/data/ch9/nonlinear.csv.schema'
  },
  RoleARN='arn:aws:iam::178277513911:role/service-role/AmazonMLRedshift_us-
east-1_amlpackt',
  ComputeStatistics=True
)
```

Beyond the obvious parameters (`Database Information`, `DataSchemaURI`, `DataSourceId`, and `DataSourceName`), you need to find the value for the **Role ARN** identifier. Go to the **IAM** console, click on **Roles,** and then on the **AmazonMLRedshift_us-east-1_amlpackt** role in order to find the **Role ARN** string:

IAM > Roles > **AmazonMLRedshift_us-east-1_amlpackt**

▾ Summary

Role ARN   arn:aws:iam::178277513911:role/service-role/AmazonMLRedshift_us-east-1_amlpackt

The `DataRearrangement` string will depend on the nature of the datasource with a 0% to 70% split for the training datasource and a 70% to 100% for the evaluation datasource. The `SelectSqlQuery` is where we are going to do the feature engineering and create new variables as powers of *x*.

For instance, the following query generates an x to the power of 2 variable:

```
select x, power(x,2) as x2, y from nonlinear order by random()
```

This query also generates an x to the power of 3 variable:

```
select x, power(x,2) as x2, power(x,3) as x3, y from nonlinear order by
random()
```

Besides having to generate new queries for each new set or variables, we also need to generate a new schema. The original schema for the non-linear dataset is as follows:

```
{
  "version" : "1.0",
  "rowId" : null,
  "rowWeight" : null,
  "targetAttributeName" : "y",
  "dataFormat" : "CSV",
  "dataFileContainsHeader" : false,
  "attributes" : [ {
    "attributeName" : "x",
    "attributeType" : "NUMERIC"
  }, {
    "attributeName" : "y",
    "attributeType" : "NUMERIC"
  } ],
  "excludedAttributeNames" : [ ]
}
```

We modify this original schema by adding the following element to the schema attributes list for each new power of x variable:

```
{
    "attributeName" : "x{N}",
    "attributeType" : "NUMERIC"
}
```

In order to run our trials, compare different feature sets, and do cross-validation to select the best model, we need to write a set of Python functions.

Driving the trials in Python

So far, we have written sequential code in Python. Writing simple object-oriented code instead is always a time saver in the end. The code is more organized, maintainable, and less prone to becoming unusable after a while. Taking the time to write simple classes with clear initialization, instances and class methods will make your code much simpler and robust in the end. With that in mind, we will now write a `NonLinear` class for our experiment.

Let's first write down the different functions of that class that generate some of the fields that depend on the power of the polynomial regression:

- This function takes in a power p and returns the SQL query:

```
def generate_sql(self, p):
    powers = [ 'power(x,{0}) as x{0}'.format(i) for i in range(1,p+1) ]
    return 'select ' + ','.join(powers) + ', y from nonlinear order by random()'
```

- This function takes in the name of the data split (training versus evaluation) and returns the string, formatted as JSON, which will be required during the datasource creation:

```
def generate_data_rearrangement(self,split):
    if split == 'training':
        pct_begin = 0
        pct_end = 70
    else:
        pct_begin = 70
        pct_end = 100
    return json.dumps( { "splitting":
    {"percentBegin":pct_begin,"percentEnd":pct_end } } )
```

- Finally, the following function takes in the power p and returns the schema JSON string:

```
def generate_schema(self, p):
    attributes = [ { "attributeName" : "x{0}".format(i), "attributeType"
    : "NUMERIC" } for i in range(1,p+1) ]
    attributes.append({ "attributeName" : "y", "attributeType" : "NUMERIC"
    })
    return json.dumps({ "version" : "1.0",
        "rowId" : None,
        "rowWeight" : None,
        "targetAttributeName" : "y",
        "dataFormat" : "CSV",
        "dataFileContainsHeader" : False,
        "attributes" : attributes,
        "excludedAttributeNames" : [ ]
    })
```

The next three functions use the machine learning client to create the datasources, the model, and the evaluation. They are very similar to the scripts we wrote in `Chapter 7`, *Command Line and SDK*.

- The data source creation takes in a power p, and an index k for the cross-validation, and splits the nature of the datasource created. The script calls the `generate_sql` and `generate_data_rearrangement` methods:

```
def create_datasource(self, p, k, split ):
  print("Create datasource {0} {1} {2} {3}".format(p,k,split,
  self.prefix))
  return self.client.create_data_source_from_redshift(
  DataSourceId = "ds_{2}_{3}_p{0}_{1}".format(p,k,split,
self.prefix),
  DataSourceName = "DS {2} {3} p{0} {1}".format(p,k,split,
   self.prefix),
  DataSpec = {
    'DatabaseInformation': {
      'DatabaseName': 'amlpacktdb',
      'ClusterIdentifier': 'amlpackt'
    },
    'SelectSqlQuery': self.generate_sql(p),
    'DatabaseCredentials': {
      'Username': 'alexperrier',
      'Password': 'password'
    },
    'S3StagingLocation': 's3://aml.packt/data/ch9/',
    'DataRearrangement': self.generate_data_rearrangement(split),
    'DataSchema': self.generate_schema(p)
  },
  RoleARN='arn:aws:iam::178277513911:role/service-role
  /AmazonMLRedshift_us-east-1_amlpackt',
  ComputeStatistics=True
  )
```

- The create model method also takes in the power p and index k:

```
def create_model(self, p, k):
  print("Create model {0} {1} {2}".format(p, k, self.prefix))
  return self.client.create_ml_model(
  MLModelId = "mdl_{2}_p{0}_{1}".format(p,k, self.prefix),
  MLModelName = "MDL {2} p{0} {1}".format(p,k, self.prefix),
  MLModelType = 'REGRESSION',
  Parameters = self.sgd_parameters,
  TrainingDataSourceId = self.ds_training['DataSourceId'] ,
  Recipe = json.dumps(self.recipe)
  )
```

- Finally, the create evaluation method is as follows:

```
def create_evaluation(self, p, k):
print("Create evaluation {0} {1} {2}".format(p, k, self.prefix))

return self.client.create_evaluation(
EvaluationId = "eval_{2}_p{0}_{1}".format(p,k, self.prefix),
EvaluationName = "EVAL {2} p{0} {1}".format(p,k, self.prefix),
MLModelId = self.model['MLModelId'],
EvaluationDataSourceId= self.ds_evaluation['DataSourceId']
)
```

We use `create_sql(p)` and `create_schema(p)` to render the `SelectSqlQuery` and `Data.Schema` fields when creating datasources. The model creation function uses two class items not yet initialized: `sgd_parameters` and `recipe`. The datasource creation function returns the response from the Amazon ML `create_data_source_from_redshift` function. We memorize the response in `ds_training` and `ds_evaluation` and use these items to pass on the appropriate `DataSourceId` in the model and evaluation creation functions.

The global code for running all the different evaluations is this:

```
# Initialize the object
nl = NonLinear(max_p, n_crossval, prefix)
# Run all the datasources, models and evaluations creation
nl.run_all_trials()
# Wait until the evaluations are finished and get the results
nl.get_results()
# Export the results to a csv file
nl.to_csv(filename)
# Free the resources
nl.delete_resources()
```

These functions are defined by the following:

```
import pandas as pd
import boto3
import json
import csv

class NonLinear():

  def __init__(self, max_p, n_crossval, prefix):
  self.trials = []
  self.max_p = max_p
  self.n_crossval = n_crossval
  self.prefix = prefix
```

```python
self.client = boto3.client('machinelearning')
self.sgd_parameters = {
"sgd.shuffleType": "auto",
"sgd.l2RegularizationAmount": "1.0E-06",
"sgd.maxPasses": "100"
}

self.recipe = {
"groups" : {},
"assignments" : { },
"outputs": ["ALL_INPUTS"]
# "outputs": ["quantile_bin(ALL_NUMERIC,200)"]
}

def run_all_trials(self):
for p in range(1,self.max_p+1):
for k in range(self.n_crossval):
self.trials.append( self.run_trial(p,k) )

def run_trial(self, p, k ):
self.ds_training = self.create_datasource(p, k, 'training')
self.ds_evaluation = self.create_datasource(p, k, 'evaluation')
self.model = self.create_model(p,k)
self.evaluation = self.create_evaluation(p,k)
return {
"p": p,
"k": k,
"ds_training_id": self.ds_training['DataSourceId'],
"ds_evaluation_id": self.ds_evaluation['DataSourceId'],
"model_id": self.model['MLModelId'],
"evaluation_id": self.evaluation['EvaluationId'],
"rmse": None
}

def get_results(self):
results = []
for trial in self.trials:

waiter = self.client.get_waiter('evaluation_available')
print("Waiting on evaluation {0} to finish ".format(
trial['evaluation_id'] ) )
waiter.wait(FilterVariable='DataSourceId', EQ=trial['ds_evaluation_id'] )

response = self.client.get_evaluation( EvaluationId=trial['evaluation_id']
)
rmse =
float(response['PerformanceMetrics']['Properties']['RegressionRMSE'])
trial["rmse"] = rmse
```

```
results.append(trial)
print("Evaluation score {0}".format(rmse))
self.trials = results

def delete_resources(self):
# Now delete the resources
print("Deleting datasources and model")
for trial in self.trials:
response = self.client.delete_data_source(
DataSourceId = trial['ds_training_id']
)
response = self.client.delete_data_source(
DataSourceId = trial['ds_evaluation_id']
)
response = self.client.delete_ml_model(
MLModelId = trial['model_id']
)

def to_csv(self, filename):
print("exporting to csv {0}".format(filename))
keys = self.trials[0].keys()
with open(filename, 'w') as output_file:
dict_writer = csv.DictWriter(output_file, keys)
dict_writer.writeheader()
dict_writer.writerows(self.trials)
```

The integral code is available on GitHub at `https://github.com/alexperrier/packt-aml`
.

Interpreting the results

The following graph shows the different RMSE obtained for the five cross-validations and the different polynomial degrees (1 to 5):

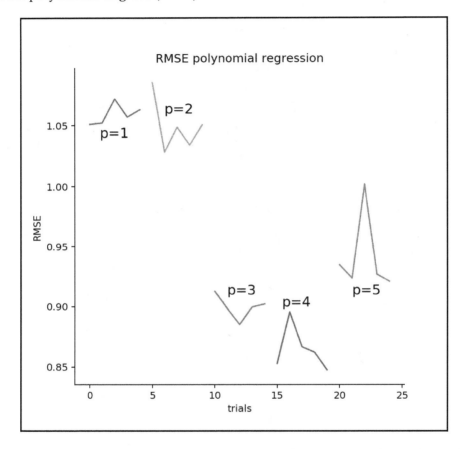

We see that the best fit is obtained for the polynomes of degrees 3 and 4. In the end, the overall RMSE of our models based on polynomial regression models is not good compared to the RMSE obtained with quantile binning. Polynomial regression gives RMSE values at best around 0.85, while the RMSE with quantile binning was found to be around 0.15. Quantile binning, as it is done by Amazon ML, beats polynomial regression by a large factor.

Summary

In this chapter, we saw how to use Redshift as a datasource for Amazon ML. Although RDS could also have been used to create datasources, Redshift is much easier to use with Amazon ML as all the access configuration is taken care of by the AWS wizard.

We have shown how to use simple SQL queries on Redshift to carry out feature engineering and implement a polynomial regression approach on a highly non-linear dataset. We have also shown how to generate the required SQL queries, schemas, and recipes to carry out the Monte Carlo cross-validation.

In the next chapter, we will build on our Redshift integration and start streaming data using the AWS Kinesis service.

9
Building a Streaming Data Analysis Pipeline

In this final chapter of the book, we will build an end-to-end streaming data pipeline that integrates Amazon ML within the Kinesis Firehose, AWS Lambda, and Redshift pipeline. We extend the Amazon ML capabilities by integrating it with these other AWS data services to implement real-time Tweet classification.

In a second part of the chapter, we show how to address problems beyond a simple regression and classification and use Amazon ML for **Named Entity Recognition** and content-based recommender systems.

The topics covered in this chapter are as follows:

- Training a twitter classification model
- Streaming data with Kinesis
- Storing with Redshift
- Using AWS Lambda for processing
- Named entity recognition and recommender systems

In the chapter's conclusion, we will summarize Amazon ML's strengths and weaknesses.

Streaming Twitter sentiment analysis

In this chapter, our main project consists of real-time sentiment classification of Tweets. This will allow us to demonstrate how to use an Amazon ML model that we've trained to process real-time data streams, by leveraging the AWS data ecosystem.

We will build an infrastructure of AWS services that includes the following:

- **Amazon ML**: to provide a real-time classification endpoint
- **Kinesis firehose**: To collect the Tweets
- **AWS Lambda**: To call an Amazon ML streaming endpoint
- **Redshift**: To store the Tweets and their sentiment
- **S3**: To act as a temporary store for the Tweets collected by Kinesis Firehose
- **AWS Cloudwatch**: To debug and monitor

We will also write the necessary Python scripts that feed the Tweets to Kinesis Firehose.

Popularity contest on twitter

All good data science projects start with a question. We wanted a social network question not tied to a current political or societal context. We will be looking into the popularity of vegetables on twitter. We want to know what the most popular vegetables on twitter are. It's a question that could stand the test of time and be adapted to other lists of things, such as fruits, beverages, weather conditions, animals, and even brands and politicians. The results will surprise you... or not.

We will start by training a binary classification Amazon ML model using a large public twitter sentiment analysis dataset.

There are many available sentiment analysis libraries that can, with a few lines of code, and given a piece of text, return a sentiment score or a polarity (positive, neutral, negative). `TextBlob` is such a library in Python. It is available at `https://textblob.readthedocs.io`. Built on top of **NLTK**, `TextBlob` is a powerful library to extract information from documents. Besides sentiment analysis, it can carry out some aspects of speech tagging, classification, tokenization, named entity recognition, as well as many other features. We compare `TextBlob` results with our own Amazon ML classification model. Our goal, first and foremost, is to learn how to make these AWS services work together seamlessly. Our vegetable popularity contest on social media will follow these steps:

1. We start by training a twitter sentiment classification model on Amazon ML and creating a real-time prediction endpoint.
2. We set up a Kinesis Firehose that stores content on S3.
3. We write a simple Python script called a `producer` that collects the Tweets from the twitter API and sends them to Kinesis. At this point, Kinesis Firehose stores the Tweets in S3.

4. We move on from storing streaming data in S3 to storing streaming data in Redshift. To do so, we must launch a Redshift cluster and create the required tables.

5. Finally, we add an AWS Lambda function to our pipeline in order to interrogate our Amazon ML classification endpoint.

6. Throughout the project, we use AWS CloudWatch to check the status and debug our data pipeline.

We end up with a collection of Tweets, with two types of sentiment scoring that we can compare. We will look at the ranking of vegetables according to the two methods, their variability, and the inter-rate agreement between the two methods, and we will try to assess which one is better. It's worth noting at this point that we refrain from any involved text processing of Tweets. Tweets are a very specific type of textual content that contains URLs, emoticons, abbreviations, slang, and hashtags. There is a large number of publications on sentiment analysis for twitter that explore different preprocessing and information extraction techniques. We will not use any particular feature extraction technique and restrict ourselves to a simple bag-of-words approach. Our comparison between sentiment analysis via Amazon ML and TextBlog is a proof of concept, not a benchmark.

The training dataset and the model

The first step in our project is to train a sentiment analysis and classification Amazon ML model for Tweets. Fortunately, we have access to a rather large twitter sentiment dataset composed of over 1.5M Tweets tagged 0/1 for negative/positive sentiments. The dataset is available at `http://thinknook.com/twitter-sentiment-analysis-training-corpus-dataset-2012-09-22/`. This dataset is an aggregation of two twitter sentiment analysis datasets:

- **University of Michigan Sentiment Analysis** competition on Kaggle: `https://inclass.kaggle.com/c/si650winter11`
- **Twitter Sentiment Corpus** by *Niek Sanders*: `http://www.sananalytics.com/lab/twitter-sentiment/`

This Twitter **Sentiment Analysis** Dataset contains 1,578,627 classified Tweets. Each row is tagged with 0/1 for negative/positive sentiment. We use a sample of that dataset (approximately 10%, 158K Tweets) to train a classification model in Amazon ML. We load the dataset on S3, and train and evaluate a binary classification model using the Amazon ML service. We apply no specific text transformation on the texts. The recipe is as follows:

```
{
  "groups": {},
  "assignments": {},
  "outputs": [
      "ALL_BINARY",
      "ALL_TEXT"
  ]
}
```

We set the model to have mild L2 regularization and 100 passes. Training the model takes a bit of time (over 10 minutes) to complete, probably due to a large number of samples in play. The model evaluation shows pretty good overall performances with an AUC of 0.83. Roughly two-thirds of the Tweets are properly classified by the Amazon ML model. The predictions are smoothly distributed across the range of class probabilities, as shown by the model's evaluation graph:

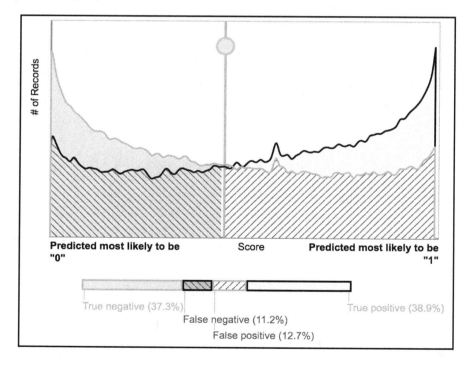

We now create a real-time prediction endpoint from the model's page by clicking on the **Create endpoint** button at the bottom of the page:

The endpoint URL is of the form `https://realtime.machinelearning.us-east-1.amazonaws.com`. We will use that endpoint to classify new Tweets through requests from the Lambda service. Let's test whether our Amazon ML classifier works as expected with the following Python script:

```
import boto3
client = boto3.client('machinelearning')
client.predict(
    MLModelId = "ml-ZHqxUjPNQTq",
    Record = { "SentimentText": "Hello world, this is a great day" },
    PredictEndpoint =
"https://realtime.machinelearning.us-east-1.amazonaws.com"
)
```

The sentence `Hello world, this is a great day` returns a score of *0.91* for the probability that the sentence is positive, and classifies the sentence as *1*, while a `Hello world, this is a sad day` sentence returns a probability of *0.08*, and classifies the sentence as 0. The words `great` and `sad` are the words driving the sentiment classification. The classifier is working as expected.

Let's now switch our attention to the Kinesis service.

Kinesis

Kinesis is a multiform service organized around three subservices: **Streams**, **Firehose**, and **Analytics**. Kinesis acts as a highly available pipeline to stream messages between data producers and data consumers.

- Data producers are sources of data coming from streaming APIs, IoT devices, system logs, and other high volume data streams
- Data consumers will most commonly be used to store, process data, or trigger alerts

Kinesis is able to handle up to 500 Terabytes of data per hour. We use Kinesis at its minimal level and with its most simple configuration. Readers interested in the more complex usage of Kinesis should read the AWS documentation at `https://aws.amazon.com/documentation/kines is/`. A good overview of the different concepts and elements behind AWS Kinesis on the blog post at `https://www.sumologic.com/blog/devops/ki nesis-streams-vs-firehose/`.

Kinesis Stream

Kinesis Stream is used to collect streaming data given by a producer and processed by a consumer. It's the simplest of the three Kinesis services as it does not store the data in any way. Kinesis Stream mainly acts like a buffer, and the data is kept available between 24 hours to 168 hours. An IoT device or a log service would typically act as the producer and send data to the Kinesis stream. At the same time, a consumer is running to process that data. Consumers services that trigger alerts (SMS, e-mails) based on event detection algorithms, real-time dashboards updated in real time, data aggregators, or anything that retrieves the data synchronously. Both producer and consumer must be running simultaneously for the Kinesis stream to function. If your producer and consumer are scripts running on your local machine, they must both be running in parallel.

It is possible to add processing to the incoming data by adding an AWS Lambda function to the stream. The whole data pipeline will now follow these steps:

1. A custom application or script sends records to the stream (the producer).
2. AWS Lambda polls the stream and invokes your Lambda function when new records are detected.
3. AWS Lambda executes the Lambda function and sends back the record, original or modified, to the Kinesis Stream.

We will not be using Kinesis Streams since we want to store the data we are collecting. Kinesis stream is a good way to start with the Kinesis service.

Kinesis Analytics

Kinesis Analytics is AWS's most recent add-on to the Kinesis mix. Kinesis Analytics allows you analyzing real-time streaming data with standard SQL queries. The idea is to go from querying a static representation of the data to a dynamic one that evolves as the data streams in. Instead of using AWS Lambda to process the data via a scripting language, the goal is to process the data in SQL and feed the results to dashboards or alerting systems. We will not be using Kinesis Analytics, but instead, focus on Kinesis Firehose.

Setting up Kinesis Firehose

We will focus on the Kinesis Firehose service, which offers two important features: data received can be fed to an AWS Lambda function for extra processing, and the resulting data can be stored on S3 or on a Redshift database.

We will start by setting up a Kinesis Firehose delivery stream that stores data on S3 without any Lambda functionality:

1. Go to the Kinesis Firehose dashboard at `https://console.aws.amazon.com/fir ehose/` and click on **Create Delivery Stream.**
2. Fill in the following fields:
    - **Destination**: `Amazon S3`
    - **Delivery stream name**: `veggieTweets` (or choose your own name)
    - **S3 bucket**: `aml.packt`
    - **S3 prefix**: `veggies`
3. Click on **Next**:

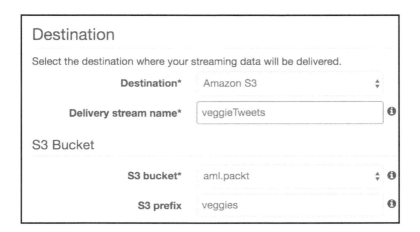

Note that the **S3 prefix** field corresponds to a folder in your S3 bucket. You should now go to S3 and create a `veggies` folder in your bucket. Mimic the setup from the next screenshot:

1. For the moment, we will keep the **Data transformation with AWS Lambda** disabled.
2. Enable **Error Logging,** since we will need to debug our data delivery errors with CloudWatch Logs.
3. For the **IAM** role, select **Firehose Delivery IAM Role**. You will be taken to the IAM service and guided through the creation of the required role. You can choose an existing policy and create a new one. The Role/Policy wizard will handle the details. Click on **Allow** to be redirected to the initial Firehose configuration screen.
4. Click on **Next**, review the details of the Firehose delivery stream, and click on **Create Delivery Stream**.

We now have a Kinesis Firehose delivery stream that will, once we send data to it, store data in the S3 **packt.aml/veggies** location. We now need to create a producer script that will send the data to the Kinesis Firehose service.

Producing tweets

A Kinesis producer can take many shapes as long as it sends data to the Kinesis Stream. We will use the Python Firehose SDK and write a simple script that collects Tweets from the twitter API, filters some of them, and sends them to the Kinesis Firehose. We use the Python-Twitter library.

 There are several Twitter API Python packages available on GitHub. Two of the more popular ones, `Twitter` and `Python-Twitter` (`https://pypi.python.org/pypi/python-twitter/`) share the same import calls `import twitter`, but not the same method calls, which can lead to confusion and time being wasted.

The Python-Twitter package offers a `GetSearch` method that takes either a query string `term` or a `raw_query` as a parameter for the Twitter search:

- The query string (`term`) corresponds to the keywords you would write down on the Twitter website search bar; for instance, `term = brocolli OR potato OR tomato`.
- The `raw_query` parameter takes for input the parameter part of the URL once you've hit the search button: the string after the `?` in the URL. You can build advanced queries from the twitter advanced search page `https://twitter.com/search-advanced`. For instance, our search for "*brocolli OR potato OR tomato*" translates to a `raw_query = q=brocolli%20OR%20potato%20OR%20tomato&src=typd`. We use the `raw_query` parameter in our call to the search API.
- To obtain your own Twitter development API keys, go to `https://apps.twitter.com/` and create an application.

We first define a class that initializes the access to the twitter API. This class has a `capture` method, which runs a search, given a raw query. Save the following code in a `tweets.py` file:

```
import twitter
class ATweets():
    def __init__(self, raw_query):
        self.twitter_api = twitter.Api(consumer_key='your own key',
            consumer_secret= 'your own key',
            access_token_key='your own key',
            access_token_secret='your own key')
        self.raw_query = raw_query

    # capture the tweets: see
```

```
http://python-twitter.readthedocs.io/en/latest/twitter.html
    def capture(self):
        statuses = self.twitter_api.GetSearch(
            raw_query = self.raw_query,
            lang = 'en',
            count=100, result_type='recent', include_entities=True
        )
    return statuses
```

Given this class and a `raw_query` string, gathering Tweets consists in initializing the `ATweets` class with the `raw_query` and applying the capture method on the instantiated object as such:

```
tw = ATweets(raw_query)
statuses = tw.capture()
```

Here, `statuses` is a list of Tweets, each containing many elements. We only use a few of these elements. Now that we can gather Tweets from the `Twitter` API, we need a producer script that will send the Tweets to Kinesis. The producer Python script is as follows:

```
from tweets import ATweets
import json
import boto3

# The kinesis firehose delivery stream we send data to
stream_name = "veggieTweets"

# Initialize the firehose client
firehose = boto3.client('firehose')

# Our own homemade list of vegetables, feel free to add seasoning
vegetables = ['artichoke','asparagus', 'avocado', 'brocolli','cabbage',
'carrot', 'cauliflower','celery', 'chickpea', 'corn','cucumber',
'eggplant','endive', 'garlic', 'green beans', 'kale', 'leek', 'lentils',
'lettuce','mushroom','okra', 'onion','parsnip', 'potato','pumpkin',
'radish','turnip', 'quinoa', 'rice', 'spinach', 'squash' , 'tomato',
'yams', 'zuchinni']

# Loop over all vegetables
for veggie in vegetables:
 # for a given veggie define the query and capture the tweets
 raw_query = 'f=tweets&vertical=default&l=en&q={0}&src=typd'.format(veggie)
 # capture the tweets
 tw = ATweets(raw_query)
 statuses = tw.capture()
 # and for each tweet, cleanup, add other data and send to firehose
 for status in statuses:
```

```
# remove commas and line returns from tweets
clean_tweet = ''.join([s for s in st.text if s not in [',', 'n']])
# and build the record to be sent as a comma separated string followed by
a line return
record = ','.join([str(st.id), st.user.screen_name,veggie, clean_tweet]) +
'n'
# send the record to firehose
response=firehose.put_record(DeliveryStreamName = stream_name,
Record={'Data': record} )
```

Save that code to a `producer.py` file in the same folder as the `tweets.py` file.

As you may have noticed, we restricted the Twitter search to English Tweets by specifying `lang = 'en'` in the call to `GetSearch`. However, that did not produce the expected results, and many non-English Tweets were returned. In a later version of the producer script, we add the following conditions to the Tweets themselves before sending them to the Firehose, actually filtering out non-English tweets shorter than 10 characters or those send as retweets:

```
(st.lang=='en') & (st.retweeted_status is None) & (len(st.text) > 10):
```

We are now ready to run our producer script. One last important detail to pay attention to is that calls to the Twitter API are capped. If you call the API too often, you will have to wait longer and longer between your requests until they are allowed to go through. There are reliable ways to deal with these restrictions, and it's easy to find code online that show you how to delay your API calls. We will simply use the `watch` command line with a delay of 10 minutes (600 s) between calls. The `watch` command simply executes whatever command you write afterwards, every nth second. To run your producer code, launch a terminal, and run the following command:

```
$ watch -n 600 python producer.py
```

Every 10 minutes, tweets will be captured and sent to Kinesis Firehose. To verify that both your script and delivery stream work, go to your S3 bucket and the `aml.packt/veggies` folder. You should see files piling up. The files are saved by Kinesis in subfolders structured by date/year/month/day and hour. The filenames in the last subfolder follow a format similar to `veggieTweets-2-2017-04-02-19-21-51-1b78a44f-12b2-40ce-b324-dbf4bb950458`. In these files, you will find the records as they have been defined in the producer code. Our producer code sends comma-separated data formatted as tweet ID/twitter username/vegetable/tweet content. An example of such as record is as follows:

```
848616357398753280,laurenredhead,artichoke,Artichoke gelatin dogs. Just one
of many delicious computer-algorithm generated recipe
titles:https://t.co/mgI8HtTGfs
```

We will now set up Redshift so that these tweets and related elements end up stored in an SQL database.

The Redshift database

We saw how to create a Redshift cluster in Chapter 8, *Creating Datasources from Redshift*, we won't go through the steps again. For our vegetable contest project, we create a vegetable cluster and a `vegetablesdb` database. Wait till the endpoint for the cluster is ready and the endpoint is defined, and then connect to your Redshift database via this `Psql` command:

```
$ psql --host=vegetables.cenllwot8v9r.us-east-1.redshift.amazonaws.com --
port=5439 --username=alexperrier --password --dbname=vegetablesdb
```

Once connected to the database, create the following table with this SQL query:

```
CREATE TABLE IF NOT EXISTS tweets (
  id BIGINT primary key,
  screen_name varchar(255),
  veggie varchar(255),
  text varchar(65535)
);
```

Note that there are no `blob` or `text` data types in Redshift SQL. We defined the tweets as `varchar(65535)`, which is probably far too large, but since we used `varchar` and not `char`, the volume occupied by the data shrank to the actual length of the text and not the whole 65KB. In that table, we only capture the ID of the tweet, the tweet itself, what vegetable the tweet was associated with, and the screen name of the person writing the tweet. We disregard any other tweet elements.

Adding Redshift to the Kinesis Firehose

This part is delicate as several pieces from different services must fit together:

- The data structure, table declaration, and Kinesis Redshift configuration
- The data fields aggregation and subsequent parsing
- The role and associated policies

The fields of the Redshift table that stores the data need to be synchronized in three different places:

1. The Redshift table with a proper definition of fields.
2. The script that sends the data to Kinesis. Depending on how the record sent to Kinesis is aggregated together and later parsed by Redshift, the script must concatenate the same number of fields in the same order as the ones defined in the Redshift table. For instance, when we write `record = ','.join([str(st.id), st.user.screen_name, veggie, clean_tweet]) + 'n'` in the script, it implies that the table has four fields with the right types: `int`, `varchar`, `varchar`, and `varchar`.
3. The columns as defined in the Kinesis Firehose definition.

For that last point, we need to go back to the Firehose dashboard, create a new stream, and define it as a Redshift-based delivery stream. Click on **Create Delivery Stream**, and select Redshift as the destination. Follow the different screens and fill in the following values:

- **S3 bucket**: Your own bucket
- **S3 prefix**: We keep the prefix veggies
- **Data transformation**: Disabled for now
- **Redshift cluster**: `Vegetables`
- **Redshift database**: `Vegetablesdb`
- **Redshift table columns**: ID, `screen_name`, veggie, text (**this one is important**)
- **Redshift username**: The username you access Redshift with
- **Redshift COPY options**: Delimiter ',' (**very important too**)

Once created, your Kinesis Firehose stream should resemble the following screenshot:

Details	Monitoring	S3 Logs	Redshift Logs			Delete Delivery Stream

Cancel

Delivery stream name*	veggieStream		Redshift cluster*	vegetables
S3 bucket*	aml.packt		Redshift database*	vegetablesdb
S3 prefix	veggies/		Redshift table*	tweets
IAM role*	firehose_delivery_role		Redshift table columns	id,screen_name, veggie,tb_polarity,
Data transformation*	● Disabled ○ Enabled		Redshift username*	alexperrier
			Redshift password*	········
S3 buffer size (MB)*	5		Redshift COPY options	delimiter ','
S3 buffer interval (sec)*	60		Retry duration (sec)*	30
S3 Compression	UNCOMPRESSED		COPY command	COPY tweets (id,screen_name, veggie,tb_polarity, text) FROM 's3://aml.packt/<manifest>' CREDENTIALS 'aws_iam_role=arn:aws:iam::<aws-account-id>:role/<role-name>' MANIFEST delimiter ',';
S3 Encryption	No Encryption			
Status	ACTIVE			▸ View instructions
Error logging	● Enable ○ Disable			

Notice the `COPY` command in the bottom right corner of the screen, which is reproduced here:

```
COPY tweets (id,screen_name, veggie,tb_polarity, text) FROM
's3://aml.packt/<manifest>' CREDENTIALS 'aws_iam_role=arn:aws:iam::<aws-
account-id>:role/<role-name>' MANIFEST delimiter ',';
```

This command indicates how Redshift will ingest the data that Kinesis sends to S3, what fields it expects, and how it will parse the different fields (for instance, separated by a comma). There are other potential `COPY` formats including JSON or CSV. We found this one to be simple and working. It's important that the way the record is defined and formatted in the producer script (four variables separated by commas) corresponds to the COPY part of the `table name (name of the four fields)` command with the right definition of the delimiter `','`.

This COPY command is also a good way to debug the pipeline when the data is not getting recorded into the database. Psql into the database, and run the same query in order to get useful error messages on why the queries are failing.

It's now time for a word on role-based access control.

Setting up the roles and policies

There are two types of access control in AWS: key based and role based. Key based is much easier to set up but cannot be used to make Kinesis, Redshift, and S3 talk to each other, as AWS indicates at `http://docs.aws.amazon.com/redshift/latest/dg/copy-usage_notes -access-permissions.html`:

With role-based access control, your cluster temporarily assumes an IAM role on your behalf. Then, based on the authorizations granted to the role, your cluster can access the required AWS resources. An IAM role is similar to an IAM user, in that it is an AWS identity with permission policies that determine what the identity can and cannot do in AWS. However, instead of being uniquely associated with one user, a role can be assumed by any entity that needs it. Also, a role doesn't have any credentials (a password or access keys) associated with it. Instead, if a role is associated with a cluster, access keys are created dynamically and provided to the cluster. We recommend using role-based access control because it provides more secure, fine-grained control of access to AWS resources and sensitive user data.

We must create the right role for your user to be able to access Redshift, and then we must give it the necessary policies.
There are three steps:

1. First, authorize Amazon Redshift to access other AWS services on your behalf. Follow the instructions at: `http://docs.aws.amazon.com/redshift/latest/mgm t/authorizing-redshift-service.html`

2. Second, attach the role in clustering. Take a look at `http://docs.aws.amazon.co m/redshift/latest/mgmt/copy-unload-iam-role.html`.

3. Finally, using the console to manage IAM role associations, perform the following steps:
   1. Go to Redshift, and click on Manage **IAM Roles.**
   2. Select from the available roles.
   3. Wait for the status to go from **Modifying** to **Available**.

Roles and policies in AWS, when trying to have different services connect with one another, can be challenging and time consuming. There is an obvious need for strict access control for production-level applications and services, but the lack of a more relaxed or loose generalized access level to allow for proof of concepts and pet projects is definitely missing from the AWS platform. The general hacking idea when facing role-related access problems is to go to the **IAM Role** page and attach the policies you think are necessary to the role giving you trouble. Trial and error will get you there in the end.

If all goes well, when you run the producer script, you should see the following happening:

- Files and date-based subfolders are created in the `{bucket}/veggies` folder
- Graphs and queries should show up or be updated in the Redshift cluster page
- On the Firehose delivery stream page, check the **S3 Logs** and **Redshift Logs** tabs for error messages
- Your `vegetablesdb.tweets` should start filling up with rows of content.

If that's not the case and you are not seeing tweets in your database, it's time to start debugging.

Dependencies and debugging

Connecting up the different services -- Firehose, Redshift, S3 is not a straightforward task if you're not a seasoned AWS user. Many details need to be ironed out, and the documentation is not always clear, and sometimes, too complex. Many errors can also happen in a hidden fashion, and it's not always obvious where the error is happening and how to detect it, let alone make sense of it. Of all the bugs and problems we had to solve, these were the most time-consuming ones.

Data format synchronization

If you send some data to Redshift, it needs to be parsed by Redshift. You are sending a string formatted as `id,` `username,` `sentiment,` `tweet` or a JSON string `{id: 'id',` `username:'twetterin_chief',sentiment: '0.12',tweet:'Hello world it's a` `beautiful day'}`. You need to make sure that the Redshift configuration in Kinesis follows the format of your data. You do so in the Kinesis-Redshift configuration screen with the two following fields:

- The **Redshift table columns**
- The **Redshift COPY options**

Debugging

When you run your producer, and the data does not end up in the redshift table, you should remember that there is a delay. That delay is set when you create the Kinesis delivery stream, and is set, by default, to 3,600 seconds. Set it to a minimum of 60 seconds if you want to avoid long waits. These are the places to check when your data is not streaming in your database:

1. **Check S3**: The S3 prefix corresponds to a folder in the bucket you have defined. If there are errors, you will see a new subfolder called `errors` or `processing` `errors`. Click through the subfolders until you reach the actual error file, make it public (there's a button), download the file, and examine it. It will sometimes contain useful information. The error subfolder also contains a manifest file. The manifest file is useful to reprocess failed files.

2. Connect to your Redshift database, and check the `STL_LOAD_ERRORS` table with `select * from STL_LOAD_ERRORS`. If the problem is caused by an SQL-based error (probably parsing related), useful information will show up there. The error messages are not always explanatory though. In our case, that table was showing the first tweet Redshift failed to ingest, which helped a lot in figuring out what was wrong. In the end, the problem we were facing was that some characters were taken as column delimiters by Redshift. We removed these characters from the tweets directly in the producer.

3. Check the **Redshift queries** page, where you will see the latest queries. If you see that the queries have been terminated instead of completed, you have an SQL-query-related problem.

4. In the end, a good debugging method is to connect to your database and run the COPY query shown in the Kinesis delivery stream recap page without forgetting to replace the account ID and the role name with the right values. This will mimic how Redshift is actually trying to ingest the data from the S3 buckets. If it fails, the related errors will bring you more information.

Preprocessing with Lambda

We would now like to send the tweets for sentiment classification to our Amazon ML model. In order to do that, we will enable the data transformation available in the Kinesis Firehose delivery stream page and use a Lambda function:

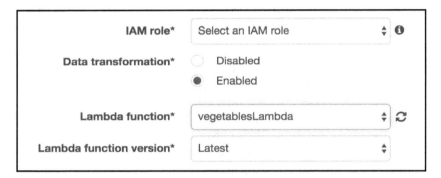

AWS Lambda is a data-processing service that allows you to run scripts (in a variety of languages, including Python 2.7, but not Python 3). It is used in conjunction with other services, such as Kinesis, as a data processing add-on. You can divert your data stream, send it to Lambda for processing, and, if you wish, have the result sent back to the initial stream. You can also use Lambda to call other services, such as sending alerts or using other storage services.

The main default of AWS Lambda is that the choice of packages you can import into your Python script is limited. Trying to import packages, such as `scikit-learn`, NLTK, or for that matter, any package not already available, is rather complex. For a guide for how to use `scikit-learn` on AWS Lambda, go to `https://serverlesscode.com/post/deploy-scik itlearn-on-lamba/` or `https://serverlesscode.com/post/deploy-scikitlearn-on-lam ba/`. This significantly restricts what can be done out of the box with Lambda. Our use of AWS Lambda is much simpler. We will use AWS Lambda to do the following:

1. Catch the data from Kinesis Firehose.
2. Parse the data and extract the tweet.
3. Send the data to Amazon ML real time end point.
4. Extract the classification score from the response.
5. Send back the data along with the classification score to the Kinesis Firehose delivery stream.

Go to AWS Lambda, and click on **Create Lambda Function**. Then perform the following steps:

1. Select the **Blank Function** blueprint and the **Python 2.7 runtime**.
2. Do not configure a trigger.
3. Fill in the **Name** as `vegetablesLambda`, and select **Python 2.7 Runtime**.

Finally, paste the following code in the inline editor:

```
from __future__ import print_function

import base64
import boto3
import logging

logger = logging.getLogger()
logger.setLevel(logging.INFO)

ml_client = boto3.client('machinelearning')

print('Loading function')

def lambda_handler(event, context):
  output = []
  for record in event['records']:
    payload = base64.b64decode(record['data'])
    payload = payload.split(',')
    tweet = payload.pop(4)
```

```
            predicted_label, predicted_score = get_sentiment(tweet)

            payload.append(str(predicted_label) )
            payload.append(str(predicted_score) )
            payload.append(tweet)
            payload = ','.join(payload)

            output_record = {
              'recordId': record['recordId'],
              'result': 'Ok',
              'data': base64.b64encode(payload)
            }
            output.append(output_record)
            return {'records': output}
```

The `lambda_handler` function is triggered automatically by the Kinesis Firehose. It catches
and parses the message (aka the payload) `event['records']`, extracts the
tweets, and calls a `get_sentiment()` function that returns a sentiment score and a
sentiment label. Finally, it adds the sentiment numbers back to the record, rebuilds the
payload, and sends it back to Kinesis. The `get_sentiment()` function sends the tweet to
our Amazon classification endpoint and returns the `predicted_label`, and
`predicted_score`. It is defined in the following script:

```
def get_sentiment(tweet):

    response = ml_client.predict(
        MLModelId = "ml-ZHqxUjPNQTq",
        Record = { "SentimentText": tweet },
        PredictEndpoint =
"https://realtime.machinelearning.us-east-1.amazonaws.com"
      )
    predicted_label = response['Prediction']['predictedLabel']
    predicted_score =
response['Prediction']['predictedScores'][predicted_label]

    return predicted_label, predicted_score
```

Since we added two new elements to the payload, we also need to add them to the Redshift table and to the Kinesis-Redshift configuration. To recreate the `tweets` table in Redshift, run the following query:

```
drop table if exists tweets;
CREATE TABLE IF NOT EXISTS tweets (
 id BIGINT primary key,
 screen_name varchar(255),
 veggie varchar(255),
 ml_label int,
 ml_score float,
 text varchar(65535)
);
```

At the Kinesis level, change the **Redshift table columns** field to id, screen_name, veggie, ml_label, ml_score, text.

Analyzing the results

We now have a complete pipeline of streaming data that is caught, transformed, and stored. Once you have collected a few thousand tweets, you are ready to analyze your data. There are a couple of things that remain to be done before we can get the answers we set out to find at the beginning of this chapter:

- What are the most popular vegetables on twitter?
- How does `TextBlob` compare to our Amazon ML classification model?

Our simple producer does not attempt to handle duplicate tweets. However, in the end, our dataset has many duplicate tweets. Broccoli and carrots are less frequent Tweet subjects than one could expect them to be. So, as we collect about a hundred tweets every 10 minutes, many tweets end up being collected several times. We also still need to obtain a sentiment score and related classes from `TextBlob`.

We will now download our collected dataset of tweets, remove duplicates, and use the `TextBlob` classification.

Download the dataset from RedShift

The right way to download data from Redshift is to connect to the database using Psql and use the `Unload` command to dump the results of an SQL query in S3. The following command exports all the tweets to the `s3://aml.packt/data/veggies/results/` location using an appropriate role:

```
unload ('select * from tweets') to 's3://aml.packt/data/veggies/results/'
iam_role 'arn:aws:iam::0123456789012:role/MyRedshiftRole';
```

We can then download the files and aggregate them:

```
# Download
$ aws s3 cp s3://aml.packt/data/veggies/results/0000_part_00 data/
$ aws s3 cp s3://aml.packt/data/veggies/results/0001_part_00 data/
# Combine
$ cp data/0000_part_00 data/veggie_tweets.tmp
$ cat data/0001_part_00 >> data/veggie_tweets.tmp
```

The `veggie_tweets.csv` file is not comma separated. The values are separated by the | character. We can replace all the pipes in the file with commas with the following command line:

```
$ sed 's/|/,/g' data/veggie_tweets.tmp > data/veggie_tweets.csv
```

We are now ready to load the data into a pandas dataframe:

```
import pandas as pd
df = pd.read_csv('data/veggie_tweets.csv')
```

Note that we could have also used | as a delimiter when loading the pandas dataframe with `df = pd.read_csv('data/veggie_tweets.tmp', delimiter = '|', header=None, names = ['id', 'username', 'vegetable', 'ml_label', 'ml_score', 'text'])`.

Sentiment analysis with TextBlob

`TextBlob` gives you sentiment analysis, scoring, and classification in a couple of Python lines. For the given a text, initialize a `TextBlob` instance, and retrieve its polarity with these two lines of code:

```
from textblob import TextBlob
print(TextBlob(text).sentiment)
```

The `TextBlob` sentiment object has a polarity and a subjectivity score. The polarity of a text ranges from -1 to +1, negative to positive, and the subjectivity from 0 to 1, very objective to very subjective. For instance, the sentence `I love brocoli` returns `Sentiment(polarity=0.5, subjectivity=0.6)`, while the sentence `I hate brocoli` returns a sentiment of `Sentiment(polarity=-0.8, subjectivity=0.9)`. We can add the `TextBlob` sentiment whenever we process the tweet, either within the producer or once we've downloaded the dataset with these simple lines:

```
from textblob import TextBlob
df['tb_polarity'] = 0
for i, row in df.iterrows():
    df.loc[i, 'tb_polarity'] = TextBlob(row['text']).sentiment.polarity
```

Each row of our dataframe now also has a sentiment score.

Removing duplicate tweets

In all Twitter-based NLP analysis, you end up dealing with bots, even when collecting tweets about vegetables! In our dataset, we had many versions of promotion tweets where the text was the same across tweets, but the links and users were different. We remove duplicate tweets by first removing the URL from the tweets and then using the `drop_duplicates` Pandas method.
Noting that all URLs in Tweets start with `https://t.co/`, it's easy to remove all URLs from the Tweets. We will create a new tweet column without URLs in our dataframe. We enter the following line, which, given a tweet, returns the tweet without URLs:

```
' '.join([token for token tk in tweet.split(' ') if 'https://t.co/' not in tk])
```

When working with pandas dataframes, a very practical way to create new columns based on some operation on other columns of the dataframe is to combine the apply method with a Lambda function. The overall pattern to create a `new_column` from `existing_column` is:

```
df['new_column'] = df[existing_column].apply(
                lambda existing_column : {
                    some operation or function on existing_column
                }
            )
```

We apply this pattern to create the `no_urls` column containing the tweets with no urls:

```
df['no_urls'] = df['text'].apply(
                lambda tweet : ' '.join(
                    [tk for  tk in tweet.split(' ') if 'https://t.co/'
not in tk]
                )
            )
```

The `no_urls` columns no longer contain any URLs. We can now remove duplicates based on this column with the following line:

```
df.drop_duplicates(subset= ['no_urls'], inplace = True)
```

This removed about 30% of our tweets.

And what is the most popular vegetable?

It's interesting to compare the sentiment score distributions between our Amazon ML model and `TextBlob`. We can see in the following plot that our Amazon ML model is good at separating positive and negative tweets, while `TextBlob` has a more centered distribution. In fact, a significant portion of tweets were scored as 0 (neutral) by `TextBlob`. We removed them from the histogram:

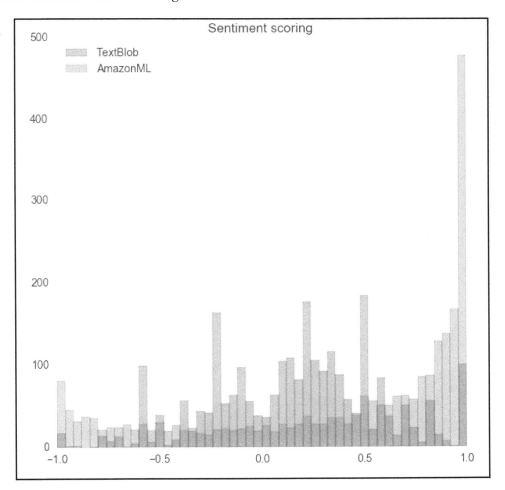

According to our Amazon ML model, the most popular vegetables on Twitter are green beans, followed by asparagus and garlic. According to `TextBlob`, **cauliflower** is ranked fourth favorite, followed by **leeks** and **cucumber**. The following plot shows the 10 vegetables with the larger amount of tweets and their respective sentiment scores obtained with `TextBlob` and our own Amazon ML binary classifier:

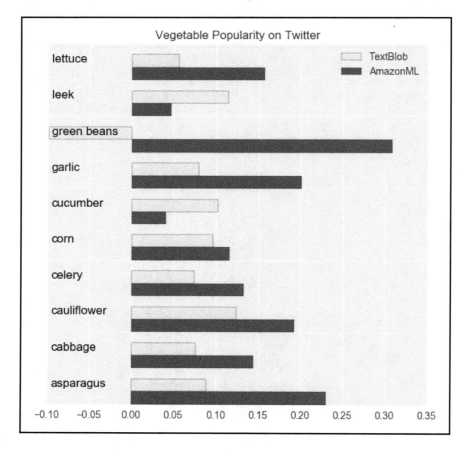

The striking result is that green beans are the least popular vegetables according to `TextBlob`. It so happens that `TextBlob` gives a negative *-0.2* sentiment score to the word `green`. So the phrase `green beans` directly scores *-0.2*.

Our Amazon ML model seems to be more reliable than `TextBlob`. After all, green beans are bound to be more popular than cauliflower!

Going beyond classification and regression

Although Amazon ML is set to solve classification and regression problems, the service can also be used for other supervised data science problems. In this last section, we looked at two classic problems: Recommender systems and named entity recognition.

- **Making recommendations**: A recommender system seeks to predict the rating or preference that a user would give to an item. There are several strategies to build recommender systems:
- **Collaborative filtering**: This involves using the behavioral patterns of similar users to predict a given user's preferences. It's the other people also bought this approach.
- **Content-based filtering**: This is the strategy where the features of a certain content are used to group similar products or content.

To use Amazon ML for recommendations, you can frame your solution as a content-based recommendation problem. One way to do this is to extract features for your products and users and build a training dataset where the outcome is binary: the user either liked the product or did not. The recommender system is transformed into a binary recommendation problem.

Named entity recognition: Named entity recognition seeks to locate and classify entities in the text into predefined categories, such as the names of persons, organizations, locations, and so forth. Amazon ML can also be used for named entity recognition problems. The idea is to use single words, and extract features as training data. Potential features could include the following:

- The word itself
- `ngram()` or `osb()` of the context around the word, such as the previous and subsequent three words.
- Prefixes and suffixes
- The predicted class of the previous three words
- The length of the word
- Whether the word is capitalized?
- Whether the word has a hyphen?
- The first word in the sentence
- The frequency of the word in your dataset
- Numeric features -- is the word a number?
- Part of speech of the word or surrounding words

Some of these feature extraction methods are available in Amazon ML; others will need external processing.

Summary

In this chapter, we leveraged the power of the AWS ecosystem to build a real-time streaming data classification pipeline. Our pipeline was able to classify streaming tweets using an Amazon ML classification endpoint. The AWS data ecosystem is diverse and complex, and for a given problem, there are often several possible solutions and architectures. The **Kinesis-Lambda-Redshift-Machine Learning** architecture we built is simple, yet very powerful.

The true strength of the Amazon ML service lies in its ease of use and simplicity. Training and evaluating a model from scratch can be done in a few minutes with a few clicks, and it can result in very good performances. Using the **AWS CLI** and the SDK, more complex data flows and model explorations can easily be implemented. The service is agile enough to become a part of a wider data flow by providing real-time classification and regression.

Underneath the simple interface, the machine learning expertise of Amazon shines at many levels. From the automated data transformations, to the tuning of the stochastic gradient algorithm, there are many elements that drive the overall performance of the models. A good balance between user control over the models and automatic optimization is achieved. The user can try several types of regularization and data transformations to optimize the models and the feature set, but the overall feeling is that using the default parameters would often work as well.

The service simplicity has some drawbacks, mostly in terms of limited data transformation and the absence of any embedded cross-validation mechanisms, which are central to a data science workflow.

In the end, Amazon ML is a useful regression and classification service that brings machine learning automatization closer. What matters in a data science project, as in any other software project, is the true costs of ownership. Compared to a home-grown solution, Amazon ML wins in terms of ease of use, maintainability, resources costs, and often performance.

Index